THE USES OF
MANUSCRIPTS
IN LITERARY
STUDIES

THE USES OF MANUSCRIPTS IN LITERARY STUDIES

ESSAYS IN MEMORY OF Judson Boyce Allen

Edited by

Charlotte Cook Morse
Penelope Reed Doob
Marjorie Curry Woods

Studies in Medieval Culture, XXXI
WESTERN MICHIGAN UNIVERSITY
Medieval Institute Publications

1992

Library of Congress Catologing-in-Publication Data

The Uses of manuscripts in literary studies : essays in memory of
 Judson Boyce Allen / edited by Charlotte C. Morse, Penelope B.
 Doob, Marjorie C. Woods.
      p.   cm. -- (Studies in medieval culture ; 31)
     Includes bibliographical references.
     ISBN 1-879288-13-3 (hard). -- ISBN 1-879288-14-1 (pbk.)
     1. Literature, Medieval--Criticism, Textual. 2. English
literature--Middle English, 1100-1500--Criticism, Textual.
 3. Manuscripts, English (Middle) 4. Manuscripts, Medieval.
 5. Transmission of texts.   I. Allen, Judson, Boyce, 1932- .
 II. Morse, Charlotte C., 1942-   .   III. Doob, Penelope Reed.
 IV. Woods, Marjorie Curry, 1947-   .   V. Series.
 CB351.S83 vol. 31
 [PN162]
 940.1 s--dc20
 [809'.02]   92-5904
                                                          CIP

Cover design by Cynthia Tyler
Printed in the United States of America

Contents

Introduction

Judson Boyce Allen loved his work and encouraged other scholars by his enthusiasm for theirs. He had an unusually wide range of interests, from the specialized study of manuscripts through the interpretation of particular literary texts to the broadest issues of literary theory. The last he got from his study at Johns Hopkins University and the first from Oxford University. R. W. Hunt guided his study of manuscripts, and the result, as Judson himself explained, was that he had the rare experience for a young American of reading a number of medieval texts for the first time not in modern editions but in manuscripts, an experience that forever marked his sensibility as a scholar. Beryl Smalley, another of his mentors, helped him to find in the friars she herself had studied a way to bring theoretical literary issues into conjunction with the study of manuscripts and the reading of texts. First came *The Friar as Critic*, and then, in his last book, *The Ethical Poetic of the Later Middle Ages*, a major assault, from a new position, on the conventional claim that there was no literary theory in the Middle Ages. By the time Judson published *The Ethical Poetic* he had met Alastair J. Minnis, whose early career Hunt and Smalley had also influenced and who, like Judson, was discovering literary theory in the *accessus ad auctores* in medieval manuscripts. For the first time, Judson had a colleague whose interests nearly mirrored his own, and the two carried on a dialogue in person and by post. Judson would have relished Alastair J. Minnis and Brian Scott's *Medieval Literary Theory and Criticism, c.1100–c.1375* (with David Wallace), a volume of translated texts with introductions.

Introduction

Judson's academic life was not easy. He did have the support of his wife Jacqueline who expertly managed their household and moved it willingly to New York or Europe for visiting or sabbatical years. Yet the kind of research he was doing and the quality of his writing should have earned him a major research university appointment earlier in his life. That the appointment to the University of Florida came so late explains why Judson formally taught so few professing medievalists (of the contributors to this volume, only R. Allen Shoaf). Even though Judson singly had very many of the skills needed to train young medievalists, he sent his Wake Forest and Marquette students to larger Ph.D. programs so they would encounter a range of scholars and kinds of expertise: Al Shoaf went to Cornell for his Ph.D.; Ann W. Astell (*The Song of Songs in the Middle Ages* 1990) to the University of Wisconsin, Madison.

Most of the contributors to this volume first met Judson either at a conference or in a library, two of his favorite places. Judson valued conferences as young or relatively isolated scholars do, as opportunities for company, as times to ask questions, to discuss work, and to trade ideas. Conferences were times for fun, for jokes, for hymns, and, at Kalamazoo from 1974 onwards, for dancing.

In formal presentations Judson sometimes urged his own most engaging theories with a preacherly conviction that some of his audience found overstated. In conversation, however, Judson was quite willing to discuss or debate to try to get nearer to the truth of things. Judson created a sense of the audience for scholarly work, making us eager to hear about the work of others and to share our own. He had a gift for affirming a community that works to draw out doubt and supply reassurance and that salves the pricks of pride with wise affection.

Judson always arranged social occasions at conferences and kept an open door. He knew what other people were doing, and he liked to introduce people who had common interests. He made sure that young scholars met their distinguished elders. He delighted in hearing his colleagues puzzle over scholarly problems or bat around arguments for books or revel over the latest gems mined from old books and manuscripts. I remember one of Judson's gatherings at which Larry Benson was worrying an apparently simple question, "What is a book?," and another year when Martin Irvine first explained to me his work on grammatical manuscripts.

Conversations were at once intense, learned, and amusing—even sometimes hilarious, as when the Falstaffian R. E. Kaske was recruiting a young scholar to Cornell for graduate study by comically denigrating the virtues of other programs, such as Harvard's, while extravagantly praising his own. Larry Benson took up Harvard's defense with equal verve, while Judson served as referee and instigator of third-party interjections. What emerged was a brilliant, parodic history of trends in the study of English literature in twentieth-century America.

A tradition most faithfully observed during MLA conventions was the singing of hymns to close an evening of scholarly camaraderie. Judson and his Southern Baptist friends and others, too—including O. B. Hardison, Patrick Gallacher, and Joseph Wittig—would sing. Singing hymns expressed the joy of community and also wryly recognized the affinity of the American South with the spiritual temper of the Middle Ages. Judson grew up in an intellectual center of the Southern Baptist Church (a Church now split in two), the son of a theologically learned Baptist preacher and publisher. For him and for many other Southern medievalists, represented in this volume by R. Allen Shoaf, Cynthia Bland, and me, coming from Flannery O'Connor's "God-haunted" South makes the Middle Ages seem less strange in its spirituality than it seems to some other medievalists; there is for us, as there was for Judson, a resonance of the South's God-ordered world in medieval literature and the pleasurable recognition of echoes in medieval religious writing of things heard in our youths.

That Judson Allen became the main sponsor of the farewell dance at Kalamazoo began in the accident of a hot night in a room too small to accommodate all his guests. The group moved down to a lounge, Penelope Doob supplied the tapes she used to stay awake driving from Toronto, and the event began. In the years afterward, Judson and John Alford personally arranged for the dance, until it became altogether a part of the annual Medieval Congresses. The dance became for Judson a way to invite everyone to share his exuberant pleasure in several intense days of medieval scholarship, and it served, as the dance traditionally has, as an image of harmony.

Judson's other favorite place was the library, most particularly any library with manuscripts and a rich range of early printed books of medieval texts. No doubt the Bodleian was the most special library for him, but he also appreciated Continental libraries because, as he once explained to Penelope Doob, they offer a wider variety of the odder kinds of manuscripts that were once in England but were spirited away to the Continent in the course of the Reformation. Judson spent a year working in Poitiers, one of the oldest Church centers in Western Europe, and another year at the Vatican Library in Rome, as well as several years in Oxford.

Libraries were not simply places for solitary study, but places for meeting other scholars. As anyone knows who works with manuscripts, having someone else to aid in the deciphering of a difficult hand or to look with you at particular problems is welcome. Josephine Koster Tarvers first met Judson at the Bodleian. She and Cynthia Bland, who already knew Judson, were then graduate students from Chapel Hill on their first independent quest for manuscripts and in Judson they found a ready friend and guide. Together they celebrated the discovery of new texts. When Jo thanked Judson for introducing her to medievalists around Oxford that summer as if she were one, Judson responded with raised eyebrow, "If you are a serious enough student to come and look at manuscripts, then you *are* a serious medievalist—like the rest of us." Judson had a gift for taking people seriously, even including some medievalists who hardly ever looked at manuscripts.

Work with manuscripts extends beyond the walls of libraries, of course. Marianne Briscoe holds a vivid memory of Judson directing her to her study, after a day at the Newberry Library and dinner, to help her decipher a hand in a manuscript that she was finding hard to read. At different times, Cynthia Bland and I joined Judson on his expeditions around London in search of manuscripts to buy for the University of Florida, for the purpose of teaching paleography. Judson invited us to examine manuscripts with him, a most enjoyable form of instruction.

The difficulties of Judson's academic life made him especially understanding of a younger generation of medievalists whose positions in the profession were insecure, often for many years. He was a sympathetic listener, always keen to encourage the best in his friends. His faith in the value of our projects helped us to keep working, even at projects that would not mature quickly and so are problematic in the American context that demands early publications. Penelope Doob, Marjorie Woods, Cynthia Bland, Marianne Briscoe, Martin Irvine, R. Allen Shoaf, Josephine Tarvers, and I, among the contributors here, feel a personal debt to Judson, in addition to the debt all of us owe to Judson as a scholar and critic.

Several of the contributors here are engaged in larger projects that meet the conditions of an ideal project, as Judson defined it, that is, a project centered on new work with manuscripts that will yield insights into critical or poetic theory and have implications for practical criticism. Such projects extend over decades and are realized in a variety of publications, from various points of view. Here I think of Alastair J. Minnis's work on the author, so close to Judson's own; of

Martin Irvine's work on grammatical texts; of Christopher Baswell's work on Virgil manuscripts; and of Jorie Woods's work on Geoffrey of Vinsauf's *Poetria nova* and its commentaries. Jo Tarvers's work on prayers, Cynthia Bland's work on late medieval grammatical texts, Kathryn Kerby-Fulton's work on apocalyptic prophecies, John Fyler's work on Genesis commentaries, and Marianne Briscoe's work on preaching manuals also meet the conditions for an admirable project. Penelope Doob's exploration of labyrinths, Al Shoaf's work on major medieval and Renaissance texts, and my edition of Chaucer's *Clerk's Tale* are less dependent on work with manuscripts than Judson's ideal project would be, but to us as well manuscripts have provided inspiration, information, and arguments. All of us would agree with Judson in recognizing how intellectually challenging it is to study the works of a manuscript culture, so unlike in both obvious and subtle ways the print and electronic culture that is our own.

As we remember Judson's advice to us, his pithy comments, his enthusiasm for ideas and information, and his generosity, we realize that Judson is still weaving bonds between us and among us. We try to remember, always, what Judson taught us of our obligations and debts to each other and of our work as a communal enterprise. We remember the charity and humility Judson so often brought to his dealings with us.

In 1985 Judson came to his last International Medieval Congress at Kalamazoo and, though he was quite ill, he read his paper, talked to his friends, and danced his last dance. Penelope Doob, Jorie Woods, and I, with the help of John Alford, went to Judson to ask what kind of memorial volume he would like to have and promised that we would follow his wishes. He gave us the title for the sessions we have organized at Kalamazoo and for this volume, *The Uses of Manuscripts in Literary Studies*, a title that clearly defined the kind of work Judson himself had done, the kind of work he had so generously fostered, and the kind of work he deeply believed holds the greatest promise for enriching medieval studies. Characteristically, he encouraged us to keep the matter of contributors open to any scholar whose work conformed to the rubric he gave us. He wanted to encourage manuscript studies as the basis for medieval literary criticism and theory.

In the event, the contributors to this volume include several of us who knew Judson well and others who knew him slightly or not at all in person. Closest of all was Al Shoaf, Judson's student at Wake Forest, later his confidante, and now his successor at the University of Florida, Gainesville. Others of us knew Judson from conferences, libraries, and correspondence. All of us know Judson through his work.

Judson Boyce Allen earned the tributes we here present to his memory. He earned them not as a formal teacher—except from Al Shoaf—but as friend, mentor, colleague, and scholar. We have all benefitted from Judson's intellectual and social generosity and we will continue to benefit from the model of professional behavior that Judson held out to us.

Charlotte Cook Morse

*

This collection opens with R. Allen Shoaf's essay on the book as an idea, a conception constrained by the reality of manuscript books but also opened out from the manuscript book to extend to the stony heart.

Marjorie Curry Woods takes up the theoretical problem posed by word and meaning in different versions of a commentary on Geoffrey of Vinsauf.

Introduction

Marianne G. Briscoe re-evaluates the uses of manuals on preaching, *artes praedicandi*, which seem not to have been formally part of university curriculum; she suggests how the manuscript evidence points to certain ways these manuals were used.

Penelope Reed Doob offers a brief review of how two ideas of the labyrinth require a rewriting of modern ideas of the labyrinthine journey to account for its uses in medieval literature.

Martin Irvine, Christopher Baswell, Alastair J. Minnis, John M. Fyler, and Cynthia Renee Bland conjoin manuscript materials with the elucidation of fourteenth-century vernacular texts, many of them Chaucer's. Martin Irvine looks at the formal problem of the manuscript page with glosses and its implications for theory and practical criticism, especially as manifest in Chaucer's dream vision poems. Christopher Baswell shows how specific glosses in Virgil manuscripts can illuminate particular Chaucerian texts, while illustrating especially through the Wife of Bath how marginal voices move to the center of the text, voices which will in turn be displaced. Working from *accessus ad auctores* and considering Juan Ruiz, Dante, and John Gower, Alastair J. Minnis explores how medieval vernacular poets who presented themselves as lovers—types without authority—began to claim for themselves the category of *auctour*. John M. Fyler takes the figure of the Tower of Babel, with its implications for attitudes toward language, which leads him into analysis of the *Canon's Yeoman's Tale*. Cynthia Renee Bland uses the earliest grammatical text with English evidence to discuss the tradition of teaching grammar, especially as it casts light on the interpretation of Chaucer's words.

Kathryn Kerby-Fulton explores English manuscripts that contain apocalyptic prophecy to try to reconstruct what kinds of texts Langland could have known, and in what manuscript context he might have read them; she finds that religious prophecies often occur in miscellanies containing other literature known to Langland.

xvi

Introduction

Charlotte Cook Morse finds in the rubrics accompanying manuscript texts of Petrarch's story of Griselda two interpretive directions that these rubrics gave to early readers of the Griselda: one group invites non-gender-specific application of Griselda's example while another encourages the more familiar application of the tale to women alone.

Josephine Koster Tarvers addresses women as writers and readers of manuscripts, bringing together information that points toward the possibility of writing a new history of the later Middle Ages, one giving a more accurate reflection of women's participation in the making of late medieval culture.

The cover of this book has been designed by another of Judson's friends, the calligrapher Cynthia Tyler.

*

The editors wish especially to thank Thomas H. Seiler, Managing Editor of Medieval Institute Publications, and Juleen Audrey Eichinger, Production Editor, for their work in bringing this volume to publication. The publishers thank the Bodleian Library, University of Oxford, for permission to reproduce the manuscripts which appear here as Plates 1 and 2 in Martin Irvine's essay; the manuscript that appears as Plate 3 is reproduced by permission of the Syndics of Cambridge University of Library. We are grateful to Otto Gründler, Director of the Medieval Institute at Western Michigan University and also director of the annual International Congress on Medieval Studies, for making possible the sessions at recent congresses devoted to the memory of Judson Boyce Allen. We thank R. Allen Shoaf and Robert Worth Frank, Jr., for making available to us the bibliography of Judson Allen's work that appeared first in the memorial issue of *The Chaucer Review* (21.2 [1986]: 90–92). We wish also to thank everyone who participated, in whatever way(s), in the Congress sessions.

Dante's Comedy, the Codex, and the Margin of Error

R. Allen Shoaf

> It is part of the reality of a work of art
> that around its real theme it leaves an
> area that is indefinite.
>
> *Hans-Georg Gadamer*

Of all medieval poets Dante is probably the one to whom the form of the book matters most.[1] For Dante, the book is "good to think with." Recall only the famous image in the last canto of *Paradiso*:

> Nel suo profondo vidi che s'interna,
> legato con amore in *un volume*,
> ciò che per l'universo si squaderna:
>   sustanze e accidenti e lor costume
> quasi conflati insieme, per tal modo
> che ciò ch'i' dico è un semplice lume.
>
> *Para* 33.85–90 (emphasis added)

> In its [the Eternal Light's] profundity I saw—ingathered
> and bound by love into one single volume—
> what, in the universe, seems separate, scattered:
>   substances, accidents, and dispositions
> as if conjoined—in such a way that what
> I tell is only rudimentary.[2]

The universe itself is a codex, and if the leaves, like the Sybil's (*Para.*

1

33.65–66), are randomly scattered in man's fractured vision, in God's transcendent and unifying vision they are bound together in the perfect codex, the divine idea of the book.

If this is the most famous example of Dante's thinking with the book, it is still only one of many such examples which vary considerably. For example, if this one is thematic, where the form of the codex is thematized in the imagery of the poem, there is another that is structural, where, given the codex and its form, structures that are both vertical and horizontal are possible, and these can be iconic or dynamic and retrospective or anticipatory.

An excellent example of structural thinking with the book, an example that is vertical and iconic and retrospective, occurs in the two cantos 30 of *Purgatorio* and *Paradiso*. Here, in a context of elaborate mirror and Narcissus imagery, Dante positions two mirror terzine:

> Così la madre al figlio par *superba,*
> com' ella parve a me; perché d'amaro
> sente il sapor de la pietade *acerba.*
> > *Purg.* 30.79–81 (emphasis added)

> just as a mother seems
> harsh to her child, so did she seem to me—
> how bitter is the savor of stern pity!

> "Non che da sé sian queste cose *acerbe*;
> ma è difetto da la parte tua,
> che non hai viste ancor tanto *superbe.*"
> > *Para.* 30.79-81 (emphasis added)

> "not that these things
> are lacking in themselves; the defect lies
> in you, whose sight is not yet that sublime."

2

I have elsewhere demonstrated (Shoaf, *Currency* 80–83) that these mirror terzine, with their reversed rhymes (*superba/acerba // acerbe/ superbe*), constitute a device by which Dante the poet can suggest that in Paradise we see the "reality" (itself, of course, a figure, a promise) that is reflected in the imperfect mirror of mortality in Purgatory. What we see, in Purgatory, when we merely see, is only reflection, as in a glass darkly—it is reversed. What we see, in Paradise, on the other hand, when seeing is reflecting—when *we* reflect—is reality (or, from Dante the poet's perspective, the promise of reality). Hence, this example suggests, Dante understands that the form of the codex entails reading both horizontally and vertically, and, thinking with the book thus, he carefully structures exact vertical intersections and horizontal nodes in his poem that serve as inter-relational loci of meaning.[3]

Yet another example of such structural thinking with the book occurs in the cantos 33 of *Inferno* and *Purgatorio*. Here, counting on the reader's vertical and retrospective reading and re-reading of his poem, Dante positions strategic repetitions of the imagery of stone ("pietra").[4] My concern in the remainder of this paper is with the imagery of stone in *Purgatorio* and, as will appear in a moment, the related imagery of "anti-stone" in the *Paradiso*.

Ugolino's description of himself hearing the tower door sealed up is one of the most famous moments in the *Comedy*:

> "e io senti' chiavar l'uscio di sotto
> a l'orribile torre; ond'io guardai
> nel viso a' mie' figliuoi sanza far motto.
> Io non piangëa, sì dentro impetrai."
> *Inf.* 33.46–49

> "below, I heard them nailing up the door
> of that appalling tower; without a word,
> I looked into the faces of my sons.
> I did not weep; within, I turned to stone."

3

As Freccero, Hollander, Mazzotta, and others have shown, the moment in which Ugolino turns to stone is also the moment he ceases forever to be capable of any spiritual understanding; henceforward all he will be able to understand is a "bestial segno" (*Inf.* 32.133), such as his anthropophagism upon the shade of Ruggieri (*Inf.* 32.125–32).

A moment in *Purgatorio*, canto 33, if less famous than the corresponding moment in *Inferno*, is no less important. Beatrice acknowledges Dante's intellectual "stoniness":

> "Ma perch'io veggio te ne lo 'ntelletto
> fatto di pietra e, impetrato, tinto,
> sì che t'abbaglia il lume del mio detto,
>
>   voglio anco, e se non scritto, almen dipinto,
> che 'l te ne porti dentro a te per quello
> che si reca il bordon di palma cinto."
>
> *Purg.* 33.73–78

> "But since I see your intellect is made
> of stone and, petrified, grown so opaque—
> the light of what I say has left you dazed—
>
>   I'd also have you bear my words within you—
> if not inscribed, at least outlined—just as
> the pilgrim's staff is brought back wreathed with palm."

These lines serve many different purposes in the canticle and also in the poem, but, initially, I want to emphasize that they continue the suggestion, already strongly implied in *Inferno*, of Dante the pilgrim's resemblance to Ugolino (see also Pézard 354). Both men were reputed ("aveva voce," *Inf.* 33.85) to have been traitors, and both men were subjected to sentences of death that included their sons. If Dante expends so much of his poetic power on the Ugolino episode and its repercussions, he does so, at least in part, because of this resemblance—

4

he is also writing about himself, in some way "stony," too.

All the more interesting then is the absence of exact vertical repetition in *Paradiso*, canto 33. There is no stone, no mention of stone, in the canto recording Dante's ultimate vision. Knowing as we do the periodicity and point of the many previous vertical repetitions in all three cantos of the same number, we may incline to argue that Dante the poet deliberately omits any mention of stone from *Paradiso*, canto 33, just to insist on the difference between this moment, the ultimate moment of the vision, and the earlier experiences in *Inferno* and *Purgatorio*: not only is there no stone, there is also no repetition—Dante is here very far indeed from the "stony" Ugolino.

But such an argument would be in at least one respect incomplete. Canto 33 of *Paradiso* is one of those cantos of the *Comedy* that actually begin at the end of the preceding canto. At the end of canto 32 of *Paradiso*, St. Bernard gives Dante special directions:

> Veramente, ne forse tu t'arretri
> movendo l'ali tue, credendo oltrarti,
> orando grazia conven che s'*impetri*,
> grazia da quella [sc. Mary] che puote aiutarti.
> lines 145–48 (emphasis added)

> But lest you now fall back when, even as
> you move your wings, you think that you advance,
> imploring grace, through prayer you must beseech
> grace from that one who has the power to help you.

The passage is important for many reasons but for present purposes most especially for the curious verb "s'impetri." The verb "impetrare" means "domandare umilmente; chiedere con preghiere, supplicando; implorare" (*GDI* I: 462.3), but in form it is all but identical to "imp(i)etrare" (recall Ugolino's "impetrai," *Inf.* 33.49; and see *ED* 3:

5

393), and Dante's strategy emerges from this near identity.

If Dante is "thinking to advance" ("credendo oltrarti")—also "thinking to outrage himself"—by approaching the center of all being, or God, then, before he can commit such an outrage as to describe the indescribable (say the ineffable, paint the undepictable), "orando grazia conven che s'impetri" ("grace must be obtained by prayer"—Singleton, *Divine Comedy*) from the mother of all graces, the Virgin Mary. From her, the woman who is called the true lodestone and the "pietra in deserto,"[5] who nonetheless is never "petrosa" but only and always "pietosa," it is necessary and conventional, here in Heaven, that grace be acquired by praying.

The verb "impetrare" by its near identity with "imp(i)etrare" insists on its ultimate difference from it—there is no confusion here, in Heaven. Quite the contrary, if for the moment we feel the *im-* of "impetrare" to be a negative prefix and if we grant Dante the full possibility of the reflexive *s'*, here in Heaven, we can then argue, "it is a convention that by praying grace ("orando grazia") one is unpetrified (one un-petrifies oneself)." What Dante the pilgrim is about to do, in effect, is to cancel the similarity between Ugolino and him by praying to Mary—"ad petram, id est, Mariam, invocando fideliter auxilium hujus petrae" (Richard of St. Lawrence 421)—in such a way as to remove the stony ("s'impetri") from his heart and spirit. Indeed, as one immediate consequence of this prayer, Dante will see God.

This is not what the Italian literally says, of course, but the literal Italian is, in fact, something of a crux (cf. Singleton, *Divine Comedy*, and Sapegno), and the apparent redundancy of "orando" and "s'impetri" in the same line must remain problematic unless we accept the possibility that Dante intends here something like a semi-pun in which "s'impetri" must play a dual role. As long as we are not ourselves stony about it, the line makes perfectly good sense.

Moreover, an identical pun is probably at work in one of the

6

famous *rime petrose*, Dante's youthful rhymes to the "stony lady" (trans. Durling 612–29). These rhymes figure prominently elsewhere in the *Inferno* (canto 9), in what amounts to a crucial palinode in which Dante recalls and judges his earlier, youthful writing (see Freccero, "Medusa" 128–30). In "Così nel mio parlar," Dante writes: "questa bella petra / la quale ognora impetra / maggior durezza e più natura cruda," and Contini, for example, admits the possibility of the pun in these lines. Although he prefers here the sense "desidera e consegue" ("desires and attains"—extensions of the sense "to obtain by prayer"), he does not deny the possibility that the verb could mean in this instance "to enclose in stone."[6] It is highly probable, I think, that Dante plays the pun in *Paradiso*, canto 32, as part of the ongoing palinode in the *Comedy* to the *rime petrose* and especially, perhaps, to "Così nel mio parlar," whose "impetra" is repeated only to be cancelled ("s'impetri") in *Paradiso*.

Be that as it may, the verb "s'impetri," I would go on to suggest, interrupts the verb "s'impetrai" in *Inferno*, canto 33, breaking the *a* out and compelling a different reading. So, too, the vertical strategy at this point in the poem is one of interruption. The verb "impetrare" occurs in *Inferno*, canto 33; it occurs in *Purgatorio*, canto 33; but it does not occur in *Paradiso*, canto 33—rather in canto 32, in what we have seen is itself an interrupting form. The exact vertical repetition is interrupted in order to place the verb "s'impetri" out of sequence; then it, in turn, interrupts the verb "s'impetrai"—for there is no (literal) stoniness in heaven (no "donna petrosa," no "rime petrose," no Ugolino feeding on a Ruggieri).

Such subtleties, such distinctions as I am arguing to be at work here are among the challenges with which poetry constantly provokes us. The more poetry we know and the more we know about poetry, the more and the finer are the distinctions we are called upon to make—distinctions which interrupt the smooth surface of generalities.

7

If we refuse this call, we do so only at the terrible price eventually of stoniness: we become inflexible, biased, blind—incapable of, insensitive to, the finer discriminations of justice.

Such stoniness, Dante suggests, petrified the humanity of Pisa, for Pisa fixed the sons of Ugolino "a tal croce" (*Inf.* 33.87) for no better reason than that he "aveva *voce* / D'aver tradita . . . de la castella" ("was reputed / to have betrayed [their] fortresses," *Inf.* 33.85–86; emphasis added). The language here, "aveva voce," means more than just "was rumored," although it does mean that, too; Dante, unlike the Pisans, is discrete, discriminate, precise—his language also means what it says, "had the word." Pisa killed Ugolino and his sons because Ugolino "had the word" of having betrayed the city—Pisa killed them for a word. Rather than acknowledge that between a *vox* and a *res* intervene conventions such that there is no direct, certain access to the *res* through the *vox*, Pisa confused the *res* with the *vox*, and having the *vox*, assumed possession of the *res*. Rather than test the connection from *vox* to *res*—according to what law is he said to be a traitor? according to whose judgment is he said to be a traitor?—Pisa assumed there is no abysm between *vox* and *res*, and went on to kill a man and his sons.

But this was, in fact, to plunge into the abysm, into the miserable chaos where words and things are confused, and it was thus to resign any claim to humanity. Little wonder Dante excoriates Pisa as a "novella Tebe": it is a city of confusion, just like Thebes (Mazzotta 98), where the human, which thrives on distinctions, cannot survive.[7] Moreover, when he calls Pisa Thebes, Dante does so in a rhetorical maneuver which itself exposes the city's guilt of confusion:

> Innocenti facea l'età *novella,*
> *novella* Tebe, Uguiccione e 'l Brigata
> e li altri due che 'l canto suso appella.
> > *Inf.* 33.88–90 (emphasis added)

8

> O Thebes renewed, their years were innocent
> and young—Brigata, Uguiccione, and
> the other two my song has named above!

The repetition of "novella"—the same word with two different senses ("renewed" and "young")—posits an apparent confusion in which, quite the contrary, exist important if subtle distinctions. Thus Dante condemns Pisa in an example of the very use of language of which Pisa is incapable. Dante's own rhetoric, unlike that of Pisa, is so subtle it can discern differences even in apparent identity. And since within the walls of Florence, he himself "aveva voce d'essere un traditore," the precision of his language is also a *cri de coeur*—a cry, untainted by self-pity, against all who would kill a man's sons, not to mention the man himself, for the sake of a "voce."

Pisa's refusal to use language justly accounts, finally, for the superficially curious way in which Dante addresses the city at the opening of the vituperation. Because Pisa murdered Ugolino and his sons and in such a cruel way, she is the "vituperio de le genti / del bel paese là dove'l sì sona" ("the scandal of the peoples / of that fair land where *si* is heard," *Inf.* 33.79–80). Dante condemns Pisa not just for having scandalized Italy but also for having scandalized Italian. Because of Pisa—in whose name is inverted and hardened the beautiful "sì" (i.e., "is")—Italian is the language that must record and name the story of Ugolino della Gherardesca. Dante's grief is not only for Ugolino's sons but also for his beloved *volgare illustre*. Here at the bottom of Hell, in the ice of Cocytus, Italian is dirtied and defaced, petrified. By the same token, but reversed, in Paradise, at the moment when Dante prays for grace from Mary to see God, he and his beloved *volgare illustre* both are unpetrified ("s'im-petri")—he, by the infusion of grace; Italian, by the *flexibility* of the pun.[8]

Dante's Comedy, the Codex, and the Margin of Error

In the years just before his death, Judson Allen turned his attention increasingly to the medieval codex in order to study what I have come to think of, reflecting on our conversations and the notes he left me, as "codicological intention."[9] Although he had a healthy scepticism about nonce terms, I think Judson Allen would have probably accepted this one as at least provisionally useful. Although the author's intention in a poem is finally irrecuperable, the intention of a codex is not subject to the same degree of opacity (cf. Ahern, "Binding the Book" 800–03). What Dante meant by the image of the "un volume" will always to some extent remain a mystery. But there is no mystery to the linearity of leaves in a codex, to the creation of margins, to the appearance of interlinearity, to the beginning of a codex or to the end (however much may be missing, there is always a first and a last), to the regularity of lineation (or attempt thereat), to the need to rule and thus to count lines, to the need to gather, and the need to bind. In other words, the physical object that is the codex entails a certain set of data that are always and everywhere significant (if only limitedly so) in roughly the same way.[10]

Could not a medieval poet have drawn the same conclusion? Judson Allen wanted to argue "yes." In this brief paper, I have in fact presupposed his affirmative argument in the case of Dante's strategy in the repetition of "pietra" in cantos 33 of *Inferno* and *Purgatorio* and canto 32 of *Paradiso*. Dante manipulates "codicological intention"—as well as, obviously, numerology—in several cantos of the three canticles to structure repetitions and recurrences whose meanings we may subsequently (and endlessly) debate but whose articulation we can hardly doubt or dispute.

Several consequences of this argument repay consideration. Although numerological thinking plays a vital role in vertical repetitions in the *Comedy*, most especially perhaps in the mirror verses in cantos 30 of *Purgatorio* and *Paradiso*, even in this latter case, the

10

codex is also crucial since the verses presuppose the *superimposition* of one book over the other.[11] Not until one places one book over the other (as I first did in the winter of 1980) will one begin to see how lines cohere and configure between or among cantos in the canticles. Moreover, this experience, which is spatial and to some extent tactile, presupposes that interruptability which I have suggested is thematized in the case of the repetition of "pietra": one stops reading and looks up or back or forward or down to assimilate spaces and loci into possible and, eventually, probable orders of significance. And it is this consequence of "codicological intention" that is perhaps most revealing of Dante's "thinking with the book."

The codex is structurally unstable, by definition indeterminate. If sentences can only be read left to right (in Occidental languages anyway), the codex can be read in any direction one pleases. (Is this not also one of Joyce's primary insights, enabling his fictions, especially *Finnegan's Wake*?) If the codex entails a set of data, always and everywhere significant in roughly the same way, by that very determinacy, the codex generates within itself a space of maximal indeterminacy.[12] Codicological intention, in other words, always presupposes error. In the codex there is always a margin of error.

Dante and, after him, Chaucer are the medieval poets most fascinated by this margin of error. Both of them are poets of error, writing of that wandering which can, though it does not always, lead to truth (both are men fascinated, we know, with Aeneas). Seen in this way, Dante's writing can easily be understood to accommodate such "error" as the lapsed repetition of "pietra" in canto 33 of *Paradiso*. Not to accommodate such error, always and everywhere to insist on the same structure of vertical repetitions, would itself be "stony," rigid and inflexible. Dante, in short, is himself a reader also of his poem and of the codex in which it is transcribed, and as he reads, he "errs" towards the truth, finding in his margins of error the way to the truth.

NOTES

1. See, esp., Curtius's classic discussion ("The Book as Symbol" 326–32) and Singleton's discussion of the "book of memory" in *La Vita Nuova* (25–54); on Singleton's discussion, see now also Harrison 5–13; see, further, Gellrich, esp. 157–66; finally consult the informative articles by Ahern.

2. For quotations and translations of the *Comedy* I cite Mandelbaum.

3. Other widely recognized vertical repetitions are in the three cantos 15 (fathers and father imagery) and 26 (fire and boundary imagery).

4. This imagery has been the object of much scrutiny recently—although even so there is probably still more to be learned and said about it. See the classic essays by Freccero, "Bestial Sign" and "Medusa: The Letter and the Spirit"; and consult Hollander's important contribution to understanding the Scriptural background of the imagery. In "Ugolino and Erysichthon" I provide source material and commentary on the related, crucial imagery of hunger and especially cannibalism. I take this opportunity to announce that I plan to correct and augment my note, "Dante and Peraldus," which also discusses imagery of hunger and thirst, in my book-in-progress, *The Crisis of Convention in Dante's "Comedy."*

5. These and other figurative titles are frequently applied to Mary in the commentaries: see, e.g., Richard of St. Lawrence, ed. Borgnet 36: 420–21; Garner of Langres, *Sermo* XI in PL 205.642, 645; John of Howden, "Viola," ed. Raby, 411, line 18; and consult further, Salzer 497, 504n2, and 567.

6. My summary of Contini's argument is from *ED* 3: 393, *sub voce*: "Ugualmente, in *Rime* CIII 3, il Contini, che pur preferisce dare al verbo il senso di 'desidera e consegue,' non esclude che possa valere 'racchiudere in pietra, inchiudere saldamente.' . . ."

7. I am at present preparing a study of the numerous words in the *Thebaid* which carry Statius's emphasis on Thebes as the city that destroys distinctions. The list includes *confusio, turba, limes, par, impar, miscere, sociam, conturba,* etc. Perhaps the easiest

12

way to illustrate, briefly, the emphasis and its importance is to note that the epic opens
with it: "limes mihi carminis esto / Oedipodae *confusa* domus" ("let the troubled [lit.
'confused'] house of Oedipus set a limit to my song," *Thebaid* I.16–17 [emphasis
added], trans. J. H. Mozley, Loeb Classical Library, 2 vols. [Cambridge: Harvard UP,
1928], 1: 340–41). From the very beginning, Statius is in doubt as to how to limit, to
demarcate, to separate and to distinguish the matter of Thebes; it itself is confused, as
well as the historical city and its inhabitants. For the rest of the epic, Statius will suffer
the same doubt as he searches for a way to write what is unspeakable.

8. Note, in this regard, how the occurrence of "impetrato" in *Purgatorio* mediates
between the occurrences in *Inferno* and *Paradiso*: Dante replies to Beatrice's criticism
of his intellect, that it is "impetrato," by affirming that "Sì come cera da suggello, / che
la figura impressa non trasmuta, / segnato è or da voi lo mio cervello" ("Even as wax
the seal's impressed, / where there's no alteration in the form, / so does my brain now
bear what you have stamped," *Purg.* 33.79–81). Dante's brain and intellect, the lines
suggest, have already begun to be more like wax than like stone—more flexible, in
other words, if also therefore evanescent.

9. See Allen, "Langland's Reading"; also "A Distinction of Stories," esp. 98–110; cf.
Bruns.

10. My argument here touches, I know, on a number of issues currently being debated
by scholars and theorists concerned with problematics of orality and textuality. I hope
to address these issues in the book-in-progress from which this paper is drawn, *The
Crisis of Convention in Dante's "Comedy."*

11. The *Comedy*, I am aware, doubtless circulated in many different degrees of binding,
from fascicles or *quadernetti* (Ahern, "Binding the Book" 800) to complete codices
containing the whole poem. I am assuming that in fascicle binding as in any of the
intervening bindings, readers could have superimposed one part of the text over
another. For MSS. that contain one canticle without the other two, see Petrocchi, 1: 57
ff.

12. At this point, it might appear that Ahern and I disagree. From the earlier image of
the Sybil's leaves scattered and lost on the wind (*Para.* 33.65–66), he argues (Ahern,

13

Dante's Comedy, the Codex, and the Margin of Error

"Binding the Book" 801–02) that Dante's figure of the "un volume" articulates the poet's desire to avert the same fate for his *Comedy*: Dante does not want his *Comedy* scattered, condemned to disorder. In fact, I completely agree with this insight. Indeterminacy such as I am describing is not the same thing as disorder, and I am not making any case for disorder. The fate of the Sybil's leaves could not possibly promote indeterminacy, only chaos. Indeterminacy, in other words, is a function of the codex, a function of binding. It is only when the poet's order is fixed in the codex that the margin of error emerges to define by its counterposition the conditions of truth in the text. The graph must be fixed for the sign to be free; and indeterminacy is not the absence of meaning but its limit—hence an integral part of it. See further Shoaf, *Currency* 149.

14

R. Allen Shoaf

WORKS CITED

Ahern, John. "Binding the Book: Hermeneutics and Manuscript Production in *Paradiso* 33." *PMLA* 97 (1982): 800–09.

———. "Dante's Last Word: The *Comedy* as a *liber coelestis*." *Dante Studies* 102 (1984): 1–14.

———. "Singing the Book: Orality in the Reception of Dante's *Comedy*." *Annals of Scholarship* 2 (1981): 17–40.

Allen, Judson Boyce. *A Distinction of Stories: The Medieval Unity of Chaucer's Fair Chain of Narratives for Canterbury*. Columbus: Ohio State UP, 1981.

———. "Langland's Reading and Writing: *Detractor* and the Pardon Passus." *Speculum* 59 (1984): 342–62.

Bruns, Gerald L. "The Originality of Texts in a Manuscript Culture." *Inventions: Writing, Textuality, and Understanding in Literary History*. New Haven: Yale UP, 1982. 44–59.

Curtius, Ernst Robert. *European Literature and the Latin Middle Ages*. Trans. Willard R. Trask. New York: Harper and Row, 1963.

Durling, Robert M., trans. *Petrarch's Lyric Poems: The "Rime sparse" and Other Lyrics*. Cambridge: Harvard UP, 1976.

Enciclopedia Dantesca. 6 vols. Rome: Istituto della Enciclopedia Italiana, 1970–78. (*ED*)

Freccero, John. "Bestial Sign and Bread of Angels: *Inferno* XXXII and XXXIII." *Dante: The Poetics of Conversion*. Ed. Rachel Jacoff. Cambridge: Harvard UP, 1986. 152–66.

———. "Medusa: The Letter and the Spirit." *Dante: The Poetics of Conversion*. Ed. Rachel Jacoff. Cambridge: Harvard UP, 1986. 119–35.

15

Dante's Comedy, the Codex, and the Margin of Error

Gadamer, Hans-Georg. *Truth and Method*. New York: Seabury Press, 1975.

Garner of Langres. *Sermones*. Ed. J-P. Migne. *Patrologia Latina*. Vol. 205.

Gellrich, Jesse. *The Idea of the Book in the Middle Ages: Language Theory, Mythology and Fiction*. Ithaca: Cornell UP, 1985.

Grande Dizionario Italiano. (*GDI*)

Harrison, Robert P. *The Body of Beatrice*. Baltimore: Johns Hopkins University P, 1988.

Hollander, Robert. "*Inferno* XXXIII, 37–74: Ugolino's Importunity." *Speculum* 59 (1984): 549–55.

John of Howden. "Viola." *The Oxford Book of Medieval Latin Verse*. Ed. F. J. E. Raby. Oxford: Clarendon, 1961.

Mandelbaum, Allen, trans. *The Divine Comedy of Dante Alighieri*. New York: Bantam, 1982, 1984, 1986.

Mazzotta, Giuseppe. *Dante, Poet of the Desert*. Princeton: Princeton UP, 1979.

Pézard, André. "Le Chant des Traitres (*Enfer*, XXXII)." *Letture dell' "Inferno."* Ed. Vittorio Vettori. Milan: Mazorati, 1963. 308–42.

Petrocchi, Giorgio. Ed. *La "Commedia" secondo l'antica vulgata*. 4 vols. Società Dantesca Italiana. Milan: Mondadori, 1966–67.

Richard of St. Lawrence. *De Laudibus Beatae Virginis Mariae* (attributed to Albertus Magnus). Albertus Magnus, *Opera Omnia*. Vol. 36. Ed. Borgnet. Paris: Vives, 1898.

Salzer, Anselm. *Die Sinnbilder und Beiworte Mariens in der deutschen Literatur und lateinischen Hymnenpoesie des Mittelalters*. Linz: Jos. Feichtingers Erben, 1893.

16

Sapegno, Natalino. Ed. *La Divina Commedia.* 3 vols. Florence: "La Nuova Italia" Editrice, 1982.

Shoaf, R. A. *Dante, Chaucer, and the Currency of the Word: Money, Images, and Reference in Late Medieval Poetry.* Norman: Pilgrim Books, 1983.

———. "Ugolino and Erysichthon." *Dante and Ovid: Essays in Intertextuality.* Ed. Madison U. Sowell. Binghamton: MRTS, 1991. 51–64.

———. "Dante and Peraldus: The *aqua falsa* of Maestro Adamo (A Note on *Inferno* 30.64–69)." *Quaderni d'italianistica* 10 (1989):311–13.

Singleton, Charles S. *An Essay on the "Vita Nuova."* 1949; Baltimore: Johns Hopkins UP, 1977.

———, trans. *The Divine Comedy.* 3 vols. in 6. Bollingen Series LXXX. Princeton: Princeton UP, 1970–75.

In a Nutshell: Verba *and* Sententia *and Matter and Form in Medieval Composition Theory*

Marjorie Curry Woods

Two of the greatest medieval poets, Geoffrey Chaucer and Alan of Lille, have left us statements in their own poems about how to be good medieval readers of poetry. Chaucer's Nun's Priest succinctly counsels his listeners to "Taketh the fruyt, and lat the chaf be stille" (NPT 3443), while in *De planctu Naturae* Alan of Lille's Dame Natura tells us in a more leisurely fashion that

> Poetry's lyre rings with vibrant falsehood on the outward literal shell of a poem, but interiorly it communicates a hidden and profound meaning to those who listen. The man who reads with penetration, having cast away the outer shell of falsehood, finds the savory kernel of truth wrapped within. (Chenu 99)[1]

> Aut in superficiali littere cortice falsum resonat lira poetica, interius uero auditoribus secretum intelligentie altioris eloquitur, ut exteriore falsitatis abiecto putamine dulciorem nucleum ueritatis secrete intus lector inueniat. (837.133–36)

With whatever tone of voice we understand them to be conveyed, these old chestnuts attest to the power of the image of narrative poetry as composed of *verba*, the removable covering of words, surrounding the *sententia*, the meaning. Inherited as a cliché from the late classical

19

period and the early Middle Ages, this image was crystalized in the hierarchy of subjects in the educational system of the later Middle Ages, where the study of words formed the basis of, but was then superceded by, the study of thoughts.

The kernel or nut theory of poetry was also associated with levels of maturity on the part of the reader, as we see in the beginning of a commentary on Statius' *Thebaid* attributed to Fulgentius:

> A child is happy to play with the whole nut, but a wise adult breaks it open to get the taste; in the same way, as a child you can be satisfied with the literal meaning not broken or crushed by subtle explanation, but as a man you must break the literal and extract the kernel from it if you are to be refreshed by the taste. (239)

> Diligit puer nucem integram ad ludum, sapiens autem et adultus frangit ad gustum; similiter si puer es, habes sensum litteralem integrum multaque subtili expositione pressum in quo oblecteris, si adultus es, frangenda est littera et nucleus litterae eliciendus, cuius gustu reficiaris. (180.20–181.5)

Later, both parts of this division were further divided. First the literal level, or *verba*, was divided into "letter" and "sense," while *sententia* was reserved to describe the implied meaning, the kernel, as in Hugh of St. Victor's description in the *Didascalicon*:

> Exposition includes three things: the letter, the sense, and the inner meaning. The letter is the fit arrangement of words, which we also call construction; the sense is a certain ready and obvious meaning which the letter presents on the surface; the inner meaning is the deeper understanding which can be found only through interpretation and commentary. Among these, the order of inquiry is first the letter, then the sense, and finally the inner meaning. And when this is done, the exposition is complete.

20

expositio tria continet litteram, sensum, sententiam. littera est congrua
ordinatio dictionum, quod etiam constructionem vocamus. sensus est facius
quaedam et aperta significatio, quam littera prima fronte praefert. sententia
est profundior intelligentia, quae nisi expositione vel interpretatione non
invenitur. in his ordo est, ut primum littera, deinde sensus, deinde sententia
inquiratur. quo facto, perfecta est expositio. (3.viii)[2]

And just as the literal level opened into "word" and "meaning," the
idea of the "sentence" (implied meaning or inner meaning) developed
into the various levels of allegorical interpretation so well known to us
from the works of philosophical poets such as Dante and Petrarch who
wished to justify their poems within the system of values codified by
the medieval education system.

But while the sophistication both of medieval allegorical poetry
and of the allegorical interpretation of all kinds of texts has been
studied for some time, there is now increasing evidence that poetic
sophistication at the literal level was also prized and sought in
medieval poetry. The intertwining of the histories of the rhetorical and
philosophical traditions in medieval interpretation has enriched both,
but this same intertwining has also made it difficult for us to see that,
in looking at certain kinds of texts, the rhetorical and philosophical
traditions should be examined separately.

Although medieval philosophers and theologians usually defined
the literal level of poetry as the bottom half of a larger whole, late
medieval rhetoricians and poets often saw the literal or verbal level as
an end in itself.[3] In the rhetorical tradition, *sententia* retains its
meaning of "thought," or verbal content, as opposed to *verba*, verbal
form. These are distinct, but not to be separated, as in the philosophical
tradition. As John O. Ward has said about the twelfth-century historian
Otto of Freising,

Otto clearly considers his whole book (his *Deeds*) to be history, both

21

> narrative and digression. . . . This is the confidence of the rhetorical
> historian, contrasted with the temerity of the annalist or the caution of the
> exegete, who like to keep the historical sense to the simple linear narrative,
> the first meaning of a piece of writing, and reserve interpretation to other
> senses and levels. (117)

The rhetorical tradition provided the basis for the medieval training in composition that was offered in the lower schools. Since it taught appreciation of the whole nut, that is, the whole poem, rather than just the kernel, the rhetorical tradition may be a truer guide than the philosophical one to the interpretation of the poetry of the great vernacular writers of the High Middle Ages, for whom philosophical ideas were part of their literary (and hence rhetorical) world, rather than the other way around.

In the rhetorical tradition, the relationships of the concepts of *verba* to *sententia* and matter to form, which resonate in such a value-laden way in the philosophical, or kernel, school of interpretation, have aesthetic rather than philosophical, and variable rather than fixed, meanings. This flexible sense of hierarchy and definition, so different from what seems to be valued in the philosophical tradition,[4] is strikingly displayed in the medieval lecture notes on teaching poetry that comprise one of the commentaries on Geoffrey of Vinsauf's *Poetria nova*, a verse treatise about writing rhetorical poetry that was widely used in medieval schools to teach composition. This early commentary was developed in two different versions, one intended for older and one for younger students, and nine manuscripts of it have survived.[5]

In the version intended for older students we find two contradictory statements about the comparative value of *verba* and *sententia*. In one we are told that "distinction in subtlety of words is greater than distinction of idea" ("dignitas que est in subtilitate uerborum excedit dignitatem rei") (Woods, *An Early Commentary* 1117,5). In the other,

22

which comes only a few paragraphs later, we are told that "although a beautiful thought needs a corresponding setting in words, yet the first consideration is held by the distinction of thoughts" ("quamuis pulcra sententia conpetentem exigat verborum positionem, primus respectus habetur a dignitate sententiarum") (1230,9). That these two statements contradict each other is not a sign of sloppy thinking on the commentator's part; rather, each statement makes perfectly good sense in its context, and each context draws on a different tradition of interpretation.

Each statement arises in a discussion of one of the aspects of the structure of the *Poetria nova* in which the commentator offers possible objections to the way in which the author organized his text; then the commentator counters these objections, each time ending with praise of the text as written. That these examples are not found in the version of the commentary intended for younger students may be a sign that certain kinds of complexity and perhaps certain kinds of contradictions were felt to be suitable only for older students, those who were being trained not just to understand the *Poetria nova* but to imitate it.

The first statement, that "distinction in subtlety of words is greater than distinction of idea," is a commonplace in the medieval rhetorical tradition, and its context in the commentary is a discussion of why the figure of the Maxim, or *sententia*—the same word means "thought"—is "classified among the Figures of Words rather than the Figures of Thoughts (*sententiarum*) since it resembles the Figures of Thoughts in both name and substance."[6] That is, why is *sententia* a *figura verborum* rather than a *figura sententiarum*? The commentator responds that

One may say in answer to this that just as in grammar an adjective that modifies both masculine and feminine is made masculine on account of the greater distinction of that gender, so distinction in subtlety of words is greater than distinction of idea. And on account of this the Maxim (or

23

sententia) is listed more appropriately among the Figures of Words than the Figures of Thoughts. For there is such subtlety in the conciseness of words that many things can be understood in just a few words. . . .

Ad hoc dicatur quod sicut in gramatica adiectiuum quod determinat masculinum et femininum genus conformatur masculino propter dignitatem generis, ita et hec dignitas que est in subtilitate uerborum excedit dignitatem rei. Et propter hoc magis annumeratur inter exornationes uerborum quam sententiarum. Tanta est enim subtilitas in breuitate uerborum ut in paucis uerbis multa intelligantur. . . . (1117,5–7.)

The commentator means here that words have more power than their content; he goes on to illustrate this by pointing out that in a Maxim without an attached reason, an implied reason can be inferred even when unexpressed. Faral has noted that, for medieval teachers of poetry, the Figures of Words were much more important than the Figures of Thoughts, and that Marbode of Rennes and Matthew of Vendome did not even include the Figures of Thoughts in their treatises (93).

The second example, in which thoughts are described as having greater value than words ("the first consideration is held by the distinction of thoughts"), is a commonplace in the philosophical tradition. It comes in the introduction to the section of the *Poetria nova* on the Figures of Thought, in which the commentator examines why the author of the *Poetria nova* gives not only examples but also definitions of the Figures of Thought, while he gave only examples for the Figures of Words. The commentator says,

One could argue that just as in the adornment of words he puts only the examples, so in the adornment of thoughts he should have expressed only the definitions. Or, one could argue that just as there he puts only examples, so, here, too, he should have put just the examples. . . .

To the second objection it should be said that, although a beautiful

24

thought needs a corresponding setting in words, yet the first consideration is held by the distinction of thoughts. And on account of this, he expresses the thought through definitions since they cannot be understood sufficiently through examples alone.

[V]idetur quoe sicut <in ornatu> uerborum sola exempla uerborum ponit, ita in ornatu sententiarum exprimere debuit solas <diffinitiones> sine exemplis. Item uidetur quod sicut ibi sola exempla ponit, ita et hic ponere debuit exempla sine diffinitionibus. . . .

    Ad aliud dicendum quod quamuis pulcra sententia conpetentem exigat uerborum positionem, tamen primus respectvs habetur a dignitate sententiarum. Et propter hoc eas expressit per diffinitiones quia sufficienter non poterant intelligi per sola exempla. (1230,3–4 and 9–10)

These examples of the commentator's interest in the author's motives and rhetorical purpose in structuring his work are typical. In fact, a discussion of the construction of the *Poetria nova* comprises most of the *accessus*, or introduction, to the commentary. We might have expected this discussion to be anchored in the terms *materia* and *forma*, matter and form. These terms are, indeed, used in a number of other places in the commentary in philosophical contexts, such as in the gloss on line 966, the definition of metonymy. There the commentator notes that Geoffrey "presents two kinds of metonymy of his own devising, namely when the abstract is put for the concrete and when the matter is put for the form" ("Unde auctor iste duas species de suo apposuit ingenio, scilicet quando ponitur abstractum pro concreto et cum ponitur materia pro forma") (966,8). In the version intended for older students, the commentator adds,

These two kinds [of metonymy] are in a subtle way related to each other and interchangeable. For when the abstract is put for the concrete, the form is put for the matter. When the matter is put for the form, however, only the matter can be put for the form [i.e, all instances of matter put for form are not instances of concrete for abstract]. . . .

Et ille due species subtiliter sibi adherent et conuertuntur. Cum enim ponitur abstractum pro concreto, ponitur forma pro materia. Cum autem ponitur materia pro forma, ponitur sola materia pro forma. . . . (966,9–11)

But while the introduction does discuss the *materia* (here meaning subject) of the *Poetria nova*, the commentator does not use the term *forma* to describe the complementary, to modern ears, aspect of the poem. Rather, the commentary describes two organizing principles that determine the parts of the *Poetria nova*; one of these is derived from the *materia* and the other from the instrument used to convey the *materia*, the latter being what we might refer to as the form, although the commentator does not.[7] These two organizing principles are discussed in the answer to one of the formulaic questions that make up the *accessus*. In the discussion of the first organizing principle, or structure, the commentator says that in order to answer the question, "What is treated in this book?" we should look for the book's subject, its *materia*.

The subject of this book is artful eloquence, or rhetoric, according to which art the book teaches poets to speak metrically. Whence the book principally consists of the five parts of rhetoric; these five make up the whole in such a way that if one part is missing, rhetoric cannot be complete, just as a house cannot be complete if the foundation or the walls or the roof is missing.

Materia autem huius libri est artificiosa eloquentia, scilicet rethorica, secundum quam docet poetas metrice <loqui>. Unde ex quinque partibus <eius> constat principaliter; sunt enim quinque partes rethorice que eam integraliter constituerunt, ita ut si desit una pars, rethorica non possit esse integra, sicut nec domus potest esse integra si desit fundamentum uel paries uel tectum. (*accessus* 3–4)[8]

The commentator goes on to name the five parts of rhetoric

(Invention, Arrangement, Style, Memory, and Delivery), to quote Cicero's definition of them, to show their natural order in terms of an orator's addressing a case, and to divide the *Poetria nova* into sections that deal separately with each of these parts of the rhetorical art. He says that the book "primarily consists of the five parts of rhetoric" and then adds that "all the parts of rhetoric involve, basically, Invention" ("Principaliter enim constat ex quinque partibus rethorice. Secondario constat ex sola inuentione quantum ad partes eius") (*accessus* 26–27).

But the commentator also describes a second organizing principle, or structure. He says that the instrument of the art of rhetoric is the discourse, which has six parts: Introduction, Narration, Division or Distribution, Proof, Rebuttal or Refutation, and Conclusion; he quotes Cicero's definitions of these terms and shows how the *Poetria nova* is divided into the parts of a discourse: "And the book consists, in a secondary way, of these six parts of a discourse" ("Et ex istis sex liber iste constat secondario") (*accessus* 25).

Thus, the work has both a five-part structure and a six-part structure. One is the structure of its matter (the art of rhetoric), and this is called its primary structure; the other is the structure of its form (the discourse), the instrument used to convey the matter, and this is the secondary structure.

For the commentator, both structures are to be appreciated simultaneously. For example, at the famous architectural image that begins "If a man has a house to build" (43), the commentator says,

> This section is assigned first to Invention [a part of rhetoric] and second to the Narration section of a discourse. It fits the description of either, for here he teaches how the *materia* ought first to be found, and having completed the Introduction section of the discourse, here through the Narration he sets out the work of his instruction.

> Locus iste principaliter assignatur inuentioni et secundario narrationi.

27

Verba *and* Sententia *and Matter and Form*

Conuenit enim descriptioni utriusque, nam docet hic quomodo materia
debeat primo inueniri, et, premisso exordio, hic exponit opus sue doctrine
<per narrationem>. (43,1–2.)

The other parts of both structures are introduced in the same way.
Indeed, the commentator spends a great deal of time both explaining
the dual structure of the *Poetria nova* in his introduction and then
actually showing the students the layout of this double structure as he
leads them through the *Poetria nova* in his glosses. The double form
or structure of the poem is pointed out as an aspect of the author's
control and skill—a complexity to be admired, and if possible,
imitated.

It is important to recognize that these structures are not identical
with the *dispositio*, or Arrangement, of the work, at least according to
the commentator. In his treatment of *dispositio* Geoffrey discusses two
kinds of order, natural and artificial, of which the latter, artificial order,
is more artistic and to be desired in poetry. Although these kinds of
order usually refer to the chronological order of events in a narrative,
other kinds of rearrangements of order were considered equally
artificial and, thus, artistic.

The commentator points out that the author of the *Poetria nova*
uses a mixture of natural and artificial order. For example, the discussion of the third part of the art of rhetoric, Style, takes up more than
half of the text (lines 208–1969) and consists of the discussion of
natural and artificial order, difficult and easy ornament (the tropes and
figures), the theory of conversions, and the theory of determinations.
In his introduction to the section on the theory of conversions (i.e.,
converting an idea to a different part of speech in order to convey it
more effectively or artistically), the commentator notes that Geoffrey
moves from a sophisticated concept, the adornment of verse through
the tropes and figures, back to a more basic concept. The theory of

28

conversions, he says, "is like the milky food and nourishment of boys, while [the adornment of verse] is like the solid food of those who are grown and independent."[9] In the version intended for older students, the commentator justifies this order because it is deliberate artificial order:

> Nothing is done out of order in this book. Rather, all parts are arranged according to a reasoned Artificial Order, for it is appropriate that this book, like others, be arranged according to a specific order. Note that in this book he subtly combines both orders. . . . He uses Natural Order since he follows the parts of rhetoric and the six parts of a discourse that were discussed above according to their own order, which could not be changed. He uses Artificial Order since he puts [the Theory of Conversions] afterward, which according to Natural Order ought to have been first. . . . .

> [N]il inordinate agitur in hoc libro sed omnia secundum rationabilem et artificialem ordinem disponuntur, oportet enim quod iste liber sicut alii secundum aliquem ordinem sit dispositus. . . . Naturali ordine utitur quia partes rethorice et illas sex species orationis de quibus supraductum est prosequitur <secundum> ordinem suum qui mutari non poterat. Artificiali utitur ordine quia postponit hanc doctrinam que preponi debuerat secundum ordinem naturalem. . . . (1588,9–12)

In this commentary, therefore, we find multiple concepts of the relationship of *verba* to *sententia* and matter to form, all resonating with aesthetic possibility and all at what we would call the literal level of the poem.

There seem to me to be several important uses for this information in our own criticism of medieval poetry. First, such information gives medieval sanction to the modern approaches to medieval literature that find this literature most fascinating and complex at its "literal" level. Second, I think that the kind of interpretation of dual form that the commentator describes in the *Poetria nova* should encourage us to accept layers of structure in medieval poetry that we might otherwise attempt to simplify or explain away.

In order to examine both of these uses, let us return to Chaucer, the author with whom we began. Chaucer was learned enough in the philosophical and theological tradition to parody it even while making a serious point (which is what I think that he is doing in the fruit and chaff statement quoted at the beginning), but also rhetorically adroit to a degree and with an originality almost beyond our ability to appreciate. This sophistication in composition at the literal level of Chaucer's work has been noted by John Fyler in his work on Chaucer's use of classical and medieval sources. Following Robert Hollander on Dante (214–42), Fyler has made clear the almost infinitely complex use that Dante has made of Statius and Ovid, and that Chaucer has made of Statius, Ovid, and Dante—all at the literal level of the texts. Fyler comments that "this way of using a classical text . . . demands . . . an active, free-ranging attentiveness to its literal surface" (77). He also notes that

> In [several important] fourteenth-century interpretations of an *auctor* [that is, Dante] to whom Chaucer also alludes, the dominant concern—perhaps surprisingly—is with the literal surface of the text. . . . Their literalness, moreover, copies the inclinations of Dante himself. As Robert Hollander has forcefully argued, Dante seems not to have been much influenced by medieval allegorical commentaries on the classics. Instead the *Commedia* is characterized by "acutely literal translations or references to the *Aeneid* and other classical works." (81)

Finally, Fyler notes that "Chaucer uses Dante, then, as he uses the classics, attending to the narrative surface. . ." (85). Spearing makes a telling point with regard to the sophisticated use of the literal level in the *Book of the Duchess*, and the commentary on the *Poetria nova* that I have been quoting emphasizes that sophistication at the literal level was valued and taught for its own sake.

But what about some of the other aspects of Chaucer's work that trouble us, the places where we know that he is doing something, but are still not sure, or at least there is no general consensus about, just what this might be? Return for a moment to The Nun's Priest's Tale, Chaucer's barnyard fable. Near the end of the tale but before the fruit and chaff statement, at the beginning of his parody of the Apostrophe to Friday (one of the most famous passages in the *Poetria nova*), Chaucer apostrophizes Geoffrey of Vinsauf and asks for inspiration in his own parody of an apostrophe to follow. In the *Poetria nova* itself, the discussion of apostrophe comes in the section on amplification, which is very amplified; it is followed by a very abbreviated section on abbreviation. The shortness of Vinsauf's section on abbreviation has bothered some modern critics, leading them to conclude that medieval authors were interested only in amplification.[10] But as the commentary I have quoted earlier points out,

> Since he is teaching about Abbreviation he does so briefly, just as above he delayed a long time on the seven methods by which material is amplified. And he does this so that the text and the teaching reinforce each other in everything.

> Quos quia <de> breuitate docet sub breuitate restringit, sicut et supra in illis septem modis quibus ampliabatur materia, diutius est immoratus. Et hic agit ut in omnibus res et doctrina sibi conueniant (690,2–3)

In an unpublished lecture, Margaret Nims has argued that one way of looking at The Nun's Priest's Tale is to see it as a parody of a school exercise in *amplificatio*, and to see the work that precedes it, The Monk's Tale (a collection of short narratives), as a parody of school exercises in *abbreviatio*.[11] But taking what has been said in the commentary about Geoffrey of Vinsauf's own treatment of ab-

31

breviation— that it is appropriately brief—we should now go back to The Monk's Tale and take another look: we find an example of abbreviation run amok. Rather than generating conciseness, the exercise generates endless garrulity. The Knight, foreseeing the endless amplification of abbreviation to come, interrupts. In these two tales we have examples of *abbreviatio* and *amplificatio* of the same length flanking each other, but compulsive, tedious abbreviation of the most sensational aspects of the lives of great personages cheek by jowl with exuberant, entertaining amplification of a day in the life of a rooster. Here not only abbreviation and amplification but also the proper form and the proper matter for each are parodied.

Medieval writers and their audiences had an almost limitless capacity and appetite for this kind of parody. Yet verbal and structural complexity is not always humorous, as we can see from a final example, also from the *Canterbury Tales*—all of them. I hope that I have already demonstrated that in medieval literature *materia* may have its own structural requirements, and that the instrument which the author chooses to convey the material may have different structural requirements. These two structures may be treated in their usual, "natural" order or more artistically; or the two orders may work together contrapuntally to great effect. If we approach the *Canterbury Tales* from this perspective, we may be able to reconcile conflicting modern approaches by allowing them to exist simultaneously.

Thus, the announced instrument of telling in the *Canterbury Tales*, the symmetrical, circular pattern of two tales for each teller on the way up and two on the way back, with the postulated narrative ending with a festive evening in the same hostel where it began, provides us with one organizing principle of the work, albeit an unfinished one. But the structural demands of the evolving *materia* itself, the themes that connect fragments, invoke their referentiality, and progress with an increasingly tense focus that finally annihilates poetic form and narrative matter altogether, all generate a second, linear structure that ends with The Parson's Tale and Chaucer's Retraction (Woods, "Poetic Digression" 622–23).

These two structures are a source of constant debate among modern scholars about their relative strength and importance, but a knowledge of medieval acceptance of and even particular delight in dual organizing structures can help us to realize that the resonance between the two may have provided Chaucer's audience with a special kind of pleasure. In addition, we might also learn to see the interruptions and rearrangements of the tales that the tellers themselves seem to bring about as not just a new kind of narrative and social realism, but as a kind of artificial order that affects both structures. This artificial order is enhanced, rather than destroyed, by the alterations or confusion of the scribes, for in whatever state of completion we believe the *Canterbury Tales* to have come down to us, and in whatever manuscript order we read them, Chaucer repeatedly calls our attention to these structures, both of which function at the literal level of the poem, and to the rearrangements to which they are subject in the development of his work. Because artificial order is defined by what it is not, rather than what it is, any deviation has a potential artistic function (and in most cases, a modern critical advocate—e.g., Owen, and Allen and Moritz).

The *Canterbury Tales*, more than any other group of framed narratives that have come down to us from the Middle Ages, demand interpretation of the arrangements of the parts and their relation to the whole, while at the same time the tales force us (as they seem to have forced their early scribes) to speculate about other arrangements, which in turn produce new interpretations. Chaucer's new kind of "artificial order" is one solution to the fear of scribal mishandling that he articulates so evocatively at the end of the more tightly-structured, and hence more vulnerable, *Troilus and Criseyde*: "So prey I God that non myswrite the, / Ne the mysmetre for defaute of tonge" (5.1795–96). Similar fears are expressed in "Chaucers Wordes unto Adam, His Owne Scriveyn," in which Chaucer chides Adam that "I mot thy werk renewe, / It to correcte and eke to rubbe and scrape, / And al is thorugh thy negligence and rape" (5–7). The theme of the impermanence and elusiveness of words and thoughts, of matters and forms, permeates Chaucer's works. It is fitting that the *Canterbury Tales*, his last long work, takes it power from these very qualities.

NOTES

1. English translations are taken from the relevant translations listed in Works Cited and precede the Latin originals for intelligibility; Latin texts are taken from the Latin editions cited in Works Cited.

2. In the most influential modern study of the allegorical interpretation of medieval works, D. W. Robertson paraphrases Hugh as follows in order to clarify the seemingly contradictory medieval terminology: "[T]he exposition of a text involves the examination of three things: the *letter*, the *sense*, and the *sentence*. A study of the letter involves the techniques of grammatical analysis. The sense is the obvious or surface meaning of a text, and the sentence is its doctrinal content or 'higher' meaning. . . . The purpose of exposition is to arrive at the *sentence*, since a text which has no third level does not require explanation. Following this convention, it became customary after the twelfth century to speak of the import of a text, whether sacred or profane, as its *sentence*. It should be remembered, however, that an older convention used only two terms: *letter* and *sense*. . . . The result of allegorical interpretation might be called either *sense* or *sentence*. The latter term was somewhat more popular during the fourteenth century" (315–16).

3. This medieval emphasis on the literal level of the poem in the rhetorical tradition is an outgrowth of earlier developments in interpretation which had their roots in twelfth-century biblical commentaries, developments that were themselves influenced by "the introductions to the *artes* which were being elaborated in the twelfth century on the basis of classical and late antique models" (Smalley 216). A parallel development took

34

place in rabbinical commentaries (Signer 333–37), and these developments in biblical commentaries influenced attitudes toward literary texts and authorship (Minnis). See also Lorenz on the exposition of the literal meaning of the works of Aristotle in the universities of Central Europe during the second half of the thirteenth century and the fourteenth century (210–11). But in the medieval universities, the literal sense was taught in addition to, and usually as further support of, the allegorical meaning of a text. See Fletcher on the emphasis on teaching the literal level of the text in humanist reforms of the universities (3 and 8).

4. Not that philosophical and theological commentators were unaware of the attraction of textual difficulty and irresolvability in the classroom; see Smalley on Stephen Langton (221).

5. The four thirteenth-century manuscripts of the commentary have been edited (Woods, *An Early Commentary*), and this edition also includes a short description of four of the later manuscripts (xlviii–xlix). The ninth, a fifteenth-century manuscript at Fulda (Landesbibliothek MS. C8), was identified after the edition went to press. A tenth manuscript, Metz, Bibl. Munic. MS. 516, dating from the fourteenth century, was destroyed during World War II. For a discussion of other differences between the two versions and the implications of these differences for our understanding of medieval methods of teaching composition, see Woods, "Classical Examples." The Latin text of the *Poetria nova* can be found in Faral 198–262; for an English translation see Margaret F. Nims, trans., *Poetria Nova of Geoffrey of Vinsauf* (Toronto: Pontifical Institute of Mediaeval Studies, 1967).

6. "Queritur autem quare hec exornatio, scilicet sententia, annumeretur inter exornationes uerborum et non sententiarum, cum tamen exornationibus sententiarum conueniat et nomine et re" (1117,4).

7. The terms *forma tractatus* and *forma tractandi*, common in many medieval *accessus* including those of other commentaries on the *Poetria nova*, are not found in any manuscript of this commentary. Several of the later manuscripts of the commentary are, however, lacking an *accessus*.

8. Note the architectural metaphor here, so important in the *Poetria nova* itself and quoted from it in Chaucer's *Troilus and Criseyde* (1.1065–69).

35

9. "Itaque <ista> doctrina est quasi lacteus cibus et nutrimentum puerorum; illa autem superior est quasi cibus solidus perfectorum et discretorum" (1588,3). Chaucer's *Treatise on the Astrolabe* is entitled "Brede and milke for children" in several manuscripts (*Complete Works* 3: lix; *Riverside Chaucer* 1195).

10. Frank's book on the *Legend of Good Women* has, however, generated new interest in abbreviation.

11. See Travis for other kinds of parodies of school exercises in The Nun's Priest's Tale.

Marjorie Curry Woods

WORKS CITED

Alan of Lille, *De planctu naturae*. Ed. Nicholas Häring. *Studi medievali* 3rd ser. 19.2 (1978): 797–879.

Allen, Judson B., and Theresa A. Moritz. *A Distinction of Stories: The Medieval Unity of Chaucer's Fair Chain of Narratives for Canterbury*. Columbus: Ohio State UP, 1981.

Chaucer, Geoffrey. *Complete Works of Geoffrey Chaucer*. Ed. Walter W. Skeat. 6 vols. Oxford: Clarendon, 1894.

———. *The Riverside Chaucer*. General ed. Larry D. Benson. Boston: Houghton Mifflin, 1987. All quotations are taken from this edition.

Chenu, M. D. *Nature, Man, and Society in the Twelfth Century*. Trans. Jerome Taylor and Lester K. Little. Chicago: U of Chicago P, 1968.

Faral, Edmond. *Les Arts poétiques du xiie et xiiie siècle: Rechèrches et documents sur la technique littéraire du moyen âge*. Paris: Sieul, 1924; rpt. 1962.

Fletcher, John M. "Change and Resistance to Change: A Consideration of the Development of English and German Universities During the Sixteenth Century." *History of Universities* 1 (1981): 1–35.

Frank, Robert Worth, Jr. *Chaucer and the Legend of Good Women*. Cambridge, Mass.: Harvard UP, 1972.

Fulgentius. *Fulgentius the Mythographer*. Trans. Leslie George Whitbred. Columbus: Ohio State UP, 1971.

———. *Fabili Planciadis Fulgentii V.C. Opera. . . .* Ed. Rudolf Helm. Leipzig: Teubner, 1898.

Fyler, John. "*Auctoritee* and Allusion in *Troilus and Criseyde*." *Res Publica Litterarum* 7 (1984): 73–93.

37

Verba *and* Sententia *and Matter and Form*

Hollander, Robert. *Allegory in Dante's Commedia*. Princeton: Princeton UP, 1964.

Hugh of St. Victor. *Didascalicon: A Medieval Guide to the Arts*. Trans. Jerome Taylor. New York: Columbia UP, 1961.

———. *Didascalicon: De Studio Legendi*. Ed. Charles Henry Buttimer. Washington, D.C.: Catholic UP, 1939.

Lorenz, Sönke. "LIBRI ORDINARIE LEGENDI: Eine Skizze zum Lehrplan der middeleuropäischen Artistenfakultät um die Wende vom 14. zum 15. Jahrhundert." *Argumente und Zeugnisse*. Ed. Wolfram Hogrebe. Studia Philosophica et Historica 5. Frankfurt am Main: Peter Lang, 1985. 204–58.

Minnis, A. J. *Medieval Theory of Authorship: Scholastic Literary Attitudes in the Later Middle Ages*. London: Scolar P, 1984.

Owen, Charles A., Jr. "The Alternative Reading of the *Canterbury Tales*: Chaucer's Text and the Early Manuscripts." *PMLA* 97 (1982): 237–50.

Robertson, D. W. *A Preface to Chaucer: Studies in Medieval Perspectives*. Princeton: Princeton UP, 1962.

Signer, Michael. "St. Jerome and Andrew of St. Victor: Some Observations." *Studia Patristica* 18 (1982): 333–37.

Smalley, Beryl. *Study of the Bible in the Middle Ages*. Notre Dame: U of Notre Dame P, 1964.

Spearing, A. C. "Literal and Figurative in the *Book of the Duchess*." *Studies in the Age of Chaucer*. Proceedings No. 1, 1984: *Reconstructing Chaucer*. Knoxville: New Chaucer Society, U of Tennessee, 1985. 165–71.

Travis, Peter. "*The Nun's Priest's Tale* as Grammar School Primer." *Reconstructing Chaucer*. Knoxville: New Chaucer Society, U of Tennessee, 1985. 81–91.

Ward, John O. "Some Principles of Rhetorical Historiography in the Twelfth Century."

Marjorie Curry Woods

Classical Rhetoric and Medieval Historiography. Ed. Ernst Breisach. Studies in Medieval Culture 19. Kalamazoo: Medieval Institute Publications, 1985. 103–65.

Woods, Marjorie Curry. "Classical Examples and References in Medieval Lectures on Poetic Composition." *Allegorica* 10 (1989): 3–12.

———. *An Early Commentary on the* Poetria nova *of Geoffrey of Vinsauf.* Garland Medieval Texts 12. New York: Garland, 1985.

———. "Poetic Digression and the Interpretation of Medieval Literary Texts." *Acta Conventus Neo-latini Sanctandreanae.* Ed. I. D. McFarlane. Medieval & Renaissance Texts & Studies 38. Binghamton: MRTS, 1986. 617–26.

How Was the ars praedicandi *Taught in England?*

Marianne G. Briscoe

In the period marked by the end of the twelfth century and the beginning of the sixteenth century, specialists in preaching produced hundreds of works known today as *artes praedicandi* or manuals on the art of preaching. The English were particularly prolific manual writers. The motive for this outpouring of instructional material remains unclear. The possibility that the *artes* were used as textbooks in medieval schools of theology or in other venues for religious study has long interested specialists in the history of rhetoric. The complementary manuals or *artes* on grammar and poetic seem to have had clear roles in the university course of study, so it would seem appropriate that the *artes praedicandi* would have been used in a similar manner. Richard Schoeck has suggested that this was the case at Oxford. James J. Murphy, countering the theories on rhetorical instruction in English universities advanced by John Matthews Manly in *Chaucer and the Rhetoricians*, concluded, "the *ars praedicandi* was not taught at all . . . since preaching was learned after completion of formal education" ("Literary Implications" 120). Murphy and Schoeck went on to debate this issue in several articles in scholarly journals.[1] At present, there seems to be no convincing evidence that the preaching manuals were part of the course of study in English (or indeed in any Continental) universities; nor is there any suggestion that they were used in cathedral schools or other centers of instruction. The question remains, however, how these obviously instructional treatises were used if not in formally taught courses.

41

How Was the ars praedicandi *Taught in England?*

It is likely that instruction in preaching was needed. Preaching went on virtually every day in England in the Middle Ages. This seems clear from the great numbers of sermons and sermon collections surviving from the era. Most contain sermons designated for particular days. One typical style of collection, usually titled *sermones dominicales*, provided a sermon for each Sunday of the year. Another, often called the *sanctorale* or *sermones de sanctis*, supplied sermons for each saint's day. In combination with other collections, these compendia suggest that late medieval practice envisioned at least one sermon to be delivered each day by mendicants or in major places of worship.

Frequency and quality of preaching were, in addition, regular concerns of the papacy as the Church sought to quell heresy and strengthen the faith and morals of the laity. Emphasis on the obligation of the priest to preach dates from the earliest days of Christianity. In the Middle Ages Gregory the Great's *Cura pastoralis* (Part 2, Chapter iv; PL 77.13–128) addressed the need for regular preaching as did Rabanus Maurus' *De institutione clericorum*, and the Carolingian *Admonitio generalis*, A.D. 789 (*MGH*, Leges, II, 1). Canon X of the Fourth Lateran Council (A.D. 1215) ordered sermons for the laity at least four times per year. In England, Archbishop John Peckham's *Constitutions* (A.D. 1281) repeated this mandate and even specified the texts to be preached:

quotuordecim fidei articulos; decem mandata decalogi; duo praecepta evangelii, scilicet, geminae charitatis; septem opera misericordiae; septem virtutes principales; ac septem gratiae sacramenta.

the fourteen articles of faith, ten mandates of the decalogue, two precepts of the evangelist, that is the twin charities; the seven works of mercy, the seven principal virtues, and the seven sacraments of grace. (Wilkins 51)

42

Marianne G. Briscoe

Preaching was without doubt the most important and regularly exercised form of rhetorical expression in the Middle Ages. In view of these circumstances, it is indeed surprising that we have little idea how preaching was learned. We do have a substantial body of *artes praedicandi* which suggests that considerable effort was devoted to promulgating a theory of preaching and to raising the standards of pulpit oratory. Despite this legacy, we have made little progress in understanding how these manuals were used or for whom they were intended. This negative itself needs probing, for we need to understand why the *artes praedicandi* were written at all and how they were used if they were not intended for classroom use. A quick review of the genre can help set the context for considering the matter.

The *ars praedicandi* first appeared in the late twelfth century. While traditional scholarship believes that Alan of Lille wrote the first fully conceived manual about 1198, others would give that distinction to Thomas of Salisbury (also thought to be Thomas Chobham [Morenzoni]) or Alexander of Esseby (or Ashby). Alan's work was followed by a veritable preaching manual "industry" that flourished for almost two hundred years. Today we know of about two hundred different medieval preaching manuals surviving in some four hundred manuscripts. The *ars praedicandi* remained a vigorous genre until well into the Renaissance (for MSS. see Caplan, *Mediaeval artes* and *Supplementary hand-list*; Gallick inventories early printed editions).

Preaching manuals varied in length. Robert Basevorn's, one of the longest, is ninety pages in T.-M. Charland's edition (233–323). Many, such as Simon Alcock's *De modo dividendi thema pro materia sermonis dilatanda* (ed. Boynton) or Henry of Hesse's (ed. Caplan), run to just a few leaves. Alcock's text is eight leaves in its longest manuscript exemplar (BL MS. Royal 8 E.XII). The Latin text of Henry of Hesse, also known as Henry of Langenstein, runs for just seven pages in Caplan's edition, based on several incunabula; in manuscript exemplars, its length is hard to determine since it is conflated with other manuals. Very few of these works have ever been edited, and textual traditions and ascriptions of authorship for a great many of the manuals are tangled.

The *artes* describe how a sermon is to be composed. The shorter ones such as Alcock's and Henry of Hesse's offer rather mechanical descriptions of thematic sermon structure and a few admonitions on content and delivery style. The longer and more thoughtful ones, such as the works by Robert of Basevorn, Thomas Waleys, Jacques Fusignano, and Johannes Surgant, address the traditions and styles of preaching from the time of John the Baptist to the present, the important place of preaching in the life of the priest, the demands it places on him for proper conduct and diligent learning, and the rhetorical strategies appropriate to various classes of auditors.[2] Sometimes the manuals preceded sermon collections; see, for example, Alan of Lille's and Michael of Hungary's.[3] Most manuals at least provide short sermon passages to illustrate their points.

The first *artes praedicandi* appeared in the early years of the Church's re-emphasis on pastoral theology. Though the manuals predate the establishment of the mendicant preaching orders, the friars quickly dominated the ranks of *ars praedicandi* authors. The manuals at first considered all styles and venues for preaching. But by the mid-thirteenth century two traditions emerge, one which treats the highly embellished and complex university sermon, the other which considers the requirements of more common, pastorally focused preaching.

University statutes, lists of texts, glosses, and commentaries offer no suggestion that the *ars praedicandi* was part of the university curriculum. Yet there remain some six hundred manuscripts dating from about 1200 to 1500. The men who chose to write manuals were most often university masters of theology who were also sometimes leading figures in the mendicant orders. Thus Humbert of Romans, the first General of the Dominican order, wrote one. The fourth lector of the Franciscans at Oxford, Thomas Waleys, wrote a manual, as did William of Esseby, first Warden of Grey Friars at Oxford, and John of Wales, Regent Master of the Franciscan school at Oxford (ob. 1260).[4] Alan of Lille had been a master of theology at Paris. Other manuals were spuriously ascribed to great churchmen such as Aquinas and Bonaventure (Caplan, "A Late Medieval" and Pseudo-Bonaventure).

The known authors of the manuals were most often individuals active in advanced theological training at universities, houses of study, or cathedral schools. Furthermore, the usual explanation of "why this little book was written" most often speaks of the need of some audience to learn about preaching. Robert of Basevorn notes that he "was importuned with many insistent requests by different Religious or various Orders and at the same time by seculars."[5] Christian Borgsleben of Erfurt writes on vernacular preaching to the people because the universities teach much about holy scripture but neglect this subject—so useful for the preacher:

> Cum in his temporibus plures sint universitates, in quibus nutriuntur viri inbuti in sacris scripturis experti, sicut et in artibus habentes ex acquisita sarcina et usu scripturarum legendi sedulum modum colligendi, dictandi modo collaciones modo sermones ad populum, qui modus sermocinandi istis temporibus valde est usitatus—Consuetudinis namque est in locis studiorum ordinibus atque conventibus, ubi puerorum erat multitudo, quod lectores 2^i in philosophia vel fratres officio legentiae fungentes philosophantibus atque in artibus proficientibus collaciones breves consueverunt formare in quarum recitacione exercebantur iuvenes fratres et reddebantur animosi, patres nichilominus audientes huiusmodi collaciones vel sermones recitare perpendebant ydoneitatem fratrum ad studia in eloquencia et sedulitate proficiendi, et hic modus ad nos traditus videtur fere abolitus, quem ut valerem resuscitare, pro informacione cogitavi studentibus ad

How Was the ars praedicandi Taught in England?

Erfordiam missis tradere formam aliquam formandi collaciones et sermones atque introducciones de simplicitate mei ingenii, alciora et sublimiora manibus maiorum reservans, ut igitur rudi stilo simplices intelligant aliquid de modo colligendi, fretus auxilio divino taliter procedam. . . .

In present times there are many universities in which unlearned men are trained in holy scripture and the arts, having acquired enormous storehouses of scriptures from practice in reading and painstaking collation; men, who at this time greatly need a method of preaching, now deliver homilies or sermons to the people. It was the custom in houses of study and in convents, where there were many boys, that 2nd degree readers in philosophy or brothers proficient in the arts serving as teachers would devise short homilies which young brothers were trained to recite and repeat with vigor. The fathers, hearing these homilies or sermons, evaluated the fitness of the brother for success and diligence in the study of eloquence. It would be good to revive this tradition which seems to have been lost by us. I have thought to pass on for training students sent to Erfurt some form of my simple creation for making homilies and sermons and introductions, keeping back the complexity and subtlety from the hands of the many so that in a rude style the simple may understand something of the method of homilizing. Let me proceed in such a way relying on divine assistance. . . . (Buchwald 68–69; trans. my own)

Gerard du Pescher begins his manual, "Quesivisti a me utrum de faciendis collationibus et sermonibus possit ars specialis aliqua inveniri . . ." ("you have asked me whether a special art can be found for preparing homilies and sermons . . .") (Delorme 180; trans. my own).

So it is that, while they seem not to have had a place in the classroom, many of these *artes* were nonetheless written to help students of some sort become preachers. This should not be surprising since those who chose the theology course in medieval universities were priests destined to preach throughout their careers. Peter the Chanter put this vocation squarely in the context of theology studies in declaring

46

preaching to be the "third and crowning function of the theologian" (Baldwin 13). Most of the manuals also speak forcefully of the priest's vocation to learn, teach, and preach. Alan of Lille, for example, opens his manual with an elaborate image of Jacob's ladder, each rung a level of vocation—and the seventh and highest is preaching:

> Vidit scalam Jacob a terra usque ad coelum attingentem, per quam ascendebant et descendebant angeli (Gen. xxvii). Scala est profectus viri catholici, qui congeritur ab initio fidei, usque ad consummationem viri perfecti. In hac scala primus gradus est, confessio; secundus, oratio; tertius, gratiarum actio; quartus, Scripturarum perscrutatio; quintus, si aliquid occurrat dubium in Scriptura, a majore inquisitio; sextus, Scripturae expositio; septimus, pradicatio.

> Jacob saw a ladder reaching from earth to heaven by which angels were ascending and descending [Genesis 27]. The ladder is the progress of universal man who has been brought up from the beginning by faith to the consummately perfect man. In this ladder the first step is confession; second, prayer; third, acts of grace; fourth, study of Scripture; fifth, if some difficulty in reading Scripture arises, assistancy of a superior; sixth, exposition of scripture; seventh, preaching. (111; trans. my own)

To incept in theology, candidates had first to complete the arts course; their entire university career would take about seventeen years[6] and their theology studies would focus on the study of the Bible and the Sentences. While this course should not be characterized as purely speculative, practical, pastoral theology had but a small place in the curriculum.

Although preaching was not a subject of university study, it was, nonetheless, part of the requirements for the theology degree. The 1215 statutes of Oxford require Franciscans incepting in theology to have "publicly preached in the university." By 1303 they were required to preach this "examination" sermon either at Black Friars or Grey

Friars. In 1314 it was moved to the larger and more public St. Mary the Virgin Church and a second Latin sermon, explicitly not for "examination," was required. By 1314 a third sermon, at St. Peter's, St. Frideswide's or St. Mary's Churches, was required (Gibson 50–53, 116–18, 238, 244, 267, 268; see also Little 38–53). Corpus Christi College's 1517 statutes required theology students to preach several sermons in nearby parishes and towns (Blomfield 55). The importance of examination sermons can be seen in that those offered by Thomas Aquinas, Stephen Langton, and Thomas Chobham, among others, survive (Baldwin 112).

Since there was no place in the formal curriculum for instruction in preaching, the specter of an approaching examination sermon surely sent more than a few university students to Thomas Waleys' *De modo componendi sermones* or similar manuals for authoritative guidance. It is this market, I believe, that accounts for the increasingly subtle and complex preaching styles developed in some of the thirteenth- and fourteenth-century manuals.

But what of the sermon first mandated by the thirteenth-century Lambeth Constitutions?

> every priest having the charge of flock do four times each year . . . instruct the people in the vulgar tongue simply, and without any phantastical admixture of subtle distinction in the articles of the Creed, the Ten Commandments, [etc.] (Gasquet 8)

It, too, was served by the manuals; but these were written in a tradition increasingly separate from that of the university sermon guides. These authors advocated a simpler form of the thematic sermon, and, late in the Middle Ages, as we have seen in the dedication of Christian Borgsleben's manual, they even began to discuss vernacular preaching techniques.

48

Gerald Owst and other historians of preaching would have us imagine that these modest handbooks were ready references tucked in the cowls of mendicants who traveled the countryside preaching and shriving. Maybe they were used this way, but those that remain today surely were not. Aside from the small probability of a codex surviving such treatment, the known exemplars are generally quartos or folios, not the duodecimo or octavo formats one could carry about. Instead, the surviving manuals, at least, were copied into substantial codices of florilegia, sermon collections, and devotional works. I believe that they served students and preachers both at universities and in chapter houses and cathedral libraries.

The practice of copying texts was thriving and widespread in the late Middle Ages. Guy Lytle has observed that book collecting and the compilation of florilegia were major occupations of students at New College in the fourteenth and fifteenth centuries (209–10). A. G. Little notes that the one "labor" discussed in the mendicant statutes is scribal copying. It is just such enterprise that probably produced MS. Bodley 5 (c. 1400), with its fair hand and mistaken arrangement of the parts of Ranulph Higden's *Ars componendi sermones*; in her edition, Margaret Jennings describes MS. Bodley 5 and indicates that it contains two separate efforts to record the preaching manual (xlii–xliii). This manuscript offers, I believe, evidence of a pecia copying system gone awry. Such systems were especially common in university communities. Another manuscript suggesting its place in this university book culture is Cambridge University Library MS. Gg 6.20 (C15). Some historians believe the name Geoffrey Schale, found in the colophon, is that of the scribe. Schale was probably simply a member of a university community who made a personal collection of preaching manuals and then added a few leaves of his own notes and guidelines for preaching.

How Was the ars praedicandi *Taught in England?*

Records of book ownership also provide evidence of the distribution and use of the manuals. Little's studies of testamentary records show that Franciscans in Exeter in the thirteenth and fourteenth centuries owned a surprising number of books. They left many of them to the chapter house. Of 346 bequeathed, most were missals, but ten were practical theological manuals of one sort or another. Fully 20% of the legacies of Franciscan vicars and annuellers at Exeter were "manuals." Syon Abbey Library in 1526 cataloged at least twelve volumes containing *artes praedicandi* (Bateson 89–115).

Outside the university, we might imagine that the much maligned English parish priest consulted these preaching manuals to improve his style. Though it is unlikely that his parish maintained a library, the probability that at some time in his career the parish priest had access to instruction in preaching either through lectures or manuals is somewhat greater.

In this regard, it is important to understand that there were at least two clerical education "tracks" in England (Orme 24), tracks which I believe correspond to the two traditions of preaching manuals. The elite, intellectually or financially, could complete grammar school and go on to university to study in the arts and eventually complete a doctorate in theology. This took seventeen years, and the minimum age for the doctorate was thirty-five. It has been suggested that only the friars, with their mendicant support system, could afford such training in any numbers. Secular clergy and less talented friars patched together their education in other ways.

One important alternative route to a theological education was offered in the cathedral schools. They predated the universities as centers of theological study and continued to offer education for those who could not go to university. There was some advanced study at the cathedral, and many were examined and ordained to the priesthood at cathedrals; there were also, as mandated by the Fourth Lat-

50

eran Council in 1215, public lectures for clergy both from the cathedral and from nearby parishes. Topics seem to have emphasized very basic theology. Since concerns about the quality of preaching and confession motivated the Church to take these steps, methods of preaching and shriving may also have been reviewed in these lectures. Finally, some cathedral libraries served not only their members but also the secular clergy in the region. So, for example, in addition to its Chapter library, Exeter maintained a smaller, chained library in the choir available for consultation by all clergy in the region (Orme 24). Medieval catalogs suggest a fair representation of sermon collections and "manuals" in these Exeter libraries (Oliver 301–10, 320–76).

In 1298 Pope Boniface VIII's decree "Cum ex eo" made provision for secular clergy with parishes to go to university to study, on the condition that a substitute was found for them in their parish duties. The expenses of university study were to be borne by the parishes. Ecclesiastical records show that many clergy took advantage of this opportunity. Few ever completed degrees. But these individuals surely represented a primary reading market for the preaching manual, the catechetical manuals, and the florilegia, all of which were designed to help the practicing pastor carry out his duties.

The question about the use of these texts—most often phrased "how were the *artes praedicandi* taught?"—is a question very much like how were the florilegia or the *Pupilla Oculi* or other catechetical or penitential works taught. They weren't, in the university sense. They were contemporary responses to contemporary needs. University learning, and theological study in general, emphasized the analysis of received texts, of authorities. Glosses and summative works were built upon the foundations of these authoritative texts.

The tradition of writings on pastoral care certainly had its own elegant, authority-laden style of exposition. But it was based on new and pressing needs in the Church: first in response to the heresies,

51

then in response to the new view of the role and obligations of laymen in religious observance. The *artes* were written by university theologians to help the pastorate meet these new requirements. The elite clergy needed the *ars praedicandi* as a climax to their accredited mastery of theology—for example, for the examination sermon. The common priest needed the *ars praedicandi* even though he never had the opportunity to master theology. In this very important sense, the manuals, at least those later manuals serving the common priest, were not major parts of some rhetorical tradition, though they certainly reflect the rhetorical studies and theories of their age. They were, instead, rhetorical treatises set within and serving a devotional movement. This is a considerable step beyond our customary view that they represent a Christianization of classical Roman oratory.

NOTES

1. Schoeck, "On Rhetoric," and Murphy, "Rhetoric" and "Earliest Teaching."

2. For editions of the manuals of Robert of Basevorn and Thomas Waleys, see Charland. Jacques' work was printed in several incunable editions and many manuscripts where it often appeared with the *Manipulus curatorum* of Guy de Monte Rocheri; for a full listing see Charland 48–50; incunable editions cited there include Hain 7399 (Cologne 1476), 7400 (Cologne 1487), 8162 (Basel 1485), 8186 (Cologne 1460), and Copinger 7399 (Cologne 1480), which are further described and listed in Gallick 484. Johannes Surgant's manual is examined extensively in Roth. Printed editions include Basel 1503, 1508, and Strassburg 1520.

3. Published editions of Michael of Hungary's *Evagatorium, modus predicandi* include Hagenau 1498, Cologne 1502, Paris c. 1505.

4. Parts of Humbert of Romans' *De instructione praedicatorum* have been edited by Berthier 373–484 and by Heintke 161–65; see also "Works Cited" for full text and English translation. For Thomas Waleys, *De modo componendi sermones*, see Charland, *Artes praedicandi.* The many titles of John of Wales's treatise include *Ars praedicandi* and *Ars praedicandi sive information notabilis et praeclara de arte praedicandi.* Textual traditions for this manual are complex and not yet entirely clear. See the Caplan handlist and Charland for manuscripts and editions. A portion of this text is printed in the Quaracchi Brothers' edition of the works of Bonaventure; Gilson discusses it at length.

5. "Quia . . . cum a diversis diversorum Ordinum religiosis simul et saecularibus super hoc precibus essem magnis frequentibusque pulsatus. . . ." Trans. L. Krul in Murphy, *Three* 114; text in Charland 233.

6. Little discusses a case concerning length of study at Oxford, 37 ff. Franciscans had often been exempted from the requirement to complete the arts degree before incepting in theology. The case discussed here puts an end to that exemption. Simon 40 ff. also reviews term of study with reference to Lyte 280–84, 302.

How Was the ars praedicandi *Taught in England?*

MANUSCRIPTS CITED

Alcock, Simon. *De modo dividendi thema pro materia sermonis dilatanda*: London, BL MS. Royal 8 E.xii, ff. 53–61.

Alexander of Esseby. [*Ars praedicandi*]: Cambridge, Cambridge University Library MS. Ii.I.24, ff. 169–73. Oxford, Magdalen College MS. 168, ff. 128ᵛ–130ʳ.

Basevorn, Robert. [*Ars praedicandi*]: London, BL MS. Royal 7 C.I.

Higden, Ranulph. [*Ars componendi sermones*]: Oxford, MS. Bodley 5.

Schale, Geoffrey. [*Ars praedicandi*]: Cambridge, Cambridge University Library MS. Gg 6.20.

Thomas of Salisbury, *Summa de arte predicandi*: Cambridge, Corpus Christi College MS. 455.

WORKS CITED

Admonitio generalis (A.D. 789). *Monumenta Germaniae historica (500–1500): Legum Sectio II, Capitularia regum francorum.* Vol. 1. Ed. Alfredus Boetius. Hannover: Hahn, 1881. No. 22, pp. 52–62.

Alan of Lille. *Summa de arte praedicatoria.* PL 210.110–98.

Baldwin, John W. *Masters, Princes and Merchants: The Social Views of Peter the Chanter and His Circle.* Princeton: Princeton UP, 1970.

Bateson, Mary, ed. *Catalogue of the Library of Syon Monastery, Isleworth.* Cambridge, 1898.

Blomfield, J. C. *History of Upper and Lower Heyford.* Part VI. London, 1892.

Boynton, Mary F., ed. "Simon Alcock on Expanding the Sermon." *Harvard Theological Review* 34 (1941): 201–16.

Buchwald, Georg, ed. "Die *Ars praedicandi* des Erfurter Franziskaners Christian Borgsleben." *Franziskanische Studien* 8 (1921): 67–74.

Caplan, Harry. "'Henry of Hesse' on the Art of Preaching." *PMLA* 48 (1933): 340–61.

———. *Mediaeval artes praedicandi: A Hand-list*. Cornell Studies in Classical Philology 24. Ithaca: Cornell UP, 1934.

———. *A Supplementary hand-list*. Cornell Studies in Classical Philology 25. Ithaca: Cornell UP, 1936.

———, ed. "A Late Medieval Tractate on Preaching [Pseudo-Aquinas, *Tractatulus solemnis de arte et vero modo predicandi*]." *Studies in Rhetoric and Public Speaking in Honor of James Albert Winans*. New York: Century, 1925. 61–90.

Charland, Thomas-Marie. *Artes Praedicandi; Contribution à l'histoire de la rhétorique au moyen âge*. Paris: J. Vrin, 1936.

Delorme, Ferdinand M., ed. "L'*Ars faciendi sermones* de Géraud du Pescher." *Antonianum* 19 (1944): 169–98.

Gallick, Susan. "*Artes Praedicandi*: Early Printed Editions." *Medieval Studies* 39 (1977): 477–89.

Gasquet, F. A. "Religious Instruction in England During the Fourteenth and Fifteenth Centuries." *Historical Papers* 16. London: The Catholic Truth Society, 1894.

Gibson, Strickland, ed. *Statuta Antiqua Universitatis Oxoniensis*. Oxford: Clarendon, 1931.

How Was the ars praedicandi Taught in England?

Gilson, Etienne. "Michel Menot et la technique du sermon médiéval." *Les idées et les lettres*. Paris: J. Vrin, 1932. 93–154.

Heintke, F[ritz]. *Humbert von Romans, der fünfte ordenmeister der Dominikaner*. Berlin: Dr. Emil Ebering, 1933. Also published in *Historische Studien* 222 (Berlin, 1933).

Humbert of Romans. *De instructione praedicatorum*. Ed. M. de la Bigne. Maxima Bibliotheca Vetrum Patrum 25. Lyons, 1677.

———. *Treatise on preaching* [*De instructione praedicatorum*]. Ed. W. M. Conlon. Trans. Dominican Students, Province of St. Joseph. Westminster MD: Newman P, 1951.

Jennings, Margaret, ed. *The* ars componendi sermones *of Ranulph Higden*. Davis Medieval Texts and Studies. Davis CA: University of California P, 1990.

Little, Andrew G. *The Grey Friars in Oxford*. Oxford Historical Society 20. Oxford, 1892.

Lyte, H. C. Maxwell. *A History of the University of Oxford*. London, 1886.

Lytle, Guy Fitch. "A University Mentality in the Late Middle Ages: The Pragmatism, Humanism, and Orthodoxie [sic] of New College, Oxford." *Genèse et débuts du grande schisme d'Occident*. Colloques Internationaux du Centre Nationale de la Recherche Scientifique 586. Paris: CNRS, SUPPLY DATE. 201–30.

Manly, John Matthews. *Chaucer and the Rhetoricians*. Proceedings of the British Academy, Warton Lecture on English Poetry 17. London: The British Academy, 1926.

Morenzoni, Franco, ed. *Summa de arte praedicandi: Thomas de Chobham; cura et studio*. Corpus Christianorum, Continuation mediaevalis 82. Turnhout: Brepols, 1988.

Murphy, James J. "Earliest Teaching of Rhetoric at Oxford." *Speech Monographs* 27 (1960): 345–47.

——. "Literary Implications of Instruction in the Verbal Arts in Fourteenth-Century England." *Leeds Studies in English* 1 (1967): 119–35.

——. "Rhetoric in Fourteenth-Century Oxford." *Medium Aevum* 34 (1965): 1–30.

——, ed. *Three Medieval Rhetorical Arts*. Berkeley: U of California P, 1971.

Oliver, George. *Lives of the Bishops of Exeter, and A History of the Cathedral*. Exeter, 1861.

Orme, Nicholas. *Education in the West of England, 1066–1548*. [Exeter]: U of Exeter, 1976.

Owst, Gerald R. *Preaching in Medieval England: An Introduction to Sermon Manuscripts of the Period, c. 1350–1450*. 1926. New York: Russell & Russell, 1965.

Pseud. Bonaventure. *Ars concionandi*. In *S. Bonaventurae Opera omnia* 9 (Quaracchi, 1882–1902): 8–21.

Rabanus Maurus. *De Clericorum Institutione*. PL 107.294–420.

Roth, Dorothea. *Die mittelalterliche Predigttheorie und das Manuale curatorum des Johann Ulrich Surgant*. Basler Beiträge zur Geschichtswissenschaft 58. Basel and Stuttgard: Helbing and Lichtenhahn, 1956.

Schoeck, Richard. "On Rhetoric in Fourteenth Century Oxford." *Medieval Studies* 30 (1968): 214–25.

Simon, Joan. *Education and Society in Tudor England*. Cambridge: Cambridge UP, 1966.

How Was the ars praedicandi Taught in England?

Wilkins, D. ed. *Concila Magnae Britanniae et Hibernias*. Vol. 2. London, 1737.

Contradictory Paradigms:
The Labyrinth in Art and Literature*

Penelope Reed Doob

It is in manuscripts that medieval art and literature are most visibly and precisely juxtaposed, and this juxtaposition on the page frequently reveals information that neither art nor text could provide alone. The nature of the relationship between art and text may vary greatly. At one extreme, when there is close (and intentional) coordination between word and picture, art illuminates literature and literature art in a kind of hermeneutic circle. At the other extreme, reciprocal illumination breaks down when picture and text are completely independent, as when grotesques ornament books of hours or bizarre bas-de-page anecdotes of foxes and geese bedeck religious texts. In particularly subtle instances the apparent independence of art and word may veil complex thematic interconnections.[1] Perhaps the most challenging interrelationship between word and image, however, is found when text and art seem to have been intended as mutual glosses, parallel versions of the same statement, but close inspection reveals them to be disjunctive, and possibly quite unconsciously so. When such a conflict between verbal and visual information is recurrent, widespread, and even habitual in relation to a particular concept

---

or visual image in the work of an individual or in a culture, a study of the disjunction can be singularly informative. The torch of reciprocal illumination throws its light into the hidden recesses of an intellect or culture, and explorations of the implicit conflict between word and image yield unexpected information.

In this essay I want to show how this process operates in the case of the labyrinth or maze,[2] a common subject in texts and art of the classical and medieval periods. Literature and art of these periods characteristically espouse contradictory paradigms of the labyrinth which are silently juxtaposed in many manuscripts, suggesting much more than we would otherwise know about how medieval people understood the labyrinth. My discussion of the implications of this radical disjunction will be abstract and theoretical; for its grounding in and confirmation by actual texts and visual images, I refer readers to my recent book, *The Idea of the Labyrinth*.[3]

Classical and medieval literary tradition typically represents the labyrinth as a highly complicated three-dimensional building whose architectural intricacies have a dual effect depending on the beholder's point of view: mazes simultaneously delight those rare observers who grasp their artistic principles and bewilder strangers lost within them. Literary labyrinths contain so many vast halls, blind walls, and circuitous passages that a maze is both "inexplicable" and "inextricable" (Pliny 36.19). For Virgil, mazes have "a thousand paths, where the signs to be followed were confused by undiscoverable and irretraceable wandering" (*Aeneid* 5.590–91). Thus, labyrinths are simultaneously artistic miracles objectively worthy of admiration and subjective nightmares in which it is all too easy to lose one's way. Both the maze's elaborate artistry and the confusion it induces depend in part on a single physical characteristic: the apparently endless proliferation of choices among paths. To use a technical term, these labyrinths are *multicursal* and therefore potentially inextricable (see fig. 1). This multicursal paradigm informs most classical and medieval texts.

From time immemorial until the Renaissance, however, the visual arts unanimously present a very different paradigm. In prehistoric rock-carvings and seventh-century B.C. wine pitchers, in Roman mosaics and medieval manuscripts, the labyrinth is represented visually as a two-dimensional diagram or floor-plan.[4] The pattern depicted is always *unicursal,* containing one profoundly circuitous path that inevitably leads to the center by the longest possible path and then back out again (see fig. 2). There are no choices among paths at all; it is quite impossible for any wanderer to become lost in these extricable labyrinths whose architectural plan explicates itself.

Thus there are two distinctive contradictory models of the maze: the unicursal model of the visual arts and the multicursal model of literary tradition. (We will touch on another aspect of the difference between models—the three-dimensional, architectural image portrayed in literature vs. the two-dimensional schematic model usually depicted in art—later.) No conflict between these models is necessarily perceived or implied when one or the other paradigm appears independently: a text describes the multicursal Cretan maze, or a French cathedral nave is paved with a unicursal labyrinth design. Sometimes, however, the opposing paradigms are strikingly juxtaposed in manuscripts: taken together as they appear on a page, text and illustration paradoxically assert both the inextricable choice-driven multicursal literary model and the unicursal visual model. The unicursal visual design commonly illustrates texts referring to multicursal labyrinths: in manuscripts of Raban Maur's *De rerum naturis*, for instance, where a description of the confusing ancient labyrinths is ornamented with a unicursal design (Doob pl. 9; Kern pls. 159–60); or in Boethius' *Consolation of Philosophy* as a visual correlative to the labyrinth of logical complexity mentioned in 3pr12 (Kern pl. 183); or in Lambert of

St. Omer's *Liber floridus*, where a maze ornaments a recounting of the Cretan myth (Kern pl. 163); or in at least one French manuscript of the *Histoire ancienne jusqu'à César*, whose précis of the *Aeneid* describes Aeneas' arrival at Cumae with its Daedalian sculpture of the many-pathed Cretan labyrinth (Doob pl. 19). Even when there is no full-blown accompanying literary text, unicursal maze drawings in manuscripts may be labelled "laborintus," the word used in literature for patently multicursal mazes; or a gloss may read "domus daedali," a common synonym for "laborintus" whose naming of the great architect Daedalus instantly evokes the Cretan myth with its necessarily multicursal maze.[5]

By juxtaposing multicursal text and unicursal image, manuscripts forcefully focus our attention on the surprising and general co-existence of contradictory paradigms of the maze in the classical and medieval periods. Even more astonishing, however, is the fact that this clash of paradigms, which after all does not depend on the existence of manuscripts representing both, goes almost unnoticed by classical and medieval writers. I know of only two explicit comments on the discrepancy between the models. First, Pliny the Elder (36.19) contrasts the magnificent but confusing many-pathed labyrinth of Egypt with the far simpler labyrinth mosaics of Roman floors—mosaics that are always unicursal, and in which one cannot get lost.[6] Second, many centuries later, Boccaccio notes that

> This [Cretan] labyrinth was not made as we design ours, with circles and windings of the walls, through which anyone who goes without turning round infallibly arrives at the middle and then, continuing to follow the windings without turning, comes outside; but there was, and still is, a mountain all excavated within, made with square chambers so that each chamber has four doors, one in each side, each door leading to a similar room, so that anyone who enters grows bewildered and does not know how to get out. (Boccaccio 2: 108; my translation)

62

These comments indicate that classical and medieval people were quite competent to distinguish between unicursal visual and multicursal literary paradigms, but the fact remains that they generally did not choose to do so. Unicursal and multicursal models share a common name, and each paradigm coexists peacefully with the other.[7] Boethius, great reconciler of apparent contradictions, reports Lady Philosophy's remedy for such situations: "Let us set our arguments against each other and perhaps from their opposition some special truth will emerge" (3pr12). So too here: the baffling discrepancy between paradigms is blatantly obvious in manuscripts where visual and literary representations of mazes coincide. But it is precisely this apparent contradiction that provides a key to the classical and medieval idea of the labyrinth, thereby facilitating more accurate and sensitive readings of labyrinths in art and literature.

Let us imitate Philosophy, that artful crafter and unraveller of mazes, by setting our paradigms against each other so that from their opposition some special truth—the medieval idea of the labyrinth—will emerge. We begin by examining the formal implications of each model taken independently to see how its structure prescribes the metaphorical freight it may bear. Then, by setting the paradigms together, we can transcend their differences—differences that in a scholastic sense are accidental rather than essential—and thereby discover the features common to both paradigms. These common features define the essence of the labyrinth in classical and medieval times and constitute the principal bases for metaphorical transformations of the maze in art and literature. Theorizing about formal implications thus lays the groundwork for interpretation, although that practical application of labyrinthine theory is not the project of this essay.

To understand the implications and metaphorical possibilities of the multicursal literary model, the kind of labyrinth through which Theseus picked his laborious way, imagine the maze as an open-roofed three-dimensional structure through which people wander without seeing over the walls. Because it is multicursal, this maze offers choices between paths, as if the Herculean or Pythagorean choice between the roads to pleasure and virtue were reduplicated at every turn to create a continuous array of choices. Because a multicursal maze demands constant choice, with no end to the struggle until the unseen goal is achieved, it is a perfect emblem of intellectual and moral difficulty.

Figure 1. Design for a multicursal labyrinth. Drawing by Robert Ouellette.

Imagine being inside this maze. Your movement will be halting, as each choice requires a pause for thought. Your direction shifts constantly, as your choices lead you. You may lose confidence, retrace your steps, and take another path, for inside the maze you can't see its center until you reach it. The essence of the maze experience is therefore confusion, doubt, and frustration; even if you are lucky enough to have a guide, you may not be sure you're on the right track; indeed, you cannot be sure that there is any center at all. The multicursal maze is dangerous whether or not it contains a minotaur, for anyone who gets lost may be imprisoned forever. Thus the maze is potentially inextricable, and survival and escape may depend not only on intelligence but also on the grace of guidance—Ariadne's thread, the wings of Daedalus, instructive principles, signposting, or advice along the way.

In theory, the architect or the guide might be responsible for the maze-walker's failure or success: the maze-maker might have created a sadistic design with no path to the center, or no center at all, but classical and medieval literary maze-makers play fair. Guides may help or hinder, but finally the multicursal maze emphasizes the role of the individual who may follow or ignore advice. While maze-walkers can't choose with complete freedom, since they have to pick an existing path, their fate is more the result of free choice than it is the consequence of the architect's devious design. Therefore, while in both maze paradigms there is structure-determined wandering (*error* is the word commonly used), in a multicursal maze these *errores* usually involve errors of judgment (choosing the wrong path). Because the multicursal maze leaves significant choice to the wanderer, it highlights the individual's responsibility for his (or her) own fate. In this sense, maze-walking is analogous to the operation of free will within certain prescribed limits. Morally, the experience of multicursal mazes can be positive (if you learn or accomplish something important and transcend the confusion of the maze); it may be negative (if you

65

choose badly and remain imprisoned); or it may be neutral (the path through the labyrinth is the only way to get from A to B, but the process and goal carry no moral connotations). These characteristics of multicursal mazes make them useful analogues for processes fraught with difficult decisions and critical choices: chivalric quests, the composition or exegesis of a text, the mental attempt to organize large amounts of material (see Doob 82–92 and chs. 6–11).

In contrast, imagine being inside a unicursal maze of the visual tradition. Most mazes in the classical and medieval visual arts are represented as two-dimensional floor-plans or blueprints, so you can actually see the whole pattern and the unobstructed path to the center— you can take in the whole thing at a glance, as if looking on from above. The following exercise, therefore, depends on imagining that the diagrammatic blueprint is realized in three dimensions, so that the view of the whole, and even the view a little way ahead or behind, is blocked by walls. The unicursal maze contains only one path with no choices, no forks: the maze itself is an infallible guide to its own center, and you can follow the path steadily, even thoughtlessly. But unicursal mazes are nonetheless disorienting: their complex turnings mean that you don't know where you are going or how near you are to the end, and indeed the unicursal patterns typically found in later medieval art toy with the maze-walker by leading first almost directly to the center and then weaving a complicated path out to the periphery before allowing eventual access to the goal. Ironically, the wanderer is geographically closer to the center early in the journey than when it is almost over.[8] Multicursal mazes contain more and less direct routes to the center depending on what paths you choose, but a unicursal maze by its very nature defines the longest, most circuitous route conceivable within any given space: you're forced to cover *all* the territory between entry and center. Full of unavoidable delays, the very embodiment of enforced circuitousness, a unicursal maze is a perfect symbol of the need for patient endurance of unpredictable twists of fate.

Figure 2. Unicursal labyrinth. Design of the nave pavement labyrinth in Chartres Cathedral, c. 1194–1220. Drawing by Robert Ouellette.

The essence of the unicursal maze experience is confusion and frustration, just as in the multicursal maze. But in this case confusion arises from the maze-walker's spatial disorientation rather than from the need for recurrent choice, and the frustration arising from the design-enforced delay might appropriately be directed towards the structure and its architect. Delay is part of the nature of things in the uni-

67

cursal labyrinth, whereas in a multicursal maze it derives more from the mistakes of the wanderer.

In a unicursal maze there is no objective danger of getting lost, and it takes no skill to find the goal or exit; the labyrinth is not intrinsically inextricable, however inescapable its turnings may seem to wanderers ignorant of pattern and goal. But there are very real dangers nonetheless: there may be a minotaur threatening its own form of inextricability—sudden death; and there are also psychological dangers—immobility, despair, temptations to stop short of the goal on the intolerably long and apparently fruitless road.

Individual responsibility diminishes in a unicursal maze, whose necessary structural wanderings (*errores*) may be merely physical. But sometimes wandering in and of itself suggests moral culpability: errors, strayings from the straight and narrow. While multicursal wanderers actively determine their course, unicursal wanderers are totally dependent on the whim of the maze-maker who plotted the path they have no choice but to follow; this model, then, is inherently deterministic. If multicursal mazes insist on the importance of individual choice, unicursal patterns prescribe a universal journey for Everyman.

So far I have suggested that the unicursal labyrinth involves no choice except whether to continue. That assessment is valid when applied to anyone already inside the maze. However, this model can *imply* a crucial choice: whether to enter the maze in the first place.[9] The unicursal maze may thus represent one possible result of a single momentous decision like Hercules' choice at the crossroads. Choosing to enter a unicursal labyrinth abrogates all future decisions except a decision to retrace your steps; once in, you are committed to a terrifyingly unforeseeable course of events during which you are subject to the power of the maze and the will of its maker. Thus unicursal mazes can be prison-like even though they are not architecturally inextricable, and guides may be useful even though the most helpful ones probably stand and advise outside the door, not within the maze itself. If we count the choice to enter at all as an aspect of structure, the unicursal maze resembles a single *bivium* with lengthy and devious consequences. Analogous experiences and processes range from life itself, fatalistically and universally conceived, to the temporally linear reception of a literary text or philosophical argument (when choices of interpretation are ignored and uncomplicated reception of the literal level is emphasized). In the moral realm, the unicursal labyrinth can be positive, with connotations of patience in adversity; negative, implying persistence in folly; or neutral, as when one follows a consistent if involuted mental process or argument doggedly to its conclusion.

These, then, are some of the implications of the two paradigms so paradoxically juxtaposed in medieval manuscripts and maintained in medieval thought. At first glance, we may be overwhelmed by the differences: one paradigm contains a single path, the other many; one proves patience, the other tests intelligence; one is difficult and the other easy to penetrate or escape, at least in theory. But however suggestive and useful these differences may be for metaphor-makers, they are accidental rather than essential characteristics. As Boethius suggests, one can transcend the kinds of opposition conceptually inherent in the two models of the maze and physically represented on every manuscript page where a verbal description of the multicursal labyrinth adjoins a unicursal illustration. In this way, we may discover the essence of the medieval maze—the major features common to both models, features that make it plausible for the same word, *laborintus*, to denote both paradigms.

Overtly or covertly, texts about labyrinths insist on an important duality: with their superb design and chaotic impact, mazes cause admiration or alarm depending on the observer's point of view, above the maze or within it. Most literature highlights subjective chaos, as one would expect from the fact that most literature describes labyrinths as multicursal, enclosing, three-dimensional buildings; most art, relying on a diagrammatic unicursal pattern that can be seen whole as if from above, highlights labyrinthine order and symmetry. When a labyrinth text is illustrated by a unicursal diagram, this characteristic duality of the maze is intensified, as text asserts confusing multicursality and diagrammatic illumination asserts unicursality and artistic order. But one can also detect a similar duality in unicursal and multicursal mazes taken independently. Anyone immersed in a maze of either paradigm, unable to see the pattern whole, would be disoriented and confused, whether by repeated occasions for choice or by the dizzying turns of a single path. From above, either design might be intricate and symmetrical, an image of order containing and controlling magnificent complexity, a representation of pattern determining and consisting of paths.[10] Thus both paradigms equally exemplify *planned chaos*:[11] their artistry baffles or dazzles according to the viewer's perspective (and the architect's skill). And indeed, in art and literature alike, labyrinths may represent complex art, the confusion induced by over-complexity, or both at once.[12] Moreover, this artistry/chaos duality is relative and convertible: what bewilders one viewer delights another, and when you change your point of view, your understanding changes—rise above the maze on the wings of Daedalus and order is revealed. This conversion from chaos to clarity is described in many labyrinthine narratives (Doob chs. 6, 9–11). The first essential characteristic of the labyrinth, then, is its perspective-dependent duality: both paradigms embody artistry and chaos, each of these qualities being convertible to the other with a change in point of view. The fragmented vision is chaotic; the whole picture, revealed by the long view, is art.

The second essential characteristic is structural: both paradigms achieve their artistry and/or confusion by means of their defining *errores* and *ambages*—wanderings, enforced circuitousness. Whether there is one path or many, whether choice is paramount or ignored, whether *error* is moral or geographical, the way to the center is necessarily circuitous; all labyrinths involve digression, detour, deferral, delay, diversion. Anything essentially circuitous—a multi-episodic quest, an ornate and highly amplified text, a complex piece of logic—is labyrinthine in this sense.

Thanks to their circuitousness, labyrinths afford no easy passage: the *labor intus* of the labyrinth, the difficulty experienced within, is sometimes interpreted as difficult entry, sometimes as difficult exit (Doob 96–97). Thus the third essential characteristic involves the labyrinth's fabled impenetrability or inextricability, depending on whether you want to get in or out. Multicursal mazes are obviously difficult to enter and leave, but at first glance it's hard to see how a unicursal labyrinth could be either impenetrable or inextricable. If, however, you imagine being inside such a maze, unable to see any distance ahead or behind, unable to tell whether the center (if any) is near or far, it's clear that even unicursal mazes are *subjectively* inextricable or impenetrable so long as you are inside them and unable to determine their pattern, or even whether they are unicursal or multicursal. If you cannot choose among paths, you may feel even more constrained than if you could choose. Subjective inextricability or impenetrability, then, is the third essential feature of labyrinths, found in both paradigms to varying degrees.

While some mazes really are virtually inextricable or impenetrable, others only feel that way: the single or multiple paths of some labyrinths-*in-bono* may have been carefully designed by a benevolent master-architect to lead the elect, or perhaps every maze-walker, to a profitable goal. The circuitous path, the choices, the *errores*, all are planned to cover just the right territory to reach (and teach) something that could not have been reached (or taught) by a more direct route. The unicursal maze-architect has calculated the precise pattern of disorientation you need so you can appreciate the center when you get there. The multicursal maze-maker has foreseen alternative routes, of which some lead to failure while others test the wanderer to make him worthy of enlightenment, which may be presented as extrication from the maze, a rising above it to see its pattern, and a transformation of confusion into an understanding that would not have been possible without initial confusion. As T. S. Eliot said in a context not wholly dissimilar,

> In order to arrive at what you do not know
> You must go by a way which is the way of ignorance. (140–41)

However benevolently they may be intended, these pedagogical labyrinths are often frightening: confusion may be for your own good, but it's still confusion, and labyrinths are labyrinths precisely because they feel inextricable and aimless, whether or not the maze-walker is destined for transcendence.

Both unicursal and multicursal models are effective embodiments of this fourth essential feature of the maze: its ability to delineate, and to recreate for reader or viewer, the way of ignorance—ignorance of the path, the pattern, the goal, the maze-maker's intentions. This ignorance, this intense immersion in mazy process, generates numerous metaphors, many of them involving epistemology. Both models describe the way of ignorance, of difficult process, equally well, if with the subtle difference that a unicursal maze charts a universal and authoritative curriculum while a multicursal wanderer participates actively and selectively in his own education. In a unicursal maze, one learns by precept; in a multicursal maze, by dialectic, an art often compared to the labyrinth (Doob 87–90, 199–201, 268–70).

Set against each other in the mind as they are on the medieval manuscript page, the literary and visual paradigms with their accidental differences resolve themselves into a more privileged vision of essential commonality based on four factors: (1) the maze's dual and convertible perspective-dependent potential as simultaneous artistry and chaos; (2) its structural circuitousness, defined by *ambages* and *errores*; (3) its subjective impenetrability and/or inextricability; and (4) its wholly or partially enforced prescription of the subjective path of ignorance, of the difficult process that may eventually lead to transcendent understanding.

Such are the defining qualities of a classical or medieval labyrinth, characteristic of both paradigms. Each has an architect, kindly or malevolent, whose artistry is manifested in a circuitous design that bewilders (and perhaps instructs) the ignorant as it delights the knowing. Each seems inextricable and impenetrable, but each may occasion a conversion from confusion to perception. In these essential qualities of the maze lie the roots of most metaphorical uses of the labyrinth image in medieval literature and art alike. It is because the literary multicursal paradigm and the visual unicursal paradigm share these defining qualities that both are fitly called *laborintus*—having hardship, or exertion, or artistry, within—and that one paradigm may properly be paired with the other. Where modern eyes see conflicting paradigms in the juxtaposition of text and illumination, we must conclude that most medieval people saw accidental variations on an overarching essential theme, and a significant assertion of the labyrinth's characteristic duality as art and as confusion. I don't mean to imply that medieval people were unaware of the distinctions between the models, distinctions that were probably rather less obtrusive to them than to us, given our contemporary obsession with labyrinthine mul-

73

ticursality. On the contrary, some great artists—the author(s) of the *Queste del saint graal*, for instance, or Dante, or Chaucer—describe, and indeed structure great works upon, the differences as well as similarities between the variant models of the maze (Doob 175–91, chs. 10–11). But that is another and far longer story.

I began this essay by mentioning some of the relationships that may exist between text and visual image on a medieval manuscript page and then explored how a radical disjunction between texts about and illustrations of labyrinths could reveal more about medieval ideas of the labyrinth than any simple, straightforward, point-for-point conjunction of word and image. I then extrapolated the essential qualities that apparently define the concept *labyrinth* in the Middle Ages from an analysis of the similarities underlying the superficially paradoxical paradigms, and I worked from the abstract text/image conjunction to even more abstract and implicit hypothetical metaconcepts of the maze, using the clash of paradigms that might be visible on a manuscript page to speculate about what medieval people meant by the word *laborintus* or the visual image of the maze. Since few if any medieval readers probably went through a similar chain of thought when faced with an actual unicursal maze illustrating or accompanying a particular text in a particular manuscript, however, I would not like to close without mentioning a few things medieval readers are somewhat more likely to have thought when confronted with a maze diagram in a manuscript.

Drawings of labyrinths are often placed at the beginning or ending of complicated, sophisticated literary texts: for example, four manuscripts of Boethius' *Consolation of Philosophy* end with an illustration of a maze, as if to sum up in a single image the work's labyrinthine artistry and intellectual complexity as well as its narrative thrust—the conversion of the prisoner's perception of the world from

74

a place of disorder, futility, and time-bound linearity (the view from within the labyrinth) to an appreciation of the cosmic circles of God's eternity.[13] In these Boethius manuscripts there is, then, a specific thematic connection between text and illustration. Here and elsewhere, however, initial or terminal labyrinths may serve more generally as a scribe's seal of approval for a literary work carefully crafted, just as some cathedral labyrinths (Amiens, Reims) apparently honored the Daedalian arts of the building's commissioners and architects (Doob 121–23). Sometimes, too, the illuminated labyrinth may indicate textual difficulty: Marius Mercator recommended that marginal labyrinths be used to signal readers that certain passages in a text are particularly difficult (81), and some initial or terminal labyrinths might mark the difficulty, as well as the artistry, of a complete text.

In many cases, however, the pairing of a complex text, whether or not it deals explicitly with multicursal mazes, and an elegant, symmetrical, diagrammatic, unicursal maze might carry an optimistic if almost subliminal message. On one hand, any complicated labyrinthine text (and we must remember that labyrinths too are *textus*, woven—see *Aeneid* 5.589) is likely to involve linearity, choices of meaning, tropes, and turns of phrase—in short, *processes* in which a reader is necessarily immersed and encompassed, just as in a complex building. Reading a difficult text is very much like being inside a multicursal labyrinth, whether or not there is a guiding thread of marginal commentary, as there so often is in medieval manuscripts.[14] The diagrammatic visual image of the unicursal maze, on the other hand, does not emphasize process; instead, it depicts an artistic *product* one can take in at a glance and see whole; it is a summary, an overview, a clear assertion that the twisting, irrational path eventually creates a comprehensible pattern, that there is an attainable center, that complexity begets not only frustration but also pleasure. Visual labyrinths may mark passages and texts that are difficult when one is still within them, exploring and extracting their meaning, but the fact that these labyrinths depict an overview may well assert that confusion and difficulty can be mastered and comprehended—the lesson that the prisoner Boethius learned when Lady Philosophy's guiding threads of labyrinthine argument revealed the circles of divine simplicity. The juxtaposition of labyrinthine literature and visual labyrinths, then, can sometimes be an expressive composite emblem of the terrors and rewards of perseverance in the quest to resolve textual (or moral, or intellectual) difficulty. If a picture really is worth a thousand words, and possibly more memorable, the most enduring message of the paired paradigms in manuscripts may be the optimistic promise of order, clarity, and artistry inherent in the overview depicted by the diagrammatic unicursal maze of the visual arts.

NOTES

1. Such independence is particularly characteristic of East Anglian MSS., though it is also found frequently in northern French, Flemish, and other English MSS.: see Rickert 122–35, *Hours of Jeanne d'Évreux*, *Hours of Catherine of Cleves*, Sandler 1: 7–18.

2. These English terms, one of Greek (via Latin) and the other of Norse (via Old English) origin, are synonymous.

3. At several critical turning-points when I had almost given up hope of ever bringing my study of labyrinths to any satisfactory conclusion, Judson Allen's warm encouragement kept me going; his importance to *The Idea of the Labyrinth* and its author is recognized in a small way by that book's dedication to his memory, and by the existence of the present collection.
   Much of the present essay is a condensation and recasting of materials in *The*

Idea of the Labyrinth, particularly ch. 2, to fit the theme of this collection; my thanks to the Cornell UP for permission to rework the materials here.

Extensive examples of real and metaphorical labyrinths and labyrinthine processes in the classical and early Christian literary tradition may be found in chs. 1, 3, 8 (the *Aeneid*), and 9 (Boethius); examples from the medieval literary tradition are found in chs. 6–7, 10 (Dante), and 11 (Chaucer); examples from the visual arts are discussed in chs. 2 and 5. A wide range of visual examples is available in Kern.

4. See Doob pls. 1–3, 5, 9, 16–17, 19–23, 25; Kern chs. 4, 6–8.

5. If the Minotaur is to be imprisoned or concealed effectively, the labyrinth must be virtually inextricable. On etymologies and synonyms of laborintus, see Doob 133–44.

6. For mosaic pavements, see Matthews ch. 8; Santarcangeli ch. 9; Kern ch. 6; and Doob ch. 2.

7. That this simultaneous assertion of contradictory models goes almost unnoticed might indicate the presence of a significant *aporia* in the Derridan sense (Doob 62), but more likely, as I argue here, it reflects the operation of a medieval definition of the concept *labyrinth* that differs from modern definitions.

8. For an intriguing moral application of this idea in the *Queste del Saint Graal*, see Doob 180. The design to which I refer is the "Chartres" pattern (Kern 125–27), a circular design with four sectors and cruciform axes, represented by fig. 2 here.

9. Initial choice also exists with a multicursal maze, but its impact is diminished by the continuous sequence of important choices.

10. I am assuming that a multicursal maze, had any been drawn in classical and medieval times, would have been an adaptation of the unicursal pattern, preserving its near-symmetry as in fig. 1. Certainly manuscripts showing an exterior view of a

spherical architectural maze (e.g., Doob pl. 18) and the descriptions by Pliny and Boccaccio suggest symmetry in the multicursal design.

11. Alfred David's phrase, originally used in quite a different context, sums up the essence of the maze.

12. For example, a brilliantly ornate and labyrinthine sermon that delights the learned may lose the ignorant (Robert of Basevorn 190–91); and God's created universe is a labyrinth to us with our terrestrial perspective at the same time as it expresses superb divine order (Doob 67–69, 153–55, chs. 9–10). For related examples see Doob chs. 3 and 5–7.

13. The MSS. are Munich Clm 800, 55ᵛ (Kern pl. 184), Oxford Bodley Auct. F. 6. 4, 61aᵛ and 61bᵛ (Doob pl. 22), Cambridge Trinity Hall 12, 50ʳ (Kern pl. 185), and Florence Bibl. Laur. 78.16, 58ʳ (Doob pl. 23). See also Doob 138–39 and ch. 9. The textual contrast between labyrinth and divine circles occurs in 3pr12, and one MS.—St. Gall 825, p. 176 (Kern pl. 183)—depicts a maze at that point.

14. Sometimes, metaphorically, the role of the marginal labyrinth may be played by difficult texts themselves. Imagine a manuscript page of the biblical text of *Ezekiel* describing the Temple in Jerusalem, a highly complicated building with so many chambers, galleries, winding stairs, and passages that it is a labyrinth in its own right. Surrounding this difficult labyrinthine text about a labyrinthine building is the explanatory guiding *textus* of Jerome, describing *Ezekiel* as a textual and hermeneutic labyrinth to be solved (in the form of Jerome's commentary) only with the guidance of Christ, in an extended series of errands into, and out of, the textual maze. See Jerome 447–49 and Doob 69–71; on texts as labyrinthine, see Doob ch. 7.

Penelope Reed Doob

WORKS CITED

Boccaccio, Giovanni. *Il Comento alla Divina Commedia.* Ed. Domenico Guerri. 3 vols. Bari: Laterza, 1918.

Boethius. *Boethii Philosophiae Consolatio.* Ed. Ludwig Bieler. Corpus Christianorum Series Latina 94. Turnholt: Brepols, 1957.

Boethius. *The Consolation of Philosophy.* Trans. Richard Green. Indianapolis: Bobbs-Merrill, 1962.

David. Alfred. "Literary Satire in *The House of Fame.*" *PMLA* 75 (1960): 333–39.

Doob, Penelope Reed. *The Idea of the Labyrinth from Classical Antiquity through the Middle Ages.* Ithaca: Cornell UP, 1990.

Eliot, T. S. "East Coker." *The Four Quartets. The Complete Poems and Plays.* New York: Harcourt, 1952.

The Hours of Catherine of Cleves. Introd. and comm. John Plummer. New York: Braziller, 1966.

The Hours of Jeanne d'Évreux. Introd. James J. Rorimer. New York: Metropolitan Museum of Art; Greenwich, CT: New York Graphic Society, 1965.

Jerome. *Commentariorum in Ezechielem Prophetam.* PL 25.15–490.

Kern, Hermann. *Labirinti: forme e interpretazioni: 5000 anni di presenza di un archetipo.* Trans. Libero Sosio. Milan: Feltrinelli, 1981. Trans. of *Labyrinthe: Erscheinungsformen und Deutungen 5000 Jahre Gegenwart eines Urbilds.* 1981.

Marius Mercator. *Concilium Universale Ephesenum. Acta Conciliorum Oecumenicorum.* Tom. 1, vol. 1, pt. 1. Ed. E. Schwartz. Berlin and Leipzig: Walter de Gruyter, 1924–26.

79

The Labyrinth in Art and Literature

Matthews, W. H. *Mazes and Labyrinths: Their History and Development.* 1922. New York: Dover, 1970.

Pliny the Elder. *Natural History.* Trans. D. E. Eichholz and H. Rackham. Vol. 10. London: Heinemann, 1962.

Rickert, Margaret. *Painting in Britain: The Middle Ages.* 2nd ed. Pelican History of Art. Harmondsworth: Penguin, 1965.

Robert of Basevorn. *The Form of Preaching.* Trans. James J. Murphy. *Three Medieval Rhetorical Arts.* Ed. James J. Murphy. Berkeley and Los Angeles: U of California P, 1971.

Sandler, Lucy Freeman. *Gothic Manuscripts 1285–1385.* 2 vols. A Survey of Manuscripts Illuminated in the British Isles 5. General ed. J. J. G. Alexander. London: Harvey Miller; Oxford: Oxford UP, 1986.

Santarcangeli, Paolo. *Le livre des labyrinthes: Histoire d'un mythe et d'un symbole.* Trans. Monique Lacau. Paris: Gallimard, 1974. Trans. of *Il Libro dei Labrinti.* 1967.

Virgil. *The Aeneid.* Trans. H. Rushton Fairclough. Rev. ed. Vol. 1. Cambridge: Harvard UP, 1974.

"Bothe text and gloss": Manuscript Form, the Textuality of Commentary, and Chaucer's Dream Poems

Martin Irvine

The literary, rhetorical, and ethical implications of glosses in medieval books and of glossing as a discursive practice have become important subjects in Chaucer criticism,[1] but the form and textual status of the marginal gloss or commentary in literary manuscripts has yet to be fully investigated for what it can tell us about literary theory and textuality in the age of Chaucer. I would like to suggest here some of the ways in which the physical features of the manuscript books, specifically the form of page layout designed to present text and gloss in a system of signification unique to authoritative texts, can be investigated to provide a model of textuality that Chaucer exploits throughout his works. I shall argue that commentary, which was given its own space on the page, had a distinctive textuality, both discursively as a function of interpretive and intertextual relations and materially in the visual form of the manuscript page, and that Chaucer foregrounds the textuality of commentary in the dream poems, which function as extended glosses on texts of the *auctores*.

I would like to frame my discussion of the relationship between manuscript format and forms of medieval textuality by considering two sets of statements that characterize two different levels of textual analysis:

1) "The frontiers of a book are never clear-cut; beyond the title, the first lines, and the last full stop, beyond its internal configuration and its autonomous form, it is caught up in a system of references to other books, other texts, other sentences: it is a node within a network. . . . The book is not simply the object that one holds within one's hand. . . . [A book] constructs itself only on the basis of a complex field of discourse." (Foucault, *The Archaeology of Knowledge* 23)

   "Knowledge therefore consisted in . . . bringing into being . . . the secondary discourse of commentary. The function proper to knowledge is not seeing or demonstrating; it is interpreting. . . . Language contains its own inner principle of proliferation. 'There is more work in interpreting interpretations than in interpreting things; and more books about books than on any other subject; we do nothing but write glosses on one another' [Montaigne, *Essays* 3.13]. . . . The task of commentary can never, by definition, be completed." (Foucault, *The Order of Things* 40–41)

2) "[A]ll literary products descend into immediate experience; that is, they come to the reader in determinate forms. The most elemental of these determinate forms is the physical object. . . . [W]e must forcefully remind ourselves that discourse takes place in specific and concrete forms, and that those forms are by no means comprehended by the limits of language." (McGann, *Beauty* 95)

There are here two different conceptions of the book and the text, conceptions that interpreters of medieval texts and manuscripts have yet to appreciate in a self-conscious way. The first set of statements articulates the approach to texts in post-structuralist discourse analysis

82

and the second the orientation to texts taken by a critic of modern textual criticism and editorial methods. The second statement by Foucault points out the essentially intertextual nature of commentary, which links texts to earlier texts in an ongoing chain of interpretation and mutual presupposition. Foucault's statements parallel Roland Barthes' famous reconceptualization of the text in "From Work to Text"; the "work" is the concrete object, taking up space in a book, but the "text" exists only at the level of discourse, as a discursive productivity rather than a product or object. My investigations here assume that these conceptualizations of discourse and texts—as elements in a synchronic system and as concrete vehicles of signification—are not exclusive categories or polar opposites; rather, they are distinct levels of analysis which are, finally, mutually dependent. The concrete object of the book, in all the dimensions of its physical form, is encoded with social significance parallel to the way literary discourse is so encoded; both the concrete form (the "work") and discourse (the "text") take on intelligibility and meaning as parts of a larger configuration of meaning and social value.[2]

Furthermore, I approach the visual and physical form of manuscripts as significant in itself. The concrete object of the manuscript book thus contains many layers of information not abstractable from its physical and visual form. Differentiation among styles and levels of script and the design and layout of the page provide a grid that signifies textual values and relationships over and above any verbal content that the form makes possible. "The meaning of a text" is therefore not limited to its verbal content but is a function of all the visual codes that interpret a text in the way it appears on the page for the reader. In other words, the very form of a glossed book, independent of the text presented in that form, has a meaning, a load of ideological and cultural significance inseparable from the experience of reading a text in that form.

The necessary interplay between the two aspects of textual analysis—"works" and "texts"—becomes obvious in the study of texts in manuscript form: the text is a concrete social event that is intelligible and meaningful only in a larger system of meaning extending beyond the physical boundaries of the individual book. In other words, to understand medieval texts within manuscript culture one must proceed both archaeologically and semiologically, attending to the form of texts in their material and historical concreteness and to the larger systems of meaning, verbal and visual, through which the "works" of medieval culture became "texts," ideal bodies of discourse invested with social value. Glossed manuscripts provide an unusually explicit example of the connection between the physical and visual form of the book and the system of meaning in which it participates.

Implicit in my argument about manuscripts and textuality, therefore, is a critique of the still prevalent division in medieval studies between "philology" (broadly defined to include paleography and manuscript studies) and "theory" or "interpretation."[3] The implied critique cuts in both directions so that I can present an alternative, filling in the larger theoretical implications of paleography for the historical study of texts understood as social events with an irreducible and untranslatable material form. The disciplines of paleography and codicology have long resisted self-conscious questioning of method, presuppositions, and ideology, and specialists in these disciplines have often sought refuge in a cover or smokescreen of sheer erudition that obscures any essential theoretical point at issue. On the other hand, literary scholars and critics too often simply refer to authorities on paleography and codicology for particular details—manuscript dates, provenance, script, for example—and then return to reading a printed abstraction of a medieval text in a critical edition, a fixed text in a form unknown to medieval readers and writers that becomes the basis for all interpretation.

There are several stubborn historical facts about manuscripts and manuscript culture that the modern methods of editing and philology obscure: the fact that most medieval "texts" are not ideal, self-substantial, or self-identical verbal entities but events, "works," produced in multiple versions and in physical contexts largely unknown or inaccessible to the modern reader.[4] This irreducible textual variation from copy to copy and from physical context to context has been termed "mouvance" by Paul Zumthor, an apt term for the instability of most medieval texts, especially in the vernacular:

> any work, in its manuscript tradition, appears as a constellation of elements, each of which may be the object of variations in the course of time or across space. The notion of *mouvance* implies that the work has no authentic text properly speaking, but that it is constituted by an abstract scheme, materialized in an unstable way from manuscript to manuscript, from performance to performance.[5]

Variation and instability at the level of the signifier finds a reflex at the level of signification in medieval books designed to include glosses and commentary with a "primary" text. The various forms of page layout designed to accommodate commentary attempted to fix a text in a frame that supplied a substitute for the text—its meaning, displayed in another text—but the parallel text of commentary produces quite another effect, in which any text is subject to endless supplements, repetitions, and rewritings.

Text and gloss format thus discloses one of the most fundamental features of medieval textuality—writing as an ongoing chain of supplements and interpretations, a feature of sign systems which is now termed semiosis in modern semiotic theory. Semiosis, a term given currency by C. S. Peirce, refers to the necessity of using additional signs to interpret the meaning of other signs. Simply stated, the interpretation of a text (one set of signs) always takes the form of another text (a supplement, an additional set of signs).[6] In the terms of Foucault's statement above, "language contains its own inner principle of proliferation." Social institutions with an interest in authority—church, school, court—attempted to regulate proliferations of textual meanings, and the frame of the marginal gloss is a representation of the attempt to at once disclose and control the text. But by displaying the non-self-sufficiency of the text in the interpretive supplement, the necessity of continual interpretation, of never capturing the text once and for all, is graphically displayed. Again, in Foucault's words, "the task of commentary can never, by definition, be completed."

Furthermore, the relationship between text and commentary represented in medieval manuscripts reveals that prior texts—ordinarily authoritative texts understood to bear a surplus of meaning—are constituted as texts per se through the supplementary text of commentary. The commentary by necessity refers to an object text, and as part of a system of social and political relations this objectification of a text is a mark of authority and cultural value. Not all medieval writings were objectified in this way—many things set down on paper had a different and sometimes ephemeral cultural function—but all texts presented with an apparatus of glosses or commentary would have registered as objects of knowledge and cultural value to a reader.

The textuality of commentary can thus be defined as the textual status generated by the differential relations among object texts and the texts of interpretive discourse; in short, the sense of the text that emerges from the layout of books in the text and gloss format. This form of textuality is closely related to the principle of intertextuality, which allows us to form a corollary: the writing of any new text can be understood as an interpretation or rewriting of prior texts within a library or larger system of texts. Or in the words of Montaigne cited by Foucault above, "we do nothing but write glosses on one another."

86

The gloss was thus what I term a medieval macrogenre, a literary form embracing, and attached to, other genres, which was not only transcribed in the margins, outside the manuscript space designed for texts (literary, legal, scientific, biblical), but, as a major genre in the medieval intertextual system, was also inscribed *within* many individual texts themselves, providing principles for composition and interpretation.[7] Since the gloss or commentary was a universal practice in medieval manuscript culture, imposing a material form on textuality that endured for centuries, the relationship between the textuality of glosses and that of other medieval texts needs to be closely investigated.

The textuality of commentary is interwoven throughout many medieval works, but Chaucer's dream poems provide an especially clear disclosure of this aspect of textuality since he exploits its literary, social, and political implications in a highly self-conscious way. Thus, *The Book of the Duchess*, *The House of Fame*, and *The Parliament of Fowls* reveal that the principles of gloss and commentary function in a formally constitutive way for the composition and organization of individual texts. Chaucer's rewriting and interpreting of Ovid, Vergil, or Macrobius in a new poem is thus the formal equivalent of the supplementary text of commentary transcribed in the margins. The textual principles writ large in the practice of the marginal gloss in medieval book production are also inscribed as organizing and interpretive principles in Chaucer's works.

Text and Gloss Format

Stanley Morison has shown that the styles of script and letter design in the history of writing were functions of political and institutional authority, and the development of page layout for accommodating commentary on authoritative texts has a similar, though as yet unwritten, history. There is no paleographical or codicological study of the history of the text and gloss format, and very few general studies of manuscript format have been written.[8] My remarks here (overly general as they are) are based on my own study of manuscripts relevant to medieval *grammatica* (grammatical treatises, copies of Vergil, Ovid, Boethius, and other *auctores*, and literary compilations and florilegia) from c.700 to c.1500. Although this is not the place for a technical discussion of manuscript layout, a few general principles should be kept in mind when considering manuscript textuality and the semiotics of the manuscript page.

The text and gloss format—actually a few different forms of page layout designed to support the presentation of text and gloss on the same page—became standardized in the Carolingian era and was practiced universally throughout European scriptoria as a result of the prestige and wide dissemination of books in post-Carolingian centers of learning. Most of the earliest glossed manuscripts are texts belonging to *grammatica*—classical and Christian Latin *auctores* and grammatical treatises. Most manuscripts of the *auctores* from the Carolingian era on reveal a standard method of arranging the space on the page. The page was ruled in three unequal columns, a large central column for main text and two outer columns of varying width for glosses. Ordinarily the scribe would divide the columns with double bounding lines and rule two sets of horizontal lines, one for the text and a second in the margins for glosses. The usual ratio for ruling lines was two lines in the gloss space for every one of main text. The top and bottom margins were also laid out for commentary and often ruled in advance with the effect that the gloss formed a frame around the central text. Space was allowed between the lines of the main text for interlinear glosses and grammatical aids.

The early manuscripts of the *Glossa ordinaria* on the Bible reveal that the layout for the biblical gloss was directly adapted from that used for Latin secular *auctores*.[9] The biblical *Glossa*, like the apparatus of glosses surrounding the *auctores* and legal and medical texts, reveals that the standardization of the form and content of marginal commentary is an effect of centralized authority.

As the layout for text and gloss developed after the twelfth century, interpretive glosses began to be written between the lines also, and the grammatical division of labor between interlinear and marginal glosses was not as strictly adhered to. This feature is clearly seen in manuscripts of the books of the Bible: the *Glossa* was frequently written in both the interlinear and marginal spaces on the page (see de Hamel). An alternative and widely used format in the twelfth through fifteenth centuries was the two-column layout, in which the text was copied in two columns with an accompanying running commentary. The commentary was transcribed, often in a smaller script, following manageable sections of the main text or following lemmata. In every format that was designed to include glosses, page layout and changes in script were used to signify both the distinction between text and gloss and the inseparable textual relationship between them. The text and gloss format, and the literary methodology it represents, continued in various forms throughout the later Middle Ages and even survived in the era of the printed book.

A study of the development of text and gloss format reveals that the post-Carolingian *mise-en-page* for canonical texts was an adaptation of the methodology for reading and interpretation in *grammatica*, *disciplina* of the literary text and literary language. Of the four main methodological divisions of *grammatica* (*lectio*, *enarratio*, *emendatio*, *iudicium*), the first two are represented formally in the format of the glosses: aids for *lectio*, which supplied procedures for reading a manuscript aloud, concerned lexical, syntactical, and metrical matters and were inscribed in interlinear glosses, especially in manuscripts of poetic texts; *enarratio* or exegesis of content (*e-nar-*

ratio: out of, from the *narratio*) was copied in the margins, the interpretive frame of the text, which could be expanded in width in proportion to the length or expansiveness of the commentary. Grammatical *enarratio* was quite explicitly a supplementary discourse, a writing of the reading of a text, and not simply an internalized, meditative act. A commentary is thus an "enarrated" text, and a gloss in any format stood in a dialogic relation with the source text.[10] The layout of manuscripts in the grammatical tradition reveals a striking case of interpretive methodology crystallizing into a visual form that discloses an underlying principle of textuality.

The medieval experience of an authoritative text, therefore, ordinarily included a commentary that was transcribed in a predesigned space in the margins and between the lines. The commentary or gloss was ordinarily copied simultaneously with the "primary" text and most often from the same exemplar. Text and gloss format does not represent ad hoc reader's marginalia added afterwards and unanticipated by the design of the book. (I am not, therefore, discussing here the question of readers' responses in marginalia, which is a different, though valid, topic of textual reception.) Only authoritative or canonical texts were transmitted in this format; in fact, the chief mark of a text's status, that it was received and read as a text, a privileged linguistic object in the cultural canon, is its presentation in this format and the existence of an apparatus of accompanying commentary. The forms of layout for the marginal gloss are thus a revealing example of the interpretive function of format and page layout in the presentation of the text to a reader.[11]

A multitude of manuscripts from the age of Chaucer exemplify the text and gloss format, but I will refer to only a few here. Oxford, Bodleian Library, Rawlinson G.187 (s.xiv², Italy) (plate 1) is a copy of Boethius's *On the Consolation of Philosophy* with the commentary of Nicholas Trevet. The text was written in two columns with wide

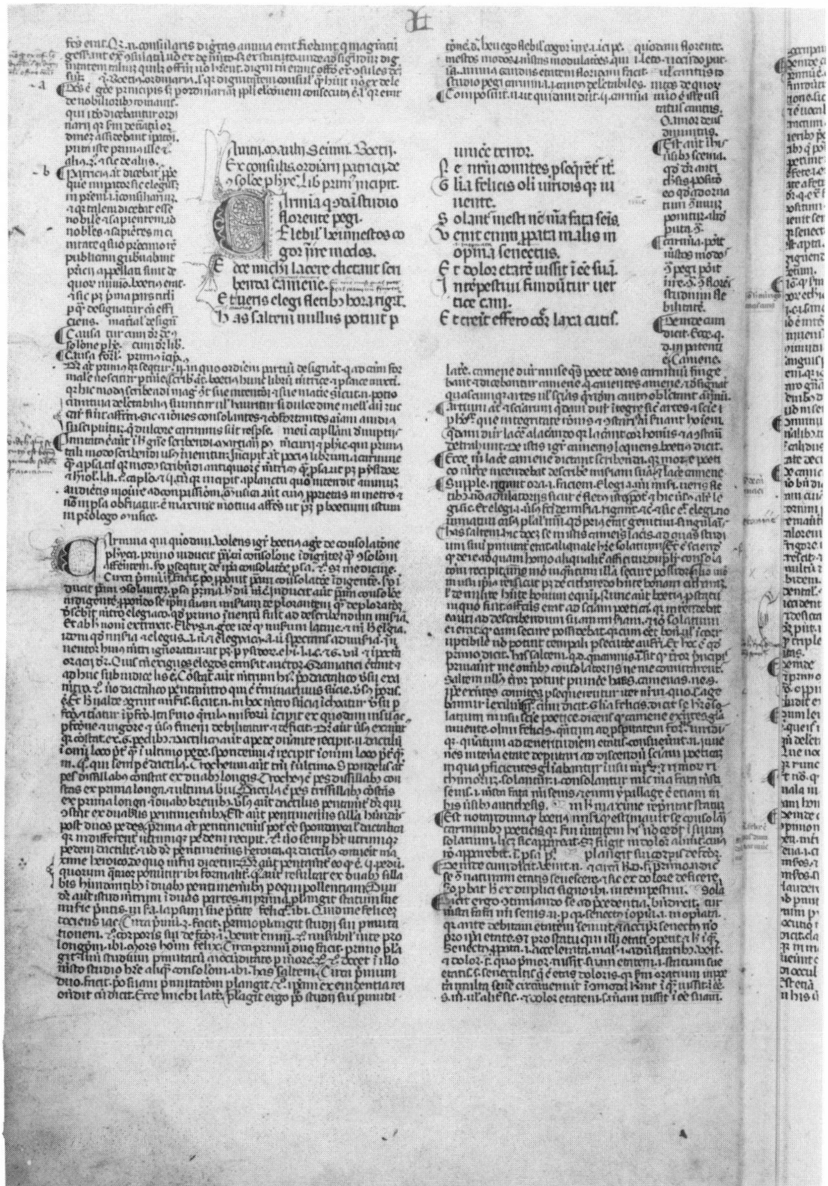

Plate 1. Oxford, Bodleian Library, MS. Rawl. G. 187, fol. 1ᵛ

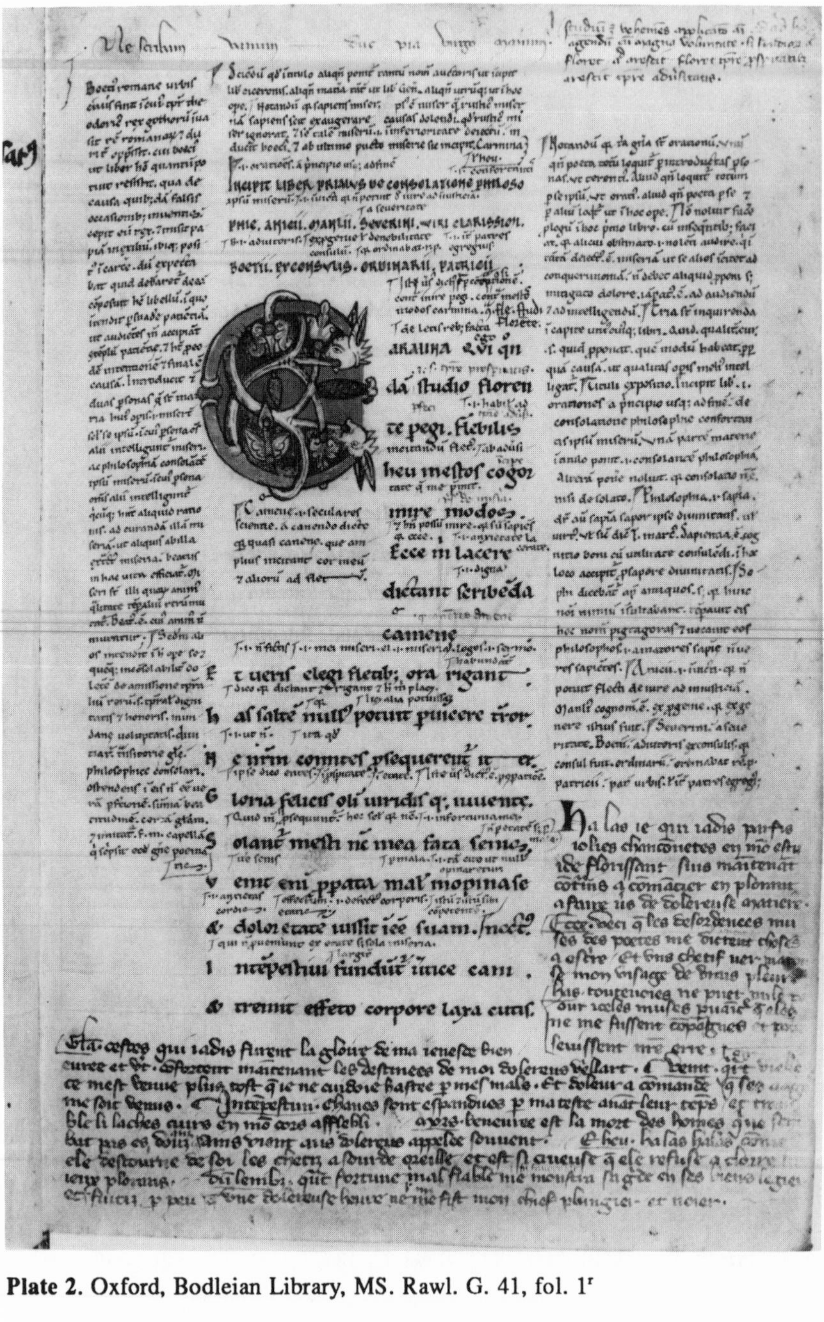

Plate 2. Oxford, Bodleian Library, MS. Rawl. G. 41, fol. 1ʳ

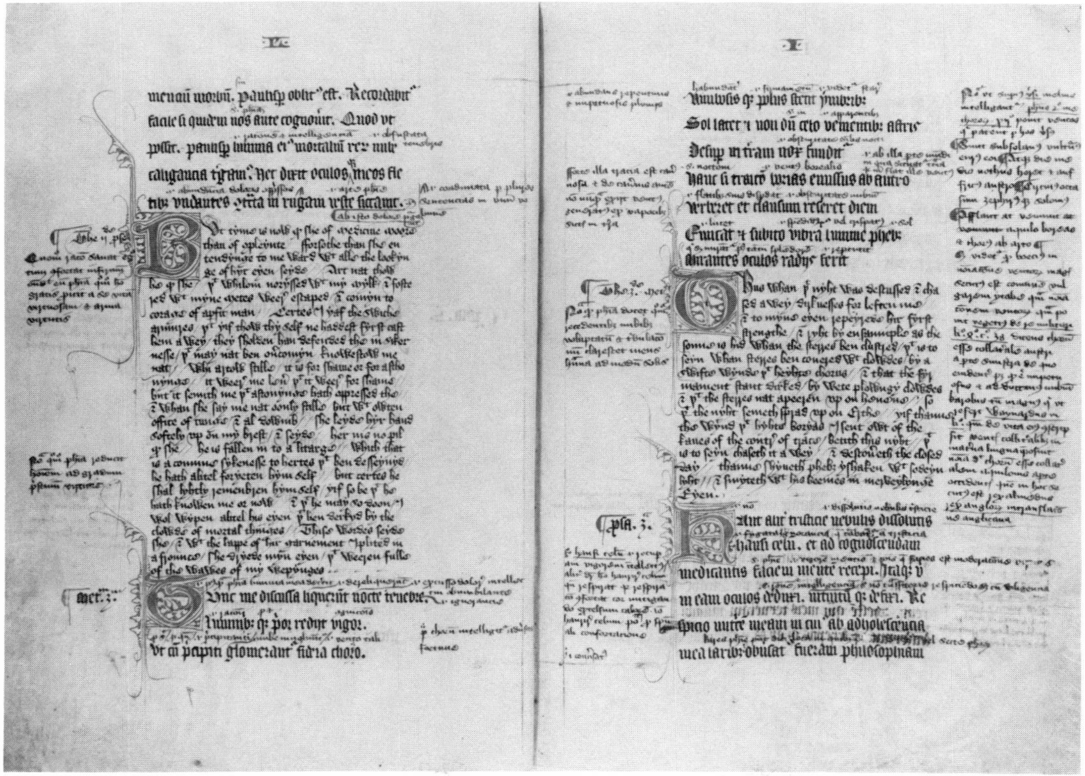

Plate 3. Cambridge University Library MS. Ii.3.21, fols. 13ᵛ–14ʳ.

margins designed for the commentary, which surrounds the text in all four margins. Similarly, Rawlinson G.41, a twelfth-century copy of Boethius written in a single column in the center of the page, contains the French translation of Boethius by Jean de Meun, which was copied at the same time as the text and functions as a gloss; then in the fourteenth century a second scribe added the commentary of Nicholas Trevet in remaining space in the side and bottom margins (plate 2). Chaucer himself may have used a copy of Boethius in this format. In Chaucer's translation of Boethius, which includes glosses derived from Nicholas Trevet and other sources, the authoritative form (*auctor-cum-glossa*) is inserted in the English version, a translation that includes its own gloss. An example in the two-column format is Cambridge, University Library, Ii.3.21 (c.1420–30), which presents Boethius's Latin text and Chaucer's translation in the gloss position. The page layout also allows for Latin glosses and headings in the margins. Chaucer's *Boece*, written in smaller script and copied on every ruled line, as opposed to every other line for the Latin text, clearly functions as a gloss on Boethius (plate 3). The status of Chaucer's translation as gloss is designated by the layout of the page and change in script.[12] Chaucer's *Boece* itself is a translation of text and gloss, glosses compiled from Jean de Meun, Nicholas Trevet, and Remigius of Auxerre (see Minnis).

The spatial separation or dislocation of text and meaning in the text and gloss format also produced a heightened awareness of the metatextual level of writing—marginality, supplementarity, and meaning becoming equivalent categories—and discloses that commentary had its own textuality, its own textual space. What is "outside" the text is its (re)written meaning. Commentaries are "marginal," in the manuscript sense of the term, written outside or after a text, and the spatial dislocation of text and meaning is recapitulated in separate commentaries written in other codices outside or after a text, supplementary books which take their place in the library next to the books they gloss. Rather than establishing a closure for the text, the interpretive frame of the gloss represents the endless process of deferral or limitless semiosis that constitutes reading, interpreting, and writing.

The textuality of commentary erases the boundary of the text as the simple ruling lines that distinguish the space of the text from the marginal space of the gloss: since the formal inscription of the text is always double (or at least open to doubling), and at times triple (if more than one set of glosses or commentary traditions are transcribed on the page), the text is dispersed on the page itself, repeated in another form, recapitulated beyond its initially written space. Borrowing a metaphor (and punning etymology) from Isidore of Seville—that writing or the letter (*littera*) is so called because letters are repeated in reading (*legens + itero*)—one can define a text as what is iterable, capable of repetition, in reading and in the writing of that reading in the interpretive text of commentary (*Origines sive Etymologiae*, 1.3.1–2). Text and gloss format is thus an icon of textual dissemination: medieval cultural practice both instituted canonicity and blurred the boundaries of a text by inscribing its meaning in a supplement that did not attempt to erase its own textuality, its own status as text. Commentary extends itself, paradoxically, as the *meaning* of an object text, but this meaning also turns out to be not the pure object text stripped of its rhetorical husk but yet another text occupying its own conventional space on the page.

Furthermore, in the accommodation of interpretive methodology in the design of the book, text and gloss format represents the institutional and social forces which regulated and authorized a canon of texts and their interpretation. This format instituted many texts, especially the authorized canon of *auctores*, as double: texts were mediated and strategically situated in a supplementary frame, an ideologically instituted reading represented simultaneously with the text to be read, a reading authenticated by the social institutions—school, university, monastery, church, court—that invested the text with meaning and authority. Thus the text and gloss format is an image of textual power authorized by a textual community. To produce books in this format is to reinscribe textual authority in the doubling or iteration of the text, disseminating textual power through its interpretive supplement.

Writing as Rewriting and Commentary

The textuality of commentary displayed in the layout of manuscripts is also disclosed in textual relations registered in literary discourse. As part of a network of intertextual relations, the macrogenre of commentary was interwoven or inscribed within other texts and other genres. The interweaving of the discursive form of commentary within individual texts functioned at two levels: 1) the formal or structural level of texts in which macro and microtextual categories of discourse are convertible and generic systems of language overlap or interanimate each other in the dialogic interplay that constitutes a text, and 2) the level of rhetorical rules for composing new texts, both the rules self-consciously articulated in *artes poeticae* and those presupposed in the library of texts that supplied the *materia* for new poems. The procedures for writing the supplementary text of commentary became a means of *inventio*, the formal techniques for discovering what can be said about a subject, and *dispositio*, the strategies for arrangement and organization, chief of which for poetry was amplification, the expansion of a theme.[13]

In medieval poetry, the convertibility of text and commentary, or new poem as commentary on earlier poems, can be readily seen in poems which reflect upon, rewrite, expand, and interpret the texts of the *auctores*, poems which, in effect, are written in the margins of prior texts, functioning as a supplement to or extended gloss on texts in the literary canon. Many medieval texts, the *Queste del saint graal* and the *Ovide moralisé*, for example, include their own glosses or are quite explicitly an extended gloss on traditional textual *materia*. The technique of glossing or *enarratio* had become recognized in the repertoire of rhetorical strategies for composition.

The notion that writing is implicitly an act of commentary was widely recognized in medieval literary theory. For example, Marie de France, in her prologue to the *Lais*, provides a definition of the textuality of commentary to which Chaucer would have readily subscribed:

> Custume fu as ancïens,
> Ceo testimoine Precïens,
> Es livres ke jadis feseient,
> Assez oscurement diseient
> Pur ceus ki a venir esteient
> E ki aprendre les deveient,
> K'i peéssent gloser la lettre
> E de lur sen le surplus mettre. (Prol. 9–16)

> The ancients had the practice—
> as Priscian testifies—
> of speaking rather obscurely
> in the books they wrote,
> so that those who were to come after
> and were to learn them
> might gloss the letter
> and supply an addition from their own understanding.

Marie's prologue is one of the most highly commented on texts in studies of medieval poetics.[14] Some have assumed that Marie is referring to a statement in Priscian's prologue to the *Institutiones grammaticae*, in which he discusses the clarity of recent interpreters of *grammatica* who have diligently clarified what was amiss in earlier Greek writers: *cuius auctores, quanto sunt iuniores, tanto perspicaciores* ("the authors of which *ars*, the more recent they are, the clearer").[15] But Priscian is talking about clarity with respect to correcting error, not interpreting obscure meaning. It is likely that Marie has no specific passage from Priscian in mind; she may be referring to Priscian more generally as a symbol of *grammatica*, the study of textual language and literature, which provided the method for interpreting texts and writing glosses. The addition of *sens*—interpretation, meaning—through the rewriting of prior texts was a recognized strategy of romance writing, and Marie's "gloser la lettre" is the equivalent of grammatical *enarratio*, for which poets of the twelfth century and later meant interpreting the *integumenta* ("oscurement diseient") of earlier poets *through* the supplementary text ("le surplus") of a new poem.[16] The textuality of commentary, the supplement that produces meaning through a second text, is thus inscribed within the genre of medieval romance from its origins.

Chaucer's Use of the Textuality of Commentary in the Dream Poems

The dream poem genre allowed Chaucer to articulate the very model of textuality that his poetry represents. The narrator whom Chaucer invented for his dream poems is distinct from models in the French tradition in that Chaucer's narrator is explicitly represented as a reader and writer, self-consciously absorbed in the *auctores* and in questioning the very grounds of writing new poems from old. Chaucer's dream poems narrate book-induced dreams: Chaucer's narrator consistently falls asleep over a book—an *auctor*—and the subsequent poem is a product of reading, rewriting, and commenting on the text "dreamed" over.[17] Indeed, Chaucer allows the dream framework to function as a metaphor for the process of writing itself, thus raising the dream frame to the metatextual level: a new poem is a "dream" about the *auctores*, an interpretive supplement to an earlier text.

An image of this process is the *somnium animale* in *The Parliament of Fowls* in which Chaucer represents Scipio Africanus, who figures in Macrobius's *Commentary on the Dream of Scipio*, the text that the narrator had just been reading and had fallen asleep over, as the guide to the narrator's journey within the dream poem. The dream frame reveals that, in literary terms, "to dream" (write a poem) is "to read" (interpret or gloss a text), that is, to write an "enarrated" text, a text that is a writing of a reading. The dream poems, therefore, embody the textuality of commentary, Chaucer's new poems functioning as gloss or supplement (Marie's "surplus").

The textuality that constitutes Chaucer's dream poems is disclosed through three closely related features of the narrative form: 1) the relationship established between prior, authoritative texts (the narrator's "olde books") and the dream-narrative of the poem (that of text and gloss, "gloser la lettre . . . le surplus mettre"); 2) the construction of the narrator and authorial "I," a reader-writer, the site where *enarratio* and *narratio* converge to produce the text of the poem; and 3) the narrative frame of the dream-vision genre itself, which becomes a metapoetic device for describing how poems are produced. I would like to discuss each of these features briefly and then turn to a more detailed examination of *The Book of the Duchess*, which, as the earliest of Chaucer's dream poems, can conveniently be studied as a paradigm of the textual relations he elaborates in the later poems.

In *The Book of the Duchess*, *The House of Fame*, and *The Parliament of Fowls*, the narrative establishes quite explicitly the relationship between itself and an "olde bok" (*PF* 19, 110).[18] In fact, the adjective Chaucer uses most often with "book(s)" is "olde," his shorthand for traditional texts, the *auctores*.[19] The enarration of the *auctor* inscribed in Chaucer's dream poems is always written through a network of intertexts from medieval romance tradition that provided the narrative possibilities available to Chaucer—the *Romance of the Rose* and the *dits* and dream poems by Machaut and Froissart (throughout Chaucer's dream poems) and Dante's *Commedia* (from *The House of Fame* on). These medieval texts supplied the discursive models through which the *auctores* were interpreted in Chaucer's poems and are the equivalent of the larger system of discourse—philosophical, theological, literary, ideological—in which glosses and commentaries participated.

Much critical attention has been paid to the status of the narrative "I" in medieval romance literature.[20] The tradition of romance poetry produced an impersonal and universal narrative "I," a speaking subject that could include biographical references, but references that could also be copied or plagiarized. The first person narrator was thus an interchangeable part of speech in the grammar of poetic discourse, a speaker of universalized experience through the linguistic form of an individual speaker. Chaucer constructed his narrators on romance models, but with a critical difference: Chaucer's first person narrators are the site of authorial intervention in the system of texts and genres that constitute the new poem. Chaucer's narrative "I" is not simply the narrator of French romance tradition but is a reader and writer who claims no direct experience of what other narrators traditionally asserted as an authentication of their first-person voice (the experience of love), and by invoking the "I" who composed the poem, as opposed to simply the "I" who experienced what the poem narrates, Chaucer blurs the distinction between the "I" as a figure of universalized experience and the "I" of the author who stands apart from the text he has written.[21] By situating the narrator among books and the mediated experience afforded through books, Chaucer constructs the narrative "I" as a glossator, the reader-writer who composes a poem only *after* reading another text, a text that the "I" supplements with a narrative of what he experiences in a book-induced dream. Chaucer's narrative "I" is thus a meta-narrator, a narrator who reflects back on the process of writing narrative.

Chaucer also converts the narrative frame of the dream-vision genre into a metatextual device that comments on the process of writing. Each of Chaucer's dream poems is based on an underlying narrative formula that was open to variation and elaboration: the introduction of the first-person narrator, the narrator's reading of an *auctor*, a narrative of the dream induced by reading a book, and a brief closing in which the narrator states that he wakes up, having recorded the text of the dream. In *The Book of the Duchess*, the narrative frame is neatly circular, the narrator awakening with the book that induced the dream-text still in his hand (1325–29). In *The House of Fame*, the references to the texts to be rewritten are made elliptically within the narrative, and the narrator dreams the text and gloss on Vergil's *Aeneid* simultaneously in Book 1. The second text that Chaucer glosses, Ovid's *Metamorphoses* 12, is never explicitly identified, but the references to the House of Fame in Book 2 are sufficient shorthand for any reader. *The House of Fame* lacks a circular closure, but one can readily be supplied by completing the narrative frame opened at the beginning. The frame of *The Parliament of Fowls* is also circular, indeed, cyclical: the narrator awakens, concluding the extended gloss on Macrobius, by stating that he will seek out other books so that he can dream another poem (695–99). The Preface to *The Legend of Good Women* is a meditation on books and writing in which the narrator dreams and then turns to books to write the collection of stories that the god of love commands him to write: "And with that word my bokes gan I take,/ And ryght thus on my Legende gan I make" (F 578–89). The narrative frame of all the dream poems thus calls attention to reading and writing, an image, as it were, of the iteration of texts in marginal glosses and commentaries.

The Book of the Duchess provides a model of the narrative form that Chaucer continued to elaborate in his other dream poems. Chaucer constructed a narrator in *The Book of the Duchess* on the model of the insomniac narrators in Guillaume de Machaut's *Le Dit de la Fonteinne Amoureuse* and Jean Froissart's *Le Paradis d'Amours*, but Chaucer invests the narrator with a highly self-conscious literary function revealed in the comic paradox that opens the poem: an insomniac narrator, clearly the "I" of the romance dream-vision genre, cannot fall asleep, that is, cannot get the poem started, since the narrator must first sleep in order to dream/write. Chaucer's ironic play with the conventions of the French dream poem thus calls attention to the dream-frame in the first lines of the poem, signalling its metapoetic function.[22]

The narrator is also constructed as a reader, and the fit of insomnia—the inability to begin a poem, the need to find the right textual matter—is resolved through the introduction of a book, the text that allows the reader-narrator to sleep and dream the poem. The narrator states that he asks someone to fetch him a book,

> A romaunce, and he it me tok
> To rede and drive the night away;
> For me thoughte it better play
> Then playe either at ches or tables.
> And in this bok were written fables
> That clerkes had in olde tyme,
> And other poetes, put in rime
> To rede and for to be in minde,
> While men loved the lawe of kinde.
> This bok ne spak but of such thinges,
> Of quenes lives, and of kinges,
> And many other thinges smale. (48–59)

The references are clearly to Ovid's *Metamorphoses*, with a version in French ("romaunce," the *Ovide Moralisé*), and to Ovid's Golden Age ("while men loved the lawe of kinde"), a suitable myth for the idealized portrayal of the Man in Black who follows love's natural law. The book contains lives of kings and queens, one of which supplies the text to be glossed in the poem. The narrator falls asleep after reading Ovid's *Metamorphoses* 11, which contains the story of Ceyx and Alcione, and the ensuing narrative, represented as a dream, rewrites the *auctor* by extending it to a contemporary rhetorical situation, the praise of a patron through a eulogy commemorating his wife's nobility.

Chaucer got the idea for the Ceyx and Alcione story from Machaut, who uses it as an exemplum for a lover's grief, but Chaucer gives Ovid's account of the Ceyx legend an essential narrative function. Chaucer converts a reference to a story in a dream-narrative to a text that induces the narrator's dream and that the dream-narrative interprets and doubles. The narrator's apparently accidental discovery of Ovid in the passage just cited does not obscure the larger intertextual strategy that Chaucer deploys through his narrator-as-reader and the dream-frame as metapoetic device. Chaucer ties reading and interpreting a book to rhetorical invention (discovery of subject matter) and to the resulting *amplificatio* of the theme to be worked out. Textual *enarratio* takes the form of another text, Ovid rewritten in another *narratio*.

The narrator is represented as awakening into a dream in which the walls and windows of his own bedroom become an image of the poet's library, the inscribed walls depicting the larger system of texts and genres through which the poem is interpreted and which the poem glosses:

> my chambre was
> Ful wel depeynted, and with glas

103

> Were al the wyndowes wel yglased
> Ful clere, and nat an hoole ycrased,
> That to beholde hyt was gret joye.
> For hooly al the story of Troye
> Was in the glasynge ywroght thus,
> Of Ector and of kyng Priamus,
> Of Achilles and of kyng Lamedon,
> And eke of Medea and of Jason,
> Of Paris, Eleyne, and of Lavyne.
> And alle the walles with colours fyne
> Were peynted, bothe text and glose,
> Of al the Romaunce of the Rose. (321–34)

The walls of the narrator's room, with scenes from the *Aeneid* and classical tradition in the windows and the "text and gloss" of *The Romance of the Rose* on the walls, portray the textuality of the poem he is engaged in writing, an extended gloss on Ovid. At the end of the poem, the narrator is represented as waking from his dream with Ovid's text still in his hand:

> Therwyth I awook myselve
> And fond me lyinge in my bed;
> And the book that I hadde red,
> Of Alcione and Seys the kyng,
> And of the goddes of slepyng,
> I fond hyt in myn hond ful even. (1324–29)

The dream-poem is thus an enarrated text: the poem Chaucer has just written is the formal equivalent of commentary transcribed in the margins. Commentary attempts to disclose or externalize some inner, potential discourse obscured by the surface rhetoric of the text. In writing a poem that instantiates the interpretation of an *auctor*, Chaucer externalizes this potential in the same way a marginal commentary discloses the meaning of a text in a spatially externalizing form. Chaucer suggests through a thin veil of allegory that writing is necessarily a rewriting, or, in semiotic terms, the interpretation of a text must always take the form of another text. Chaucer's poem is the literary expression of Ovid-as-read, the interpretation of Ovid extended to the supplementary text of *The Book of the Duchess*. Any reader schooled in the library represented in the narrator's room would interpret the episode with the Man in Black as a clever piece of rhetorical *inventio* that extends the Ceyx and Alcione story in Ovid.

Chaucer also removes the distance between authorial voice and the narrative "I" by constructing a narrator who is at once reader and writer, a reader of Ovid and the writer of the "book" that is *The Book of the Duchess*. While narrating the story of Ceyx and Alcione, the narrator both establishes the chain of sympathies that include, prospectively, those of the Knight, and constructs the narrative "I" as the voice of the author: "I, that made this book,/ Had such pittee and such rowthe/ To rede hir sorwe. . ." (96–98). The narrator states that he could not sleep, that is, find the right textual matter to begin the poem until he read the tale of Ceyx:

> For I ne myghte, for bote ne bale,
> Slepe or I had red thys tale
> Of this dreynte Seys the kyng
> And of the goddes of slepyng. (227–30)

This is a transparent allegory of the invention process at work in the poem. The narrator states that he actually falls asleep *on* the book he was reading, after invoking the god of sleep mentioned in the text: "ryght upon my book/ Y fil aslepe, and therwith even/ Me mette so ynly swete a sweven" (274–76). The narrator as "maker" of the book also becomes identified as author at the conclusion of the poem, the dream-frame finding closure in a return to the book (Ovid) that generated the book of the dream-poem. The text of the poem is, then, a record of the Ovidian dream.

The *House of Fame*, as I have argued elsewhere, is explicitly about the nature of literary discourse and the textuality of history and *auctoritas*. Chaucer also begins *The House of Fame* with a paradox that plays on dream-vision conventions: the narrator takes the stance of a radical doubter of the validity of dreams, one who doubts their hidden, interpretable discourse of truth (1.1–65). The narrator again invokes Ovid's god of sleep ("to this god that I of rede" [1.77]), falls asleep, and dreams that he awakens into a temple of poetry that contains an interpreted version of Vergil's *Aeneid* "writen on a table of bras" (1.142). But instead of representing a narrator who falls asleep over a book, Chaucer constructs a narrator who dreams in books, that is, dreams poetic discourse, playing in the margins and between the lines of Vergil and Ovid. In book 1, the reader is told to "Rede Virgile in Eneydos/ Or the Epistle of Ovyde" (1.378–79) to learn more about the conclusion to the Dido story. Although the narrator refers to the story engraved on the brass tablet as if he dreamed in images,[23] the language used to describe the dreamed narrative is finally that of *texts*: "tho began the story anoon" (1.149), "As men may ofte in bokes rede" (1.385), "The book seyth" (1.429).

In fact, the whole of book 1, the rewriting of the *Aeneid* from Dido's point of view, is an extended commentary through the intertext of Ovid's *Heroides*: Chaucer produces a Vergil Ovidized. The transition to book 2 is likewise a textual dream. The narrator is represented as emerging from the temple into a desert like the "desert of Lybye" (1.488), the Libyan desert of Dido's Carthage in the *Aeneid*. The golden eagle of book 2, who darts out of the pages of Dante's *Commedia* and plucks the narrator out of this literary desert, transfers the narrator to another text: functioning as the librarian of the labyrinthian library of *Fama*, the eagle leads the narrator to two other books,

Ovid's *Metamorphoses* read through the intertext of Dante's *Commedia*.

The main text being interpreted in books 2 and 3 of *The House of Fame* is Ovid's *Metamorphoses* 12, which contains a description of the hall of *Fama*, and the central narrative of the *House or Fame* deconstructs the received idea of *auctoritas* through the theory of speech and writing in *grammatica*. The narrative of *The House of Fame* is an allegorical journey into the labyrinth of the literary archive that attempts to reveal the structure of discourse from within the re-echoing corridors of literary discourse itself. Reading and writing are found to be practices which occur within a vast intertextual network: any text becomes part of a labyrinthian matrix that dissolves the illusion of secure knowledge of a self-evident world external to its representation in discourse. All texts are discovered to be glosses on prior texts, ad infinitum.

Chaucer returns to the formula of Text + Dream = New Poem in *The Parliament of Fowls*. In this poem, the text and gloss structure, the construction of the narrator-reader, and the dream-frame are tightly interwoven. In the fourth stanza, Chaucer refers explicitly to the semiotic process of knowledge—that new knowledge results from interpreting earlier texts in a new text—that is, to the textuality of commentary inscribed within his own poem:

> For out of olde feldes, as men seyth,
> Cometh al this newe corn from yer to yere,
> And out of olde bokes, in good feyth,
> Cometh al this newe science that men lere. (22–25)

The narrator falls asleep over "a bok . . . write with lettres olde" (19), a copy of Macrobius's *Commentarium in somnium Scipionis*:

"Bothe text and gloss"

This bok of which I make mencioun
Entitled was al ther, as I shal telle:
"Tullyus of the Drem of Scipioun." (29–31)

A summary narration of the part of Macrobius's text that relates Scipio's dream follows, the technique also used in *The Book of the Duchess* and *The House of Fame*. Chaucer's rewriting of Scipio's dream narrative foregrounds the social value of "commune profyt" (47, 75), which is the part of Macrobius's text glossed in the parliament of birds, a marriage debate, reflecting (probably) the political negotiations in the marriage of Richard II and Anne of Bohemia, resolved "by evene acord" (668).

The narrator-glossator concludes the poem with an explicit statement of the intertextual dimension of writing and the convertability of the terms reading and writing at the level of textuality:

I wok, and othere bokes tok me to,
To reede upon, and yit I rede alwey.
I hope, ywis, to rede so som day
That I shal mete some thyng for to fare
The bet, and thus to rede I nyl nat spare. (695–99 [end])

The narrator closes the poem by awakening to the reading of other books, a reading that, in the fiction of the dream frame, will induce another "dream," another poem written as a text in the supplementary space of a commentary. Chaucer's narrator-glossator discloses that the fiction of the dream is equivalent to the glossed margins of books, that is, the dream that is itself a metatext, an interpretation of an earlier text, occurs within the space of the commentary, after or outside a text. To "dream" is to supplement, to enter the space of marginality, the writing of reading. Chaucer clearly indicates his awareness of the text he has been writing: as the meaning of a text is constituted by the interplay of text and gloss in the act of reading, a text is produced by the interplay of reading and writing, in which reading, or the prior text-as-read, is formally inscribed in its own space.

In Chaucer's dream poems, the main features of the narrative form—the dream frame, the narrator, the use of a book to induce the dream—become metapoetic devices that re-inscribe the textuality of commentary within the new text of the poems. Thus the model of textuality represented in glossed books discloses fundamental structures of interpretation and writing that can be seen replicated on many different levels. Chaucer's works make explicit the metatextual and metalingual awareness produced by the interplay of text and gloss on the manuscript page, an awareness that also runs throughout medieval grammatical and semiotic theory. The commentary or gloss, therefore, is best understood as a macrogenre—a transtextual and transgeneric form—which was inscribed within other literary genres. Both the rhetorical strategies and generic form of Chaucer's dream poems suggest that his poems are, in an important sense, extended glosses on other texts (Ovid, Macrobius, and Vergil). Writing is thus constituted by *enarratio*, a writing of a reading of other texts in the cultural library. Chaucer's works reveal a writer who understood the implications of these literary principles and was able to exploit them for his own rhetorical ends.

NOTES

1. See, for example, Carruthers, Besserman, Hanning, and Schibanoff. The problem of glosses in the Chaucer manuscripts themselves is another matter. This subject is conveniently summarized by Schibanoff and by Caie. Stephen Partridge is preparing an edition of all the glosses in the Chaucer manuscripts.

2. I am especially indebted to Jerome McGann's work on this matter; see especially the studies in *The Beauty of Inflections* 67–132 and *A Critique*. McGann's approach to textual history contains many lessons for medievalists. For the social dimensions of literary form and production, see also Macherey 51–53, 75–81.

3. This division is expertly critiqued by Patterson 3–114.

4. See the special issue of *Speculum* (January 1990), edited by Stephen Nichols and devoted to the "new philology," for other approaches to the problem of texts in manuscript culture.

5. Zumthor, *Speaking of the Middle Ages* 96n49. See the discussion on 22–27 and 59–72. This notion was first presented in Zumthor, *Essai* 68–75.

6. The concept of semiosis and the understanding of texts as systems of signs had been recognized even before Augustine, although he is the source of most medieval semiotic theory. For background see Irvine, "Interpretation and the semiotics of allegory," and for additional sources see Irvine "A guide to the sources of medieval theories of interpretation."

7. I discuss a set of medieval macrogenres more extensively in "Medieval Textuality."

8. On manuscript format in general, see Bischoff 20–30 and the studies by Gilissen. On the form of grammatical manuscripts see Holtz, and on the format of glosses on the Bible see Lobrichon, "Une nouveauté." Two recent studies in *The Role of the*

Book in Medieval Culture, ed. Peter Ganz, discuss the social uses of glossed books: Lobrichon, "Conserver, réformer, transformer le monde?," 2: 75–94 and Berschin, "Glossierte Virgil-Handschriftten," 2: 129–34. Valuable studies of the effects of larger cultural practices and interpretive methods on manuscript format are Parkes, Rouse and Rouse, and de Hamel.

9. This can be clearly seen in the plates to Smalley, "Les commentaires bibliques." The *Glossa* is actually a compilation of several layers of glosses which were consolidated in the early twelfth century by scholars in the circle of Anselm of Laon and then promoted as a standard commentary in the schools of Paris from the later twelfth century on. See Smalley "Les commentaires bibliques," "Some Gospel Commentaries," and *The Study of the Bible* 46–66, and de Hamel.

10. I treat the literary theory transmitted in *grammatica* in my forthcoming book, *Grammatica: Literary Theory and Textual Culture in the Early Middle Ages*.

11. On the significance of layout and page design in manuscripts of Chaucer's and Gower's works see Doyle and Parkes 186–203.

12. On this and other *Boece* manuscripts see Machan.

13. On *inventio* see Kelly, "Topical Invention" and "Obscurity and Memory," and on amplification adapting the procedures for commentary see Gallo.

14. See Spitzer, "The Prologue to the *Lais*"; Robertson; Donovan; Pickens; Foulet and Uitti; and Hanning, "'I Shal Finde It in a Maner Glose'" 32–37.

15. *Institutiones grammaticae*, ed. Hertz, 2.1. This is the view of Donovan and Wetherbee 228–29.

16. See Vinaver and the studies by Kelly.

17. That Chaucer's introduction of a book in the dream-narrative frame is a departure from the French models has been known for some time; see Stearns. Wimsatt records no French parallels for Chaucer's reader-narrator, and Payne (114–21) finds the book and dream formula distinctive to Chaucer's poetic theory. See also Boitani, *English Medieval Narrative* 138–92 and "Old Books Brought to Life," and Neuss.

18. All references to Chaucer's works are from *The Riverside Chaucer*.

19. See *BD* 52–53; *PF* 19, 24, 110; *LGW* Prol. F/G 25, G 27, G 82.

20. See Spitzer, "Note on the Poetic and Empirical 'I'"; the essays in *Genre* 6 (1973); Zumthor, "Le 'Je' du Poète"; and Allen.

21. Note, inter alia, the following lines: *BD* 96 ("I, that made this book") and *BD* 1330–34; *HF* 109–10, Proem to Bk. 2; *PF* 15–21, 695–99; *LGW* Prol. F/G 30, F 578–79 / G 544–45.

22. Chaucer's invention of a problematic narrator, who calls the French conventions into question, has been discussed by Nolan.

23. See 1.151, 162, 174, 193, 198, 209, 212, 219, 253, 256, 433, 439, 451, 468–72.

Martin Irvine

MANUSCRIPTS CITED

Oxford, Bodleian Library, Rawlinson G.187

Oxford, Bodleian Library, Rawlinson G.41

Cambridge, University Library, Ii.3.21

WORKS CITED

Allen, Judson Boyce. "Grammar, Poetic Form, and the Lyric Ego: A Medieval *A Priori*." *Vernacular Poetics in the Middle Ages*. Ed. Lois Ebin. Kalamazoo: Medieval Institute Publications, 1984. 199–226.

Barthes, Roland. "From Work to Text." *Image, Music, Text*. Trans. Stephen Heath. New York: Hill and Wang, 1977. 156–64.

Berschin, Walter, "Glossierte Virgil-Handschriften drier *Aetates Virgilianae*." *The Role of the Book*. Ed. Ganz. 2: 115–28.

Besserman, Lawrence. "*Glosynge is a Glorious Thyng*: Chaucer's Biblical Exegesis." *Chaucer and Scriptural Tradition*. Ed. David Lyle Jeffrey. Ottawa: U of Ottawa P, 1984. 65–74.

Bischoff, Bernhard. *Latin Paleography: Antiquity and the Middle Ages*. Trans. Daibhi Ó Croinin and David Ganz. Cambridge: Cambridge UP, 1990.

Boitani, Piero. *English Medieval Narrative in the 13th and 14th Centuries*. Cambridge: Cambridge UP, 1982.

———. "Old Books brought to life in dreams: the *Book of the Duchess*, the *House of Fame*, and the *Parliament of Fowls*." *The Cambridge Chaucer Companion*. Ed. Piero Boitani and Jill Mann. Cambridge: Cambridge UP, 1986. 39–57.

113

"Bothe text and gloss"

Caie, Graham D. "The Significance of Marginal Glosses in the Earliest Manuscripts of *The Canterbury Tales.*" *Chaucer and Scriptural Tradition.* Ed. David Lyle Jeffrey. Ottawa: U of Ottawa P, 1984. 75–88.

Carruthers, Mary. "Letter and Gloss in the Friar's and Summoner's Tales." *Journal of Narrative Technique* 2 (1972): 308–14.

Chaucer, Geoffrey. *The Riverside Chaucer.* 3rd ed. General ed. Larry D. Benson. Boston: Houghton Mifflin, 1987.

De Hamel, Christopher. *Glossed Books of the Bible and the Origins of the Paris Book Trade.* Woodbridge and Wolfeboro, NH: Boydell & Brewer, 1984.

Donovan, Mortimer J. "Priscian and the Obscurity of the Ancients." *Speculum* 36 (1961): 75–80.

Doyle, A. I. and M. B. Parkes. "The Production of Copies of the *Canterbury Tales* and the *Confessio Amantis* in the Early Fifteenth Century." *Medieval Scribes, Manuscripts and Libraries: Essays Presented to N. R. Ker.* Ed. M. B. Parkes and Andrew G. Watson. London: Scolar Press, 1978. 163–210.

Foucault, Michel. *The Order of Things: An Archaeology of the Human Sciences.* Trans. of *Les Mots et Les Choses.* New York: Random House, 1970.

———. *The Archaeology of Knowledge.* Trans. A. M. Sheridan Smith. New York: Pantheon, 1972.

Foulet, Alfred and Karl D. Uitti. "The Prologue to the *Lais* of Marie de France: Towards an Interpretation." *Romance Philology* 35 (1981): 242–49.

Gallo, Ernest. "The *Poetria Nova* of Geoffrey of Vinsauf." *Medieval Eloquence: Studies in the Theory and Practice of Medieval Rhetoric.* Ed. James J. Murphy. Berkeley: U of California P, 1978. 68–84.

Ganz, Peter, ed. *The Role of the Book in Medieval Culture.* 2 vols. Bibliologia, 4. Turnhout: Brepols, 1986.

Gilissen, Léon. "La Composition des cahiers: Le pliage du parchemin et l'imposition." *Scriptorium* 26 (1972): 3–33.

———. *L'Expertise des écritures médiévales.* Ghent: Editions Scientifiques, 1973.

———. *Prolègoménes à la codicologie recherches sur la construction des cahiers et la mise en page des manuscrits médiévaux.* Ghent: Editions Scientifiques, 1977.

Hanning, Robert W. "Roasting a Friar, Mis-taking a Wife, and Other Acts of Textual Harassment in Chaucer's *Canterbury Tales.*" *Studies in the Age of Chaucer* 7 (1985): 3–22.

———. "'I Shal Finde It in a Maner Glose': Versions of Textual Harassment in Medieval Literature." *Medieval Texts and Contemporary Readers.* Ed. Laurie A. Finke and Martin B. Shichtman. Ithaca, NY: Cornell UP, 1987. 27–50.

Holtz, Louis. "La typologie des manuscrits grammaticaux latins." *Revue d'Histoire des Textes* 7 (1977): 247–69.

Irvine, Martin. "Medieval Grammatical Theory and Chaucer's *House of Fame.*" *Speculum* 60 (1985): 850–76.

———. "Interpretation and the semiotics of allegory in Clement of Alexandria, Origen, and Augustine." *Semiotica* 63 1.2 (1987): 33–71.

———. "A guide to the sources of medieval theories of interpretation, signs, and the arts of discourse." *Semiotica* 63 1.2 (1987): 89–108.

———. "Medieval Textuality and the Archaeology of the Text." *Speaking Two Languages: Traditional Disciplines and Contemporary Theory in Medieval Studies.* Ed. Allen Frantzen. Albany: SUNY P, 1990. 181–210.

——. *Grammatica: Literary Theory and Textual Culture in the Early Middle Ages.* Cambridge: Cambridge UP (forthcoming).

Isidore of Seville. *Origines sive Etymologiae.* Ed. W. M. Lindsay. 2 vols. Oxford: Clarendon, 1911.

Kelly, Douglas. *"Sens" and "Conjointure" in the "Chevalier de la charrette."* The Hague and Paris: Mouton, 1966.

—— *Medieval Imagination: Rhetoric and the Poetry of Courtly Love.* Madison: U of Wisconsin P, 1978.

——. *"Translatio Studii*: Translation, Adaptation, and Allegory in Medieval French Literature." *Philological Quarterly* 57 (1978): 287–310.

——. "Topical Invention in Medieval French Literature." *Medieval Eloquence: Studies in the Theory and Practice of Medieval Rhetoric.* Ed. James J. Murphy. Berkeley: U of California P, 1978. 231–51.

—— "Obscurity and Memory: Sources for Invention in Medieval French Literature." *Vernacular Poetics in the Middle Ages.* Ed. Lois Ebin. Kalamazoo: Medieval Institute Publications, 1984. 33–56.

Lobrichon, Guy. "Une nouveauté: les gloses de la Bible." *Le Moyen Age et la Bible.* Ed. Pierre Riché and Guy Lobrichon. Paris: Beauchesne, 1984. 95–114.

——. "Conserver, réformer, transformer le monde? Les manipulations de l'Apocalypse au moyen âge central." *The Role of the Book.* Ed. Ganz. 2: 75–94.

Machan, Tim William. "Glosses in the Manuscripts of Chaucer's 'Boece'." *The Medieval Boethius: Studies in the Vernacular Translations of* De consolatione philosophiae. Ed. A. J. Minnis. Cambridge: D. S. Brewer, 1987. 106–24.

Macherey, Pierre. *A Theory of Literary Production*. Trans. Geoffrey Wall. London and New York: Routledge, 1978.

Marie de France. *Lais*. Ed. Jean Rychner. Les Classiques français du Moyen Âge 93. Paris: Librarie Honoré Champion, 1978.

McGann, Jerome J. *A Critique of Modern Textual Criticism*. Chicago: U of Chicago P, 1983.

————. *The Beauty of Inflections: Literary Investigations in Historical Method and Theory* Oxford: Oxford UP, 1988.

Minnis, A. J. "'Glosynge is a glorious thyng': Chaucer at Work on the *Boece*." *The Medieval Boethius: Studies in the Vernacular Translations of* De consolatione philosophiae. Ed. A. J. Minnis. Cambridge: D. S. Brewer, 1987. 106–24.

Morison, Stanley. *Politics and Script: Aspects of authority and freedom in the development of Graeco-Latin script from the sixth century B.C. to the twentieth century A.D.* Oxford: Clarendon, 1972.

Neuss, Paula. "Images of Writing and the Book in Chaucer's Poetry." *Review of English Studies* n.s. 32 (1981): 385–97.

Nolan, Barbara. "The Art of Expropriation: Chaucer's Narrator in *The Book of the Duchess*." *New Perspectives in Chaucer Criticism*. Ed. Donald M. Rose. Norman: Pilgrim, 1981. 203–22.

Parkes, Malcolm B. "The Influence of the Concepts of *Ordinatio* and *Compilatio* on the Development of the Book." *Medieval Learning and Literature: Essays Presented to R. W. Hunt*. Ed. J. J. G. Alexander and Margaret T. Gibson. Oxford: Clarendon, 1976. 115–41.

Patterson, Lee. *Negotiating the Past: The Historical Understanding of Medieval Literature*. Madison: U of Wisconsin P, 1987.

Payne, Robert O. *The Key of Remembrance: A Study of Chaucer's Poetics.* New Haven: Yale UP, 1963.

Pickens, Rupert T. "La Poétique de Marie de France d'après les prologues des *Lais.*" *Lettres les Romanes* 32 (1978): 367–84.

Priscian. *Institutiones grammaticae.* Ed. Martin Hertz. *Grammatici Latini.* Ed. H. Keil. Leipzig: Teubner, 1857–80. Vols. 2–3.

Robertson, D. W., Jr. "Marie de France, *Lais, Prologue* 13–15," *Modern Language Notes* 64 (1949): 336–38.

Rouse, Richard H. and Mary A. Rouse. "*Statim invenire:* Preachers, and New Attitudes to the Page." *Renaissance and Renewal in the Twelfth Century.* Ed. Robert L. Benson and Giles Constable. Cambridge, MA: Harvard UP, 1982. 229–47.

Schibanoff, Susan. "The New Reader and Female Textuality in Two Early Commentaries on Chaucer." *Studies in the Age of Chaucer* 10 (1988): 71–108.

Smalley, Beryl. "Les commentaires bibliques de l'epoque romane: glose ordinaire et gloses périmées." *Cahiers de civilisation médiévale* 4 (1961): 15–22. Rpt. in *Studies in Medieval Thought and Learning from Abelard to Wyclif.* London: Hambledon, 1981. 17–26.

——— "Some Gospel Commentaries of the Early Twelfth Century." *Recherches de Théologie ancienne et médiévale* 45 (1978): 147–80.

———. *The Study of the Bible in the Middle Ages.* 3rd ed. Oxford: Basil Blackwell, 1983.

Spitzer, Leo. "The Prologue to the *Lais* of Marie de France." *Modern Philology* 41 (1943): 96–102.

——— "Note on the Poetic and Empirical 'I' in Medieval Authors." *Traditio* 4 (1946): 414–22.

Stearns, Marshall. "Chaucer Mentions a Book." *Modern Language Notes* 57 (1942): 28–31.

Vinaver, Eugene. "The Discovery of Meaning." *The Rise of Romance*. New York: Oxford UP, 1971. 15–32.

Wetherbee, Winthrop. *Platonism and Poetry in the Twelfth Century*. Princeton: Princeton UP, 1972.

Wimsatt, James I. *Chaucer and the French Love Poets*. Chapel Hill: U of North Carolina P, 1968.

Zumthor, Paul. *Essai de poétique médiévale*. Paris: Seuil, 1972.

——— "Le 'Je' du Poète." *Langue, texte, énigme*. Paris: Seuil, 1975. 163–216. Trans. (in part) as "Autobiography in the Middle Ages?" *Genre* 6 (1973): 29–48.

———. *Speaking of the Middle Ages*. Trans. Sarah White. Lincoln: U of Nebraska P, 1986.

Talking Back to the Text: Marginal Voices in Medieval Secular Literature

Christopher Baswell

The condescending labellers of the Renaissance did not call "our" period the *Middle* Ages because they considered it central. They did not mean middle as in China's Middle Kingdom, but Middle Ages as in transient, suspended, lost in their betweenness.[1] As scholars of the era, we ourselves are still lost in this periodization, which remains powerful in the very title with which we cheerfully inscribe ourselves—"medievalists"—even though writers such as Umberto Eco and Lee Patterson have gone to some lengths recently to make us "middle" in the Chinese rather than the Renaissance sense. With characteristic elegance, Patterson argues that "the master narrative first put in place by the Renaissance is the cause of all our woe as medievalists" ("On the Margin" 101). As this essay will try to show, however, such acceptance of a later construction (in either sense of "middle") denies, in important ways, the literary and historical dynamics of the medieval imagination. Instead, I want to explore the way that medieval edges (especially codicological) are the places that make space for new and characteristic ideas, communities, and voices in the period. When medieval thinkers and artists create themselves at the margin, I will suggest, we should feel less need nervously to assert our own scholarly centrality.

What follows here will focus on the shifting and evanescent yet powerful margin of the medieval page, arguing for its capacity both to challenge and to reform the center it surrounds. This essay will explore the manuscript's edge, both in a literal and a metaphorical sense, as a site of dynamism, uncertainty, and even danger—a place that can allow expansion, contest, subversion—in regard to the more authoritative textual center it visually defines. In particular, I want to consider the manuscript margin as the locus of creative activities by the reader that may challenge the primary text but from which, consequently, new centers of readerly attention and ultimately new texts can emerge. On such occasions the marginal becomes, not necessarily spatially but nonetheless truly, central.

To be sure, manuscript margins are also, perhaps predominantly, "safe" arenas. Frequently they provide only straightforward pedagogical explanation of the text or suspend chunks of the culture's normative learning (cosmic, scientific, philosophical, spiritual) from small details in the master text. This latter habit of encyclopedizing the *auctor*, though, generating from that text great swathes of the reading culture's erudition, is itself a kind of respectful deformation. But I will focus on places where the margin is a field of play more in rebellion than in service, and where it sometimes succeeds through diachronic processes of reinscription—the recopying and redaction which are endemic to a manuscript culture—even in usurping the voice and place of the prior, central and would-be authoritative text.

At these points, the margin provides a space where voices or preoccupations (and the textual communities implicit behind them) relatively ignored or suppressed in the primary text are able to enter into conflict with it—to talk back to the text. This can happen in very simple ways, and arguably without specific intention on the part of the glossators, as when an early manuscript receives successive but inconsistent layers of annotation.[2] The result is a manuscript that proposes to its later readers varying versions of the *auctor*. But it can happen in much more intriguing ways, as when voices from the central text quite literally leak out into the margin in a sort of textual

122

diastole or centrifugal action. And equally, if much more rarely, the voice of the margin can come to occupy a reformed center through a contrasting pattern of centripetal action or textual systole. All of these phenomena derive from the habit of medieval reading always to be at once a voicing and an inscription of that voicing: the line between speaking and reading scarcely exists (as it is a truism to assert), but at the same time the line between speaking/reading and writing is scarcely more stable.

To illustrate this argument, I draw the bulk of my examples from manuscripts in the Latin and vernacular matter of Troy, where my own research has centered, though I also reach out to other Latin commentary traditions. Then, turning to Chaucer toward the middle and again at the close of this article, I speculate about the ways in which the vernacular narrator is dramatized as a reader/writer, a figure from the margins who finds himself or herself paradoxically at the center of the page. I say "herself" because in the second half of the essay I am increasingly concerned with what I see as a gendering, in some traditions, of this contest between center and margin, *auctor* and reader, whose high point in Chaucer occurs with the Wife of Bath. I will argue throughout that there is, from the perspective of this dynamic process, no stable textual or authoritative center in the Middle Ages, only a constant differentiation resulting from the inscribed reading of *auctoritates*, an endless flow between edge and middle. Authority (textual and, by extension, social) is thus always in danger of having its silences exposed, its denials rendered public.

These arguments, as I have already hinted, proceed from two fundamental aspects of the medieval reception of texts, aspects so widely discussed and recognized that they need little more than a nod here. First, there is the highly vocal quality of the practice of reading in the period, and an almost equally vocal quality to much of the written record of acts of reading.[3] Such vocality itself, as I will

123

demonstrate, provides a crossing point where the voice of the teacher or reader can become almost coterminous with that of the *auctor* or textual *persona*. Second, there is the extreme variability of texts in a manuscript culture, a point frequently iterated in a recent issue of *Speculum* devoted to "The New Philology" (Nichols). Bernard Cerquiglini's aphorism—"Or l'écriture médiévale ne produit pas de variantes, elle est variance" (111)—is twice (and justly) quoted there (1, 25).[4] This variability, potentially generated each time that text crosses from manuscript to manuscript, is more consistently explosive at points where the text crosses other divides, such as the move from Latin to vernacular or verse to prose.[5] The Wife of Bath's Prologue, we will see, provides just such an instance of vernacular variance.

The predominantly vocal quality of reading in the period helps account for the centrifugal action, the diastolic move of the authorial or poetic voice(s) out from the center and into the space and work of the margins. Put most simply, there is a lot of *talk* in the marginalia of the schools. From ancient Rome and earlier, and until fairly recently, the lines between reading and speaking, and reading and interpretation, were not very clearly drawn if they were drawn at all. Indeed, they were virtually coterminous, as is suggested by the multiple senses of *lectio* in antiquity and the Middle Ages—at once the act of reading, reading out loud, the text which is read, its variants, its teaching and interpretation (Lewis and Short, Niermeyer s.v. *lectio*). In the last three of these senses, *lectio* encompasses both the center and the margins of the page. And as simultaneously text and reading, *lectio* helps us understand the corollary gesture that permits the entire archeology I explore here: reading, though it is a speaking, is also just as persistently a writing, by which the moment of study is inscribed in the margin, thereby creating yet further text and *lectio*.[6]

Talk around a text, and dialogue between *magister* and *discipulus*, form the most ancient of pedagogical practices. Even in this

124

most traditional sense, though, the pedagogical dialogue that forms around a text is never a neutral medium for transferring information. It is also a site of social power, as Robert Kaster has recently demonstrated for Servius in his brilliant book, *Guardians of Language: the Grammarian and Society in Late Antiquity* (169–97; see also the review by Baswell). Kaster shows how carefully Servius establishes his magisterial control over proper usage, and thus his social function and influence, *vis à vis* both the student and Virgil himself. Every inscribed reading, then, potentially records a social claim upon the *auctor*.

Formal dialogue, and more private conversation, are implicit throughout early and high medieval commentary. Sedulius Scottus in his commentary on Donatus says, "It is asked how the differences among the above definitions can be understood. . . . To which we would say . . ." ("Quaeritur etiam quomodo possit cognosci differentia in supradictis definitionibus. . . . Ad quod dicendum . . ." 35), and the explanation then follows. This can be found almost anywhere, as in William of Conches, who constantly depends on the "Queritur cur," "Queritur quare" formulas (e.g., *Glosae* 71). Such implicit dialogue (when it is not the record of real classroom talk) can also, however, give voice to struggles for dominance between master and master or student and text. William, again, regularly contrasts the wrong opinions of most of the other masters ("Dicunt igitur fere omnes . . .") with his own right view ("Nos vero dicimus hanc esse falsam sententiam . . . ," *Glosae* 118). A secondary, marginal drama of struggle for intellectual and institutional primacy thus comes to be inscribed around the edges of the authority.

Other dialogues implicit in the "Queritur cur" formula cast the student who thinks he has caught the *auctor* in a mistake against the master who has an elegant solution. In the marginalia to the *Aeneid* in MS. Oxford, All Souls 82, a *quaestio* is posed by a voice who thinks

125

that Virgil is in error at 3.21, where Aeneas is "slaughtering along that beach a gleaming / white bull to the high king of the heaven-dwellers."

> HEAVEN-DWELLERS: It is asked why Virgil, as though he did not know what should be slaughtered on which altars, had a bull sacrificed to Jupiter. That is not permitted, except to Apollo, Neptune, and Mars. Solution: Virgil was not ignorant of the fact that a bull ought to be sacrificed to Neptune and Apollo; he said "a bull to Neptune; one to you, Apollo" (*Aen.* 3.119). But in this passage he said that a bull was sacrificed to a god to whom it was not permitted, so that he could create a passage with a portent to follow. Thus he adds below, "I . . . see an awful omen, terrible / to tell." (*Aen.* 3.26)

> CELICOLUM. Queritur cur virgilius quasi quid apud quas aras mactetur ignorans, taurum iovi fecerit immolari, quem nisi apollini neptuno et marti non licebat. Solucio. Non ignorabat virgilius taurum neptuno et appoloni esse immolandum, qui ait: "taurum neptuno, tibi taurum pulcher apollo." Sed in hoc loco taurum immolari dixit deo cui non licebat ut locum faceret monstro secuturo unde subdit "horrendum et dictu video monstrum."

At a moment such as this, the *magister* is cast as the conservative defender of the epic of imperial foundation against a jarring voice that would expose cracks in Virgil's universal learning. He speaks on behalf of authority against any version of Virgil that the questioner may find implicit in the passage.[7] We will encounter a related conflict, and repression of marginal challenge, in the Wife of Bath and her last husband, the clerk Jankyn.

In this same activity of guiding (or restricting) the reception of authority, however, the *magister* may, paradoxically, generate a slippage and expansion into the margins of the very voice of the *auctor*. The *magister*, even in such simple procedures as syntactical explanation, may speak in the voice of the *auctor* or characters; he thus re-enacts the master text and spreads it outward. This creates a second, concurrent version of the *auctor* and his dramatic imagination, inscribed now in parallel in the margin. Consider an instance from the commentary on the *Aeneid* attributed to Anselm of Laon. Anselm is discussing Juno's bitter remark that she alone is prevented by the Fates ("quippe vetor fatis," 1.39) from doing her will:

> as if Juno were to say "Pallas is not prohibited by the fates from punishing the victorious Greeks. But am I unable to harm the exiled and over-whelmed Trojans?"

> q(uasi) d(icat) pallas non est prohibita a fatis grecos victores persequi. Ego vero troianis exulibus et mersis nequeo nocere?
> > (MS. London, BL Addit. 33220)

This is little more than a pedagogue's useful rephrasing to eliminate some troubles of vocabulary and word order. But it is placed in the voice of Juno herself, which lends considerable dramatic immediacy to that moment of *lectio* and doubles it, mirroring the *auctor* in the margin.

I find parallels to this gesture of marginal voicing in commentary after commentary. They are fairly frequent in Anselm and occur in Geoffrey of Vitry's commentary on Claudian's *De raptu Proserpinae* (e.g., 26). There are a great number of instances in Ralph Hexter's recent study and edition of high medieval commentaries on Ovid. A Copenhagen commentator briefly adopts the voice of the poet himself, to apologize for speaking in so much detail about coitus (*Ars Amatoria* 3.769): "For he [Ovid] says, 'It shames me to speak about coitus. But Venus commands that I speak. And because there are many ways of coitus,' he says, 'this is NOT WITH ONE FORM'" (Hexter 72; also 73 for a further example at 3.789). The commentator thus enters into and expands the implied dialogue of Ovid's poem. The marginal

127

voicing of Ovid then rejoins the central Ovid a few lines later with the lemma. Two Ovids have briefly spoken in parallel, one at the center of the page, the other at the margin.

In a Tegernsee commentary on the *Epistulae Heroidum*, a commentator repeatedly speaks directly in the voices of the characters writing the letters. This is so fully the case in the notes to *Heroides* 7, the letter of Dido, that there is virtually a second, marginal narrative in the voice of Dido, complete with second person address to Aeneas and even one intervention in the voice of Aeneas himself when Dido imagines him calling out to the gods in yet another storm on the wintry seas (Hexter 183–86; text 256–61). This level of marginal readerly involvement in the drama of the poem, by which the reader/teacher enacts the character being read, and the resultant capacity of the authority to generate doubled, expanded, or variant versions slipping from within, will in turn become the site for a whole new poem in Chaucer's *House of Fame.*

Two unpublished marginal commentaries on the *Aeneid* from the late fourteenth century in England—just the time when Chaucer was reading and reworking the story—press this procedure even further. Both commentaries paraphrase in the voices of characters but also invent new speeches for them, to explain apparent gaps in the logic of the center text, and thus actually take on the role of the *auctor*. (For a similar Ovidian case, see Hexter 57–60.) A commentary written in Norwich often paraphrases the text directly, simplifying the syntax and clarifying the sense, but again in the voice of the characters themselves (MS. London, BL Addit. 27304).[8] Thus, when Juno asks Aeolus to raise a storm up against the Trojan fleet, he answers in the margin as well as at the center, in the note at 1.76, "Here the god of the winds responds to Juno, 'I grant your request,' giving his reasons" ("Hic deus ventorum respondet iunoni, concedo peticionem, exprimendo causas"). Later, when he encounters Venus in the Libyan desert, Aeneas speaks in the margin: "whoever you are, aid our labor, and tell us in what parts we have been cast ashore" (at 1.330: "quecumque sis adiuves nostrum laborem et doceas in quibus partibus sumus iactati"); and Venus answers in the margin: "That is, 'the celestial beings care about you and will help'" (at 1.387: "HAUT CREDO et c'. id est celestia curant de te et te adiuvabunt").

Still other notes can show the commentator's efforts to supply fuller dramatic details implicit in the *auctor*; we find these in fourteenth-century marginalia added to All Souls 82 (whose twelfth-century marginal *quaestio* was discussed above). In Book 2, for example, Aeneas disguises himself and his comrades in the armor of murdered Greeks and strongly defends the subterfuge: "If that be guile or valor—who would ask / in war?" (2.390, trans. Mandelbaum). The margin creates a dramatic situation not present in Virgil and posits an interlocutor: "In response to what someone could have said, that it wasn't good to gain victory through craft" ("Ad hoc quod aliquis posset dicere non esset bonum victoriam dolo adquirere"). In Book 3, Aeneas describes his terrifying encounter with the ghost of the murdered Polydorus. He goes on to tell briefly the story of Polydorus's death. The commentator seems to wonder what prompted the explanation, and supplies an answer that again shows a lively imaginative grasp of the dramatic situation surrounding Aeneas's book-long speech: "Because Dido could have asked about this Polydorus, therefore, since he had made some mention of him, he went on about him" (at 3.49: "Quia dido posset querere de isto polidoro ideo quia mentionem fecerat de ipso eneas ideo exequitur de ipso"). Again, when Dido mentions her early knowledge of the Trojan Teucer ("Indeed, I still remember banished Teucer," 1.619), the commentator establishes a precise dramatic context for her speech:

> Someone could have said, "How do you know Aeneas so well?" To this she would answer, "Indeed I well recollect. . . ."

Aliquis posset dicere unde cognoscis tam bene eneam. ad hoc respondet
atque equidem. . . .

Medieval textual culture, then, both speaks and writes while it
reads, and often extends the voice of the one site into the other. The
written author or author's character is enacted and even extended by
the speaking reader and (where they are, as often in the classroom,
separate) the inscription of his reading. Such a culture generates inscribed marginal sites of readerly interaction with and response to
authority—a talking next to and back to the text—and simultaneously
thereby produces expanded, potentially variant versions of authority.
The *auctor* at once needs and can be undone by such interactive
readership. And the very conferring and sustaining of a text's authority, marked by its marginalia, makes the edge of the text grow blurry
and the margin full, thereby undermining the prior center.[9] The system thus allows, though never guarantees, a recurrent divagation
through the work of reading/writing—doubling the voice, the narrative, ultimately sometimes the authority itself.

Marginal voicings of these kinds, I would thus claim, at once
construct authority and undermine it. The voice that would be mono-
phonic and authoritative, at once originary and final, is instead habitually divided into polyphony and renewed into at least some of its different (and, as we will see, sometimes prior) implicit versions, the
inevitable differences from which it is generated and which it would
have liked to leave unacknowledged and unsaid. Such mimicking or
completion in the margin forever records the moment of reading as
the surfacing of a hidden textual absence, the occultated lack or ex-
clusion that resides in the text's claim to authority and the center.

The frequently dense interpenetration, occasionally almost fusion,
of the voices of the poem and its reader/reinscriber has a profound
impact on later vernacular classicism. If the kinds of marginal voicings I have just discussed represent the centrifugal quality of the auc-

torial voice, slipping out into the margins and thus giving rise to doubling and variance, then Chaucer's narrators, in the *House of Fame* and especially in the *Legend of Good Women*, allow me to complete the implicit simile in my references to diastole and systole. The two movements, physiologically at least, are always complementary, and the one necessarily implies the other. The implicit circle of voices completes itself when a writer such as Chaucer inserts a reader/author (however socially marginal) into the center of his poems.

The immediacy, energy, and dramatic involvement of readerly experience implicit in these clamoring voices from the margin in fact have frequent analogues in "primary" texts throughout the Middle Ages and Renaissance, from William of Conches's cheerful assertion that he is Plato's "friend," to Petrarch's letters to ancient writers as if to contemporaries. But the pattern provides a particularly close model for the hyper-involved, almost overwrought Chaucerian reader of the *House of Fame*, who finds himself wandering through a textual architecture and reading, then seeing, then hearing scenes drawn inconsistently from the *Aeneid* and *Heroides*, and finally writing his memories of the event. As a marginal reader, Chaucer's Geffrey goes even further, not merely voicing the characters from the auctorial text but identifying himself, in his readerly struggles, with the worldly struggles of Aeneas. He comes out of the book/castle not knowing where he is and wandering about in a desert with as much sand as there is in Libya. The parallels continue through the three books, though the imitation of Aeneas increasingly derives from allegorized versions of the narrative.

But if it is the diastolic slippage of authorial voice to the margin and its doubling there by the *lector* that provide a model of dramatically identified readership for Chaucer, he responds to it with a systolic, centripetal gesture far more daring than any I have yet suggested. Chaucer takes "Geffrey," the marginal reader/interpreter/speaker, whose tripartite role neatly performs the senses of *lectio* I outlined above, and puts him into the center, making him the *hero* of the *House of Fame*. He is at once Aeneas and the reader of Aeneas, or perhaps—given Virgil's own emphasis on Aeneas as viewer and interpreter in the first six books of the epic—he is Aeneas *as* reader. Here the marginal figure, and his mind, become the subject of the center of the page.

This gesture of centripetal appropriation, of making the drama and *variances* of the margin a subject of the page's center, is not limited to Chaucer's early career, the period we tend to associate with his more overt and playful explorations of the problems of literary reception and interpretation. Rather, Chaucer even more dramatically inscribes the dynamic of center and margin, the permeable line between text and reader, and the role of the reader in generating a new center, in the Prologue to his *Legend of Good Women*.[10] He writes into his dream what is nearly an allegory—a fair term here—of the entire process of marginal diastole-systole I have already described. His narrator is a constant reader "of these olde appreved stories" (F Prologue 21; all quotations are from the *Riverside Chaucer*), who writes only from the gleanings left him by earlier lovers. Yet this humble marginal figure is the voice of the Prologue, making what is unused by earlier and more empowered poets—the variants they left behind—into his own work.

But in this framework, Chaucer does something even more audacious, making *himself* actually the commentated and challenged *auctor* whose prior text, the *Troilus*, is deformed and conflictingly appropriated by those divisive readers, Cupid and Alceste. Cupid sees the narrator as a consciously hostile writer, translating poems which are "heresye ayeins my lawe" (F 330) and willfully composing others: "And of Creseyde thou hast seyd as the lyste, / That maketh men to wommen lasse triste, / That ben as trewe as ever was any steel" (F

132

332–34). Alceste is more willing to credit stupidity and pressures of
the marketplace, and less willing than Cupid to think of Chaucer as an
original *auctor*:

> And eke, peraunter, for this man ys nyce,
> He myghte doon yt, gessyng no malice,
> But for he useth thynges for to make;
> Hym rekketh noght of what matere he take.
>   Or him was boden maken thilke tweye
> Of som persone, and durste yt nat withseye;
> Or him repenteth outrely of this.
> He ne hath nat doon so grevously amys
> To translaten that olde clerkes writen,
> As thogh that he of malice wolde enditen
> Despit of love, and had himself yt wroght. (F 362–72)

This marginal performance by the garden gods gives voice to
their reading and talks back, angrily then condescendingly, to the
prior text. Instead, the gods emphasize the positive version of courtly
eroticism that Chaucer's version of the Troilus story denied. And
theirs is finally a reinscribed reading, too, for the backtalk of the gods
in turn issues in a new central text: the Legends themselves. In the
Legend, then, poetry is not just the product of marginal variance on
the part of the writer but the product of readers insisting that the auth-
or reshape the thematics of his work. Readers invade (or denigrate)
the role of *auctor* and try to reduce Geffrey to something little more
than a scribe, merely transmitting the substance of their will. This of
course is the posture Chaucer develops in the General Prologue of the
Canterbury Tales, where he claims only to "reherce as ny as evere he
kan" (A 732).

In the dazzling complexity of these two settings, Chaucer strives
to contain the entire polyphony and inevitable production of variance

that, I have suggested, characterizes his readerly culture, and he strives to subsume it to his own ultimate and controlling voice. He acknowledges the versions that readership will always generate, yet forestalls them by containing those variant readings at the center of the page, in the individual poem. He produces a fictive marginal *pre-*text at once to generate and to justify his new central text: the Legends. And yet, since so many of those Legends notoriously reflect a reader at once bathetic and inept, other marginal experiences behind the fictional margin continue to peek out. A poem that is so much about the problem of truth in the reading and writing of ancient stories contains those very agents—readers both variant and errant—that challenge the possibility of stable and authoritative truth.

Chaucer's gesture of shifting marginal challenge back to the center is indeed daring, but it need not therefore be unprecedented. In fact, as I now hope to show, Chaucer inherited a whole tradition of annotated manuscripts and redactions of antique narrative that make space for marginal difference and ultimately return it to the center of the page. Far more than just voicing and doubling the *auctor* (for all the subversive potential even that contains), these marginalia can be seen as registering what, for medieval readers, the *auctor* lacks. At the most primitive and least inspired level, such marginalia merely register lack of clarity, simplicity, even syntactic or figural predictability in the *auctor*: it is to such situations that most glosses respond. Yet the general centripetal tendency of commentaries, their tendency to move from the margins back toward the center of the manuscript, occurs even here, as when a one-word gloss on a primary text is inserted, in a later copy, in place of the word it had glossed. Heinrich Dörrie's edition of Ovid's *Heroides*, which is unusually thorough in its documentation of medieval variant readings, contains a number of such instances.[11] On a larger scale, a commentary can become a primary text, which in turn attracts commentary. The most

134

famous instance of this is Macrobius's commentary on Cicero's *Dream of Scipio*, which in turn generated commentaries by distinguished teachers such as William of Conches (see Dronke 13–78). At each stage in this process, some relatively minor or latent topic in the prior text can be expanded in the marginal discussion (in this case, say, the topics of interpretation, dreams, numerology, or the ages of man), and when that marginal text becomes central it provides a pretext for yet further re- or de-formation.

Even more dynamic is the centripetal process, widely remarked upon, by which translators take the entire page, both center and margin, as their text, thereby introducing originally marginal, explanatory material into the newly reformed primary text. Jean de Meun did this in his translation of Boethius's *Consolation*, as did Chaucer in his. Moreover, the French product of Jean's textual systole—pulling the Latin margin into the vernacular center—was in some manuscripts complemented by further, new Latin marginalia (Palmer 365–71). I will return in more detail to another instance of such centripetal action in the case of a twelfth-century French vernacularization of the story of Dido.

At the same time, the very marginality of the margins, the secondary status of commentary, sometimes permitted them to act as repositories for doctrine that was slightly dangerous, theologically subversive and therefore unacceptable to the keepers of authoritative culture—doctrine that could and did lead to trouble when expressed in the middle of the page. In his commentaries on the *Consolation*, on the *Timaeus*, and (with greater hesitation) on Macrobius, William of Conches allowed himself to speculate on the Platonic World-Soul as the Holy Spirit, even though, as he admits in his Macrobius commentary, "it is heretical to say that the Holy Spirit is 'created,' unless perchance the word 'created' means 'sent.'"[12] In his primary text, the *Philosophia Mundi*, William pulls back from this position, attributing it to unnamed others ("secundum quosdam," 15), and sends the interested student to the safer site of the commentary—"in glossulis nostris super Platonem" (16)—for further discussion. William seems to have felt pressure to remove the question from his more authoritative writing and, in his last revision of the *Philosophia* into a dialogue form, the *Dragmaticon*, all reference whatever to the World Soul is expunged (Southern 24). But the discussion of World Soul as Holy Spirit continued to circulate, with whatever growing hesitations, in the commentaries.

Another equally though differently subversive kind of marginal text is generated in William's and in related commentaries on various Platonic passages. Very often, in regard to the *Anima mundi*, a quite limited repertory of three primary passages will be cited marginally to explain one another: the relevant *Timaeus* passage, Boethius's Book III *metrum* 9 "O qui perpetua mundi. . . ," and *Aeneid* 6.731 "quantum non noxia corpora tardunt. . . ." These form so tight an intertextual nexus that it becomes almost inevitable that the passages are read not in terms of their immediate context in the center of the page, but rather through the alternate Platonic context constructed for them in the margins.[13] The line in Virgil thus comes to be as much about Boethius or the *Timaeus* as it is about the *Aeneid*. So the passage in Virgil bulges out of its original context and is read instead in its marginal voicing, with Plato and Boethius in chorus beside it. A new center of attention (though not of the page) thus arises, focusing on a topic not primary in the prior authority, but inscribed only, paradoxically, in the margins.

An exaggerated instance of this is to be found in the twelfth-century marginal notes in a Virgil manuscript already twice mentioned, All Souls 82. Here, at the beginning of the World-Soul passage (6.724 ff.), the annotator simply quotes the opening of Boethius's *metrum* and appends to it a long passage lifted direct and unaltered from an

English commentary on the *Consolation*. So closely are the two passages linked that commentary on the one is directly adequate to the other. The firmness of this prior marginal grasp on the primary text is even more striking in this case because the All Souls annotator is otherwise wholly uninterested in spiritual or Platonic explanation. In a manuscript such as this one, the passage from the *Aeneid* thus belongs less to Virgil than to a sort of triple text which exists only in the margins of three different primary texts; the voice of Boethius is almost inevitably calling out to Virgil from the margins at this point, and the voice of Virgil from the margins of the *Timaeus*.

Beyond varying primary focus in the central text, marginal voices can also record and insist upon traditions and versions of a narrative that the central text, and the authoritative culture it upholds, positively ignore. In such cases, we can begin to see the margin giving voice to suppressed (or originally nonexistent) textual and even political communities, and viewpoints not just downplayed but wholly absent from the center of the page. This operates for the presentation of Aeneas in Virgil, for instance, and even more fully for that of Dido.

From earliest antiquity, Aeneas bore a double reputation, as the savior and refounder of the Trojan survivors but equally as a betrayer of Troy (see Callu, Reinhold, Ussani). Virgil recorded the positive version, but popular writers such as Dares and Dictys carried the counter-tradition to the Middle Ages. At a surprising number of points, the marginal commentaries acknowledge, even if they then evade, this alternate tradition. The commentary attributed to Bernard Silvestris, for example, begins by admitting that the real history ("historie veritatem") is told by Dares Phrygius, not Virgil (1). So even in a situation of traditional study, a reading of the *Aeneid* gives place, though at its edges, to a subversive history of the conqueror who was believed to stand genealogically behind most of the dynasties of western Europe.

The situation is still more striking in the case of Dido. As with Aeneas, Dido bears a double legend—the Virgilian version of the passionate, finally suicidal widow, and an equally early and widespread version of a powerful and effective queen who chooses suicide instead of being forced into remarriage (see Lord's excellent survey). I will examine here an earlier and more local Virgilian suppression. Virgil somewhat nervously skirts the full story of Dido's clever acquisition of Carthage after her flight from her murderous brother. All we get in the *Aeneid* is a two-line passage (1.367-68): "and they bought land—'Byrsa,' from the name of the exploit— / as much as they could surround with a bull's hide."[14]

But Virgil's most influential early commentator, Servius, gives a fuller story: "After her arrival in Libya," Servius tells us,

> when Dido was being driven out by Hiarbas, she asked him cunningly that she might buy as much land as a bull's hide could cover. And then, cutting the hide almost into threads, she stretched it out and took possession of twenty-two stadia.

> adpulsa ad Libyam Dido cum ab Hiarba pelleretur, petit callide, ut emeret tantum terrae, quantum posset corium bovis tenere. itaque corium in fila propemodum sectum tetendit occupavitque stadia viginti duo: quem rem leviter tangit Vergilius. . . . (124)

This story consistently finds its way into the margins of late classical and medieval Virgil manuscripts, sometimes in expanded form. Virgil's own silence about an important source of Dido's financial and political power is progressively acknowledged and subverted when the alternate version is given voice in the marginal commentaries. The medieval commentators thus open up a new narrative space for a counter-Dido in Virgil's margins, a Dido of overt mercantile cunning who succeeds in verbal negotiations with a figure of masculine militarism. An example of that systolic, centripetal action I mentioned earlier, this marginal voice of the suppressed Dido progressively re-occupies the center of the page in vernacular retellings of the Troy story from the twelfth century on, such as the *Roman d'Eneas*.

Almost as important to the redactor of the *Roman d'Eneas* as her initial wealth (emphasized in Virgil) is Dido's great skill ("grant angin," *Eneas* 393, which translates not Virgil, but Servius's "callide") in the arts of profitable trade. The French poet inserts at this point the story that has been growing in the margins of the Latin text:

> An cel païs est arivee;
> au prince vint de la contree,
> par grant angin li ala querre
> cu'il li vandist tant de sa terre
> com porprendroit un cuir de tor,
> doné l'an a argent et or;
> et li princes li otroia,
> qui de l'engin ne se garda.
> Dido trancha par correetes
> lo cuir, qui molt furent grellettes;
> de celes a tant terre prise
> c'une cité i a asise;
> puis conquist tant par sa richece,
> par son angin, par sa proëce,
> que ele avoit tot le païs
> et les barons a soi sozmis.

She arrived in this land and went to the prince of the country. With great cleverness she went to ask him if he would sell her as much of his land as the hide of a bull would enclose, and she gave him gold and silver for it. The prince, not suspecting a trick, granted it to her. Dido cut the hide into very thin thongs; with these she took so much land that she founded there

a city. Then she conquered so much by her wealth, by her cleverness, and
by her prowess, that she possessed the whole country, and the barons
submitted to her. (lines 391-406, trans. Yunck)

This episode, inserted from the margin, reflects a willingness to draw
into the center alternate marginal voices more open to the possibility
of feminine power, with their story of a queen's unnerving mercantile
cleverness practiced upon local male aristocrats.

The originally marginal voice at this point achieves parity, and
shared centrality, with the Virgilian. And the authoritative epic of
masculine, military empire must make room for a wholly different
system of power and acquisition. In this reformed center page, women
outsmart men and the dangerous power of unweaving, space-making,
verbal contract and financial exchange threatens, though only briefly,
to replace the values of armed combat. At a point like this, moreover,
the relation of margin to center arguably becomes gendered. The brief
bow to Dido's *angin* within the narrative allows a voice preoccupied
with (and approving) feminine power to slip back to the middle of the
page.

Such expansion of alternate versions or texts into (and, as we
have seen earlier, within) the margins manifests the incessant opening
up of difference that reading can produce. It allows space and voice
for alternate truths that repose in a single tradition or even in a single
set of words, at the moments when they move from one page, one
mode (writing, oral reading, reading reinscribed), or one language to
another. There exists for the manuscript culture of the Middle Ages,
then, a triangular (if not downright polyhedric) *lectio* where written
text, readership, and the marginal inscription of reading can at certain
times have almost equal power to influence the future of a text or
tradition. One or another may dominate at different times, and the real
center of attention can shift from the page center to the commentary

140

(as with the commentaries on Macrobius, the marginal text around the Platonic World-Soul, or the Dido material). And in turn, in a world where all textual reproduction requires rereading and reinscription, that shifted center of attention may also encroach upon the center of the page. In either case, margins can have great power, and initial centers of textual authority are always in danger (if not in the very process) of slippage to or from the very margins that visually create their centrality. However much a medieval *auctor* such as Geoffrey Chaucer may try to contain and manipulate this process, he writes within a system that implicitly acknowledges that it is forever disintegrating, challenged by the very kind of self-inscribing, participatory reader he mimics in his narrators.

Up to this point, I have discussed the slippage and fusion between authorial and marginal voice in some Latin manuscripts; the readerly, marginal voice in some contention with the center text, and producing potentially subversive variance from within it; and—resulting from both phenomena—the recentering of originally marginal priorities or experiences in some vernacular poems. The process, of course, does not necessarily end there, nor is the work of the margins always aimed at liberating ignored or suppressed materials from the silence of the prior text; indeed the very opposite can occur. I close with a look at another Chaucerian poem, The Wife of Bath's Prologue, where we can see a conservative, Latinate, and specifically masculine voice in the margins, attempting to reclaim control over a female reader/listener's voice that has usurped the center of the page. This marginal masculine voice attempts to redirect our readership of the new center that the usurping reader, the Wife, has produced.

Alisoun of Bath and her fifth husband have a densely codicological relationship, in which access to or simple possession of the book seems to guarantee dominance. Dominance is intimately reflected in turn by the textualization of the Wife's body, with her husband as *lector*, in her memory of the marriage. Alisoun is initially attracted to Jankyn not only for his youth and good legs but also because "so wel koude he me glose" (line 509). The term shifts only at this point in the Wife's Prologue from reading to seduction, from one form of Biblical knowing ("Men may devyne and glosen, up and doun," line 26) to the other. It seems to be Jankyn, too, who gives her the Latin euphemism—*quoniam* (line 608)—for what she has earlier named with the less learned if more appealing, French *bele chose* (lines 447, 510). And of course the famous climax of the whole Prologue hinges on the Wife's effort to get "this book of wikked wyves" (line 685) out of her husband's hands and into the fireplace, and to restore her own influence.[15]

The title she gives Jankyn's collection is part of an almost obsessive harping on the word "book" (six times in seventeen lines, 669–85). Alisoun narrates Jankyn's power to dole out enraging bits of its content ("redde" and "tolde" in various forms, lines 714, 721, 724, 739, 740, 747, 757, 765, and 789), which fix her by their unanswerable condemnation. Jankyn retreats to his authority at the center of the page, exclusively reading and telling; he refuses to move into the negotiations of dialogue with his listener which we have repeatedly seen at other margins (see also the excellent comments by Carruthers 215–16). He is thus the perfect type of the authoritarian reader, the reader in full service to the *auctor* and to the culture of male authority. He allows no talking back, no marginal scribble, and he denies the possibility of alternate versions or interpretations that may reside in his text's silences. In her frustration at being unable to talk back to his text, at being a silenced listener, the Wife attacks her real enemy, the book and its collation of Latin antifeminist diatribes.

But once her ear is boxed (with whatever ramifications for her later ability to hear books read) and the book burnt, the Wife regains two forms of access—financial and textual—which she had precariously wrested from her earlier relationships with men and had dangerously ceded to Jankyn:

> He yaf me al the bridel in myn hond,
> To han the governance of hous and lond,
> And of his tonge, and of his hond also;
> And made hym brenne his book anon right tho.
>
> (lines 813–16)

She gets her money back, yet also mnemonically retains and thus controls much of the burnt book, presumably vernacularized by Jankyn for her understanding. Alisoun has been mnemonically collecting pieces of text all her life at the many and highly verbal public rituals that fill her world, going "To vigilies and to processiouns, / To prechyng eek, and to thise pilgrimages, / To pleyes of myracles, and to mariages" (lines 556–58). The material of Jankyn's book too is now retained in the Wife's memory, even though the controlling codex is gone. Jankyn, by contrast, with his far greater dependence on the visual icon of the Latin book, is more likely to forget this stuff of his former power. In her performance for the Canterbury pilgrims, Alisoun redeploys much of this material to narrate her private history, in glorious variance from its prior context and redirected to the splendid self-affirmation that we hear. As Susan Schibanoff has recently written, "Alison's 'bookishness'—a woman's literal and metaphorical taking of texts into her own hands—dramatizes an extreme act of new reading. . ." (77). Alisoun narrates her first three marriages in language reconstructed from her memory of texts read to her during the fifth.[16] We have thus been listening to transformed and recast fragments, to raging *variance*, especially of Jerome's *Epistola adversus Jovinianum*, long before we ever encounter it as an object.[17]

The whole Prologue, then, should be seen as a marginal voicing once again finding its way to the center of the page, as the Wife still

143

talks back to Jankyn's book, producing a wildly variant and feminized reading and gloss from a memory as capacious as her ten-pound coverchiefs, and speaking for the kind of feminine power which is the unspoken obverse of misogynist authority.[18] This connects in four ways to the phenomena of marginal voicing in the manuscripts surveyed above. First, the Wife acts as a marginal figure of reader/listener, taking on but extending the *auctor*'s or his characters' voices (such as we have seen in the *Aeneid* and *Heroides* manuscripts) and ultimately usurping the center of the page (as in the *House of Fame*): it is Alisoun, not Jankyn or Jerome, talking in the middle of the Canterbury procession and at the center of the leaf in the *Canterbury* manuscripts. Second, Alisoun's is a marginal discourse in which not the expositor but the reader/listener (as in the challenging *quaestio* of All Souls 82) contests the sense of the *auctor(s)*.[19] Third, she participates in the kind of gendered, marginal challenge to the authoritative text that we witnessed in the notes about Dido's purchase of Carthage. Finally, and again similarly to the situation in the *Eneas*, her voice is generated at that point where Latin moves into the vernacular, a move which allows for an even greater variance and absorption of marginal voices. While Alison's memory of her marriages may stem from experience, it derives in this reweaving from the mode of marginal variance—terms borrowed but challenged by their hearers—that we have repeatedly seen in the manuscripts reviewed above. Chaucer thereby creates a Prologue that is wholly given to the difference produced by *lectio*, a difference explicitly talking back to the repressive silences of a male culture of authority.

The circle of voices is now complete. The originally central misogynist text, rigidly and unanswerably controlled in Jankyn's book, has become more purely gynist, and its voices, having made an extreme marginal move off the page and into memory, are redirected in service of a woman's power and vernacularized at the center of the page. Briefly, Alisoun gets to paint the lion. But the lion is painted over yet again, though in different ways, when we look at the Prologue as it is presented in two early manuscripts of the *Canterbury Tales*, Egerton 2864 and the Ellesmere manuscript.[20] For the process of marginal challenge, of systole and diastole between text and margin, does not suddenly end with Chaucer's or his character's redaction of the prior text. In a culture of manuscript transmission, it cannot end: the new center proposes new margins, and indeed receives them in Egerton and Ellesmere.

Susan Schibanoff has recently published an important study of the marginalia of Egerton and Ellesmere, focussing on their response to The Wife of Bath's Prologue and Tale. Schibanoff finds in the Egerton marginalia the work of a commentator who responds with increasingly open "outrage and indignation" to the Wife's performance (78), and especially to her adaptation and reinterpretation of Scripture. This annotator, Schibanoff shows, uses his Latin marginalia against the Wife to "shout her down and to cite chapter and verse against her. . ." (79). The Egerton marginalia repeatedly quote Biblical passages against women.[21] Moreover, even where they merely cite Biblical sources for the Wife's own lines, the Egerton glosses are "unusually full" (82) and thereby implicitly assert the glossator's prior and superior command of that most authoritative of all texts and his right to its interpretation. "Significantly, it is not the Wife's sexuality that draws the Egerton glossator's heaviest fire but her 'textuality,' her insistence on the right to interpret Scripture" (84). The notes surrounding the Wife's performance in the Egerton manuscript, then, clamorously and angrily refuse her the final word, and persistently assail her claims to Biblical access and interpretation.

The response to the Wife is rather more subtle in the notes surrounding her text in the Ellesmere manuscript.[22] Here the notes generally appear to accede to her use of Scripture in that they tend to

145

quote only as much scriptural Latin as she herself uses in her persistently partial citations.[23] Yet they simultaneously and more frequently cite her source in that most famous of patristic misogynists, St. Jerome, thereby setting up a counter-voice in the margins; and the size and format of the notes set up a bookish and Latinate response to the Wife's vernacular and oral voice.[24] The stately, illustrated Ellesmere manuscript is sprinkled fairly lightly with marginalia, some English, but rather more in Latin, until we reach The Wife of Bath's Prologue, where the marginalia are suddenly in far greater evidence than anywhere else in the manuscript.[25] Almost all are in Latin, and recall to the reader's attention, through repeated quotation, Alisoun's dependence on the *auctores* of the misogynist tradition, particularly Jerome.[26] A Latinate annotator thus attempts in these margins to recuperate male *auctoritas* from its vernacular and feminized voicing.[27] The Latin notes insistently remind the reader of its prior, more learned source in a Church Father notoriously unfriendly to most women. In this manuscript, then, the Wife's effort to repaint the lion is marginally challenged, her boast crowded and almost nudged aside by the Latin voice she has been trying to drown out. Voices prior even to Jankyn's vernacular telling murmur in the margins and restrict, if they cannot fully deny, the Wife of Bath's triumph.

Indeed, the Ellesmere manuscript as a whole has been seen as an effort to arrest the contemporary variance of the Chaucer canon. As Charles Owen recently put it, "Ellesmere is a much more formal manuscript [than Hengwrt], based on a carefully edited set of exemplars," and its director "is clearly aiming at a definitive Canterbury Tales" (6). Similarly, I think, the marginalia of this "authoritative," finalized version attempt to put a stop to the Wife's errant voice, to restore it to its marginal, variant status. Graham Caie notes that the Ellesmere glosses are carefully executed and nearly as large as the vernacular text. "In a sense it is a misnomer to call them 'marginalia' at all, and

146

one might confidently assume that the Ellesmere scribe considered the glosses to be an important part of the work as a whole" (350).[28] They seem to be straining toward the reappropriation of visual centrality.

The Wife's Prologue exists, in fact, in two simultaneous versions in Ellesmere: first, the challenged, written version on the manuscript page, its marginal notes forever trying to scrape off her paint and reassert their priority and claims to yet another center; and second, the version of oral performance, a situation in which the Wife's voice could float alone, were it not that her voice would conventionally be enacted by a man, its creator. In either alternative, Alisoun's version is always already voiced, literally inside the very tradition she would subvert. As Patterson puts it, "her very verbalizations remain unavoidably dependent, feminine respeakings of a resolutely masculine idiom" ("For the Wyves Love of Bathe" 682). Even at the center, she is always about to be marginalized.[29]

So, however, are all of us who chance to read an essay such as this. To return finally to where I began, to our own profession and its name, it is worth reminding ourselves that as members of a discipline we medievalists are relegated to the margins of the humanities as defined by our institutions. In almost any department into which we are atomized, we ourselves become marginal voices, calling out from a borderland we unhappily inherit from Renaissance definitions of the time we study, definitions whose influence continues today. I need only cite the institutionalized "mainstream" as implicitly defined by traditional humanities requirements to prove my point. But is it not possible for us, as medievalists, to perform a centripetal gesture emulating our mentor Geoffrey Chaucer, or Alisoun of Bath? Can we not learn to exploit the dynamics of the margin as did those voices I studied above, or as did—in an admittedly more metaphorical sense—the very people of the Middle Ages?

Far from considering themselves middle-men, medieval thinkers, as we all know, saw themselves in a vanguard, either as *moderni* (even dwarves see further than the giants on whose shoulders they stand) or as prophets of apocalypse. Again and again, medieval Europe defined itself and its heroes in terms of threats posed from its margins, geographical as well as temporal. Roland's nobility is established for the whole period by his rearguard defense of the southwestern boundary of Christendom. The Arthurian tradition throve at the centers of European power but placed its king's realm on an island off Europe's western coast. The crusades of Chaucer's Knight circumscribe the threatened, outermost margins of fourteenth-century Europe.

The contemporary discipline of medieval studies, especially among its historians, has itself been turning to the margins in recent years by exploring the social margins of the Middle Ages, or by rediscovering groups, originally important, which have later been marginalized for reasons of documentation or the altered preoccupations of succeeding periods. Much of John Boswell's work, to cite a prominent instance, has been devoted to studies of attitudes toward homosexuality and the fates of abandoned children in the period. Another group of scholars has made important strides in recuperating our knowledge of medieval women and their repeated struggles to resist or emerge from political and economic marginality. Criticism of medieval literature has also, increasingly, broadened its view of the text to include the entire page. In the issue of *Speculum* on "The New Philology," Stephen Nichols offers a salutary reminder that medieval texts exist very differently from ours, that texts are at the very least far more fluid in a "manuscript culture." In response to that fact, Nichols issues a call "that the language of [medieval] texts be studied not simply as discursive phenomena, but in the interaction of text language with the manuscript matrix and of both language and manuscript with the social context and networks they inscribe" (9).[30]

Christopher Baswell

If we cannot formulate our marginality in as heroic a mold as I have argued Chaucer and Alisoun do, we can nonetheless begin to see our institutional position, and the marginal struggles which we study, as peculiarly, even eerily, typical of the broader contemporary culture in which we operate. Americans are part of a domestic political culture ever more nervously, even defensively, aware of the claims of a constellation of groups previously relegated to the margins of power: women, the poor, racial minorities, gay people, the disabled. We live in a nation itself suddenly rendered internationally marginal by a re-centering of the attention of contemporary history on a line extending roughly from the medieval Hanse down to the Adriatic. And, chronologically, we find ourselves at the margin between centuries, neither fully in one nor the other, neither comfortable with the verities of mid-century nor certain of what new centers lie ahead.

As a discipline, then, we may never find ourselves central, but maybe a group so accustomed to the edges—of texts, of periods, of institutions—has something newly useful to say *from* the edge. We do a service as much political as literary when we teach our students to recognize how constructed are many centers of authority which would like to appear natural. Equally, we can help them to be aware of the silences from which any dominant culture asserts its own voice, and the role of its listeners in either aquiescing to or talking back to that silencing. In the historical study of literary reception and the production of variance, we can show them precedents for marginalized textual communities reasserting versions of experience (aesthetic or political) suppressed by a dominant culture of authority. I believe we do have a responsibility—to ourselves, our students, our culture—to profit from our marginality becoming ever more typical, and to continue to voice the variances which any dominant or authoritative culture tries to leave permanently aside.

NOTES

1. Part of this essay was presented in February 1990 to the Columbia University Seminar in Medieval Studies; I am grateful to that audience for a number of friendly criticisms and suggestions. I also record here my debt to those who have read and commented on later versions: Charlotte C. Morse, W. Duncan Stalker, M. Victoria Guerin, and my colleagues Sandra P. Prior and William Sharpe.

2. For one such instance, see Baswell "The Medieval Allegorization of the 'Aeneid'."

3. This latter trait descends, in the Latin tradition I will discuss, from the schoolroom setting in which such literature was studied, and that setting's practices of recitation, discussion, and dialogue. Writing itself, as well as poetry, was from antiquity taught not by reading but by talk: Donatus' *Ars minor* and Priscian's *Partitiones duodecim uersuum Aeneidos principalium*, to take just two influential instances, teach through question and answer. See also Bonner 127, 166, 225–27.

4. Quoted by Nichols 1, and by Suzanne Fleischman 25. Cerquiglini's book is also cited on 6, 19, 26–27, 46; it is itself a powerful voice in the margins of this issue of *Speculum*.

5. Ralph Hanna III writes eloquently of the dangers posed to authority when someone like the Wife of Bath could get hold of a translated text: "Perhaps most distressing for the conservative, Englished Latin had been cut free from the Latin tradition and its learned practice of reading. It had become 'open.' Englished texts were now consultable and interpretable, perhaps in ways unforeseen, seditious and dangerous" (11).

6. One can go further, of course, and note conversely that in the system of manuscript production, writing was also often a reading, the exemplar being copied orally as much as visually. This is not a neat circle, but a constant and usually unequal pull among the elements speaking, reading, writing, and text.

7. Kaster finds, in the *Saturnalia* of Macrobius, a similar need to place the culturally potent *auctor* beyond the reach of critique, and thereby to guarantee the values of the culture that has validated the *auctor*. Macrobius casts the grammarian Servius as guarantor of linguistic conservatism and (not coincidentally) a figure of impeccable social modesty, perfectly fitting his place at the bottom of the cultural elite; see *Guardians of Language* 171–72 and his earlier article, "Macrobius."

8. I study this commentary in detail and justify my dating and location, in a study of Virgilianism in high and later medieval England (forthcoming, Cambridge UP, 1993).

9. Servius's commentary on Virgil bears this out; it is generally thought that the commentary was transmitted through Ireland and England either wholly without the text of Virgil (and provided only with lemmata) or that the primary text, if present, was little studied. In such circumstances, Servius became the *auctor*.

10. I am grateful to Professor Robert Payne for suggesting the relevance of the Legend's Prologue to my approach.

11. See Ovid, *EH*, ed. Dörrie, IV.103 (78), where Dörrie's manuscript Ea (thirteenth century) reads *tenebrosa*, probably deriving from a gloss for the dominant reading, *latebrosa*. For a whole series of examples, see also Hall 185–89, 193–97. Windeatt identifies related phenomena in scribal intrusions into the text of *Troilus and Criseyde*; see 123–24.

12. Quoted by Southern 23. For Southern's discussion of William on the World-Soul, see 21–25.

13. For the repeated citation of Virgil's line when the World-Soul enters William of Conches' discussion of the *Timaeus*, see *Glosae* (ed. Jeauneau) 144–46, 152, 157, 174. Jeauneau quotes notes on Boethius III m. 9 which similarly cite Virgil, 144–45. For a citation of Boethius at *Aeneid* 6.731, see below.

14. "Mercatique solum, facti de nomine Byrsam, / taurino quantum possent circumdare tergo." I try to retain Virgil's wilful obscurity in my translation.

15. Patterson rightly emphasizes that the Wife's own narrative is itself initially figured in terms of her "joly body," see "For the Wyves Love of Bathe" 660, 685–86, 694–95.

16. Most recently, Hanna has studied the entire Prologue as an instance of *compilatio*, but one in which the Wife inverts the compilator's usual denial of personal voice and its concomitant assumption of an agreed truth residing in his authoritative sources. See 1–11, esp. 1–2.

17. It can be argued that the status of these echoes is more problematic than I allow. Are they actually in the Wife's own memory, recast and resituated to suit her ends, and therefore to a great extent under her (temporary) control? Are they present to her, yet nonetheless *not* a gesture of liberation, but rather the only language (even if stubbornly patriarchal and carrying with it its own prior prejudices) available to her to describe her activities? Are they, even more insidiously, present wholly without her being aware of them, as a joke between Chaucer and his Latinate (and thus predominantly but by no means exclusively male) readers, showing that the Wife, far from attaining the self-created experience she values, merely fulfills a previous and hostile literary stereotype? I am arguing from the assumption that the first of these is the dominant function, but my approach to the marginalia, below, allows the other responses also to operate, though not at the center of the page.

18. Patterson ("For the Wyves Love of Bathe") argues convincingly that a comparable transformation is being wrought in the story of Midas as told in the Wife's tale; see 656–59. Indeed, Patterson's general approach to the entire Prologue as a sermon on 1 Corinthians 7:28 casts the Wife's discourse as a long gloss—a marginal answer to Paul: "As an analysis the Prologue is a progressive series of glosses on a text, the gradual moralization of the letter *tribulatio*" (679; see 676–80).

19. And, as Hanna points out (9), it is not just Jankyn's *auctor* (Jerome, for instance) whom the Wife voices and thus usurps, but Jerome's own *auctor*, the Bible: "The Wife . . . restores the openness of the Biblical account. . . . In this retelling, the opacity of what Jesus meant . . . and the issue of how many husbands are licit . . . are opened to reading."

20. My knowledge of the Egerton MS. is based on the excellent study by Schibanoff that I discuss below; I have consulted Ellesmere and Hengwrt in the facsimiles (ed. Ruggiers and Hanna) listed in Works Cited.

21. Even at the one point where the Egerton annotator cites a positive Biblical estimate of women, Schibanoff points out, it is "not to praise women but to deny the Wife's knowledge of, and hence her right to interpret, written authority" (81).

22. In much of what follows, I differ from Schibanoff's response to the Ellesmere marginalia; where Schibanoff sees real support for the Wife's position, I find a kind of bland superiority in the annotations' quiet assumption of bookishness and literacy. But this does not deny the validity of Schibanoff's claim to a manifestation of a new readership in the Ellesmere notes: I am simply less certain than she that even such a new readership would be friendly to the Wife's backtalk.

23. See Schibanoff 75 n. 13, 77–78, 84.

24. Schibanoff argues that in quoting the *Adversus Jovinianum* the Ellesmere annotator would "invite us to compare the different ways in which the Wife and, as she calls him, the 'clerk at Rome' (WBP 672), gloss the same text." Such source annotation "invites us to consider the issues of relativity and contextuality in interpretation . . ." (85). But I think that this is less an invitation to compare than an assertion of prior and more authoritative male interpretation. There would be little "relativity," for a nervous reader, between a Father of the Church and a widow from Bath. This seems less a sympathetic response than an assertion of an imposing alternate interpretation.

25. The Wife's Prologue has forty-three marginal notes, three of which are English topic headings marking the passages about her various husbands. The next-most-annotated segment is the tale of the Franklin with twenty-nine, mostly derived, like those in the Wife's Prologue, from Jerome's *Adversus Jovinianum.* The Clerk's Tale also receives twenty-nine notes, almost all giving the parallel passages from his source in Petrarch. The Merchant's and Pardoner's Tales each have thirteen marginal notes, again mostly Latin. The Parson's Tale also has a number of marginal entries, but nearly all of these are English topic headings to help the reader through the sub-sections of the long prose text. The Man of Law's Tale gets ten notes, and all the others fewer yet.

26. Christine Ryan Hilary's notes in the *Riverside Chaucer* (864–72) record almost all of the marginalia and display their dependence on Jerome, even to the extent of citing the Bible as cited in *Adversus Jovinianum* rather than from the Vulgate.

27. The glossator will even implicitly protest an assertion in the Prologue by citing a counter-instance. The Wife claims that no clerk can speak well of women (D 689), but the glossator counters with Proverbs 31:10, where a good wife is called more precious than jewels.

28. Caie seems to me too eager to accept the recuperation of authority implicit in these notes: ". . . by means of them the glossator could ensure that the reader was not deceived by the Wife's false logic and her persuasive misinterpretations of Scripture and Jerome. . ." (351). See also Schibanoff 74–75.

29. Although I am approaching the Prologue from a codicological perspective, and thus very differently from her, I find the recent and challenging analysis by Barrie Ruth Strauss repeatedly consonant with my conclusions. We especially share a sense that the Wife's discourse is almost inevitably challenged and interwoven with a prior voice, which Strauss identifies as phallocentric: "Her insertion of addresses to women inside addresses to men exposes the major requirement of phallocentrism—that masculine discourse enclose feminine discourse" (531).

154

Christopher Baswell

30. The study of medieval texts in terms of, and as conditioned by, their presentation in manuscripts is not exactly "new," though it has been exploited to strikingly effective critical ends in quite recent books such as Sylvia Huot's *From Song to Book*. Beginning much earlier, and far more widespread in its impact on our discipline, has been the *Catalogus translationum et commentariorum* founded by Paul Oskar Kristeller and now thirty years in the making, presently under the editorship of Virginia Brown (Union Académique Internationale, Washington, D.C., 1960–present). The newness of New Philology is challenged, from another perspective, by Howard Bloch in the same issue of *Speculum*, esp. 38–46.

Talking Back to the Text

MANUSCRIPTS CITED

London, BL Additional 33220

London, BL Additional 27304

Oxford, All Souls College 82

WORKS CITED

Baswell, Christopher C. "The Medieval Allegorization of the 'Aeneid': MS. Cambridge, Peterhouse 158." *Traditio* 41 (1985): 181–237.

———. Review of Kaster, *Guardians. Envoi: A Review Journal of Medieval Literature* 1 (1989): 339–45.

Bernard Silvestris. *The Commentary on the First Six Books of the 'Aeneid' Commonly Attributed to Bernardus Silvestris.* Ed. Julian Ward Jones and Elizabeth Frances Jones. Lincoln and London: U of Nebraska P, 1977.

Bloch, R. Howard. "New Philology and Old French." *Speculum* 65 (1990): 38–58.

Bonner, Stanley F. *Education in Ancient Rome.* London: Methuen, 1977.

Caie, Graham. "The Significance of the Early Chaucer Manuscript Glosses (With Special Reference to the *Wife of Bath's Prologue*)." *Chaucer Review* 10 (1976): 350–60.

Callu, J. P. "'Impius Aeneas'? Échos virgiliens du Bas-Empire." *Présence de Virgile: Actes du Colloque des 9, 11, et 12 Décembre 1976.* Ed. R. Chevallier. *Caesarodunum* XIII bis, Numéro spécial. Paris: Les Belles lettres, 1978. 161–74.

Carruthers, Mary, "The Wife of Bath and the Painting of Lions." *PMLA* 94 (1979): 209–22.

Christopher Baswell

Cerquiglini, Bernard. *Eloge de la variante: Histoire critique de la philologie*. Paris: Seuil, 1989.

Chaucer, Geoffrey. *The Riverside Chaucer*. 3rd ed. General ed. Larry D. Benson. Boston: Houghton Mifflin, 1987.

Dronke, Peter. *Fabula: Explorations into the Uses of Myth in Medieval Platonism*. Mittellateinische studien und texte IX. Leiden and Cologne: Brill, 1974.

Eco, Umberto. "The Return of the Middle Ages." *Travels in Hyperreality*. Trans. William Weaver. New York: Harcourt Brace Jovanovich, 1986. 61–85.

The Ellesmere Manuscript of Chaucer's Canterbury Tales: A Working Facsimile. Intro. by Ralph Hanna III. Woodbridge, Suffolk; Wolfeboro, NH: D. S. Brewer, 1989.

Eneas: Roman du XIIe siècle. Ed. J-J. Salverda de Grave. 2 vols. Paris: Les Classiques français du Moyen Age, 1973.

Eneas: A Twelfth-Century French Romance. Trans. John A. Yunck. New York and London: Columbia UP, 1974.

Fleischman, Suzanne. "Philology, Linguistics, and the Discourse of the Medieval Text." *Speculum* 65 (1990): 19–37.

Geoffrey of Vitry. *The Commentary of Geoffrey of Vitry on Claudian's "De Raptu Proserpinae."* Ed. A. K. Clarke and P. M. Giles. Leiden and Cologne: Brill, 1973.

Hall, F. W. *A Companion to Classical Texts*. Chicago: Argonaut, 1970.

Hanna, Ralph, III. "*Compilatio* and the Wife of Bath: Latin Backgrounds, Ricardian Texts." *Latin and Vernacular: Studies in Late Medieval Texts and Manuscripts*. Ed. A. J. Minnis. Woodbridge, Suffolk; Wolfeboro, NH: D. S. Brewer, 1989. 1–11.

Hexter, Ralph J. *Ovid and Medieval Schooling. Studies in Medieval School Commentaries on Ovid's "Ars Amatoria," "Epistulae ex Ponto," and "Epistulae Heroidum."* Münchener Beiträge zur Mediävistik und Renaissance-Forschung 38. Munich: Arbeo-Gesellschaft, 1986.

Huot, Sylvia. *From Song to Book.* Ithaca and London: Cornell UP, 1987.

Kaster, Robert. *Guardians of Language: The Grammarian and Society in Late Antiquity.* Berkeley and Los Angeles: U of California P, 1988.

———. "Macrobius and Servius: *Verecundia* and the Grammarian's Function." *HSCP* 84 (1980): 219–62.

Lewis and Short. *A Latin Dictionary.* Oxford: Clarendon, 1975.

Lord, Mary Louise. "Dido as an Example of Chastity: The Influence of Example Literature." *Harvard Library Bulletin* 17 (1969): 22–44 and 216–32.

Mandelbaum, Allen, trans. *Virgil. The Aeneid of Virgil.* New York: Bantam, 1980.

Nichols, Stephen. "Introduction: Philology in a Manuscript Culture." *Speculum* 65 (1990): 1–10.

Niermeyer, J. F. *Mediae latinitatis lexicon minus.* Leiden: Brill, 1984.

Ovid. *Epistulae Heroidum.* Ed. Heinrich Dörrie. New York and Berlin: de Gruyter, 1971.

Owen, Charles A., Jr. "Pre-1450 Manuscripts of the *Canterbury Tales*: Relationships and Significance, Part I." *Chaucer Review* 23 (1988): 1–29.

Palmer, Nigel. "Latin and Vernacular in the Northern European Tradition of the *De Consolatione Philosophiae.*" *Boethius: His Life, Thought and Influence.* Ed. Margaret Gibson. Oxford: Basil Blackwell, 1981. 362–409.

Patterson, Lee W. "On the Margin: Postmodernism, Ironic History, and Medieval Studies." *Speculum* 65 (1990): 87–108.

——. "'For the Wyves Love of Bathe': Feminine Rhetoric and Poetic Resolution in the *Roman de la Rose* and the *Canterbury Tales*." *Speculum* 58 (1983): 656–95.

Reinhold, Meyer. "The Unhero Aeneas." *Classica et Mediaevalia* 27 (1966): 195–207.

Ruggiers, Paul, ed. *The Canterbury Tales: A Facsimile and Transcription of the Hengwrt MS with Variants from the Ellesmere MS*. The Variorum Edition of the Works of Chaucer, 1. Norman: U of Oklahoma P, 1979.

Sedulius Scottus. *Commentum Sedulii Scotti in maiorem Donatum grammaticum*. Ed. Denis Brearley. Studies and Texts 27. Toronto: Pontifical Institute of Mediaeval Studies, 1975.

Servii Grammatici qui feruntur in Vergilii carmina commentarii. 3 vols. Ed. Georg Thilo. Leipzig, 1881; rept. Hildesheim: Georg Olms, 1961.

Schibanoff, Susan. "The New Reader and Feminine Textuality in Two Early Commentaries on Chaucer." *Studies in the Age of Chaucer* 10 (1988): 71–108.

Southern, Sir Richard W. *Platonism, Scholastic Method, and the School of Chartres*. Reading: U of Reading, 1979.

Strauss, Barrie Ruth. "The Subversive Discourse of the Wife of Bath: Phallocentric Discourse and the Imprisonment of Criticism." *English Literary History* 55 (1988): 527–54.

Ussani, Vicenzo. "Enea traditore." *Studi italiani di filologia classica*, n.s. 22 (1947): 109–23.

P. Vergilii Maronis Opera. Ed. R. A. B. Mynors. Oxford: Clarendon, 1972.

William of Conches. *Glosae super Platonem*. Ed. Édouard Jeauneau. Paris: Vrin, 1965.

————. *Philosophia Mundi: Ausgabe des 1. Buchs von Wilhelm von Conches'* "*Philosophia*" *mit Anhang, Übersetzung und Anmerkungen*. Ed. Gregor Maurach. Pretoria: U of South Africa, 1974.

Windeatt, Barry A. "The Scribes as Chaucer's Early Critics." *Studies in the Age of Chaucer* 1 (1979): 119–41.

160

Authors in Love:
The Exegesis of Late-Medieval Love-Poets[1]

Alastair J. Minnis

Can one be an author and be in love? Nowadays that would seem to be a prime requirement for a writer, heterosexual love often being regarded as the peak of human experience. What author has the courage or foolishness to declare that he or she has had no experience of human love? But in the Middle Ages things were very different. An author, or *auctor*, was, to investigate the Latin etymology, not simply a writer but someone whose writing possessed authority (*auctoritas*). According to the value-system laid down by scholastic philosophy, the human love between man and woman was a dubious passion—indeed a dangerous passion if not directed into marriage. Within marriage it was, within certain limits, quite acceptable, but just as marriage was inferior to clerical celibacy, so love poetry was inferior to clerical works which addressed themselves directly towards the *summum bonum* and showed the human soul the path it should take towards that ultimate cause, goal, and destiny.

Fascinating problems arose when, in the later Middle Ages, vernacular literature reached the point at which it wished to locate and define itself in relation to the systems and strategies of textual evaluation which scholasticism had produced. But vernacular secular literature had human love as its main subject. Dante, in the *Vita nuova*, even suggested that it had its origin in human love: "The first to write as a vernacular poet was moved to do so because he wished to make his verses intelligible to a lady who found it difficult to understand

161

Latin" (25; *Opere*, ed. Moore and Toynbee 223; Reynolds 73). How, then, could such literature possibly win the approval of scholastic literary theory (as found in commentaries on *auctores*), with its strong moral bias and inbuilt prejudice against the notion that woman was man's joy and all his bliss (to borrow a phrase from Chaucer's Chaunticleer)? Clearly some vernacular poets (Dante most of all) were seeking such validation—their sense of the worth of the vernacular in general and their own writing in particular impelled them irresistibly in that direction.[2] One could not, of course, call oneself an *auctor* (Minnis, *Authorship* 12). One could, however, appropriate interpretive terms and techniques which had for generations been employed in expounding revered and ancient *auctores*; the reader could then make the obvious inferences.

There were basically two main methods of appropriation. A poet could accommodate certain formal features of commentary within the literary work itself. Commentary-prologues became models for writers' own prologues, some decorous and careful modification being necessary. This is what happened in two of the texts which will be discussed below. The elaborate introduction to John Gower's *Confessio amantis* and the Spanish prose preface to Juan Ruiz' *Libro de Buen Amor* are interesting but unmistakable variations on a standard prologue configuration frequently found at the head of commentaries on *auctores*, and in both cases the medieval introductions to Ovid, the so-called *accessus Ovidiani*, were of special importance to the vernacular writer as he created his self-image and commended his book (assuming, as is very likely, that the writer provided his own commentary). Second, a writer could provide his own work with a commentary—this being not simply a matter of *explication de texte* but more essentially a means of justification. "Reverent" and moral interpretation was an imperative of commentary on *auctores*; the authoritative text under consideration had to be shown to pertain to ethics or

162

some even higher science. When the writers of "new" commentary and "self-commentary" drew on the academic techniques of literary exposition they inherited an approach that was as prescriptive as it was descriptive. That is to say, the vocabulary and methods of medieval commentary-tradition were value-laden and value-bestowing. And it was precisely that great value, that high prestige, which John Gower wished to enlist when he equipped his *Confessio amantis* with Latin glosses and (far more obviously and thoroughly) which Dante appropriated when he produced the first major piece of self-exegesis to appear in any European vernacular, the Italian *Convivio*. Here two "modern" writers are self-consciously claiming a degree of literary authority for their own creations—Gower mainly through decorous implication and by allowing the textual apparatus to speak for itself; Dante by the direct statement with which he asserts the value of his own art and of Italian as an illustrious literary language.

Academic Prologues to Commentaries: Some Definitions

At the outset we must offer some definitions of crucial terms which will be used throughout this article, beginning with the distinction between "extrinsic" and "intrinsic" prologues to commentaries. In twelfth-century commentaries on authors the heading *extrinsecus* introduced a discussion of the place in the scheme of human knowledge occupied by the art or science relevant to one's text, while the heading *intrinsecus* introduced analysis of the text itself in accordance with headings such as *intentio auctoris, materia, modus agendi, utilitas,* and *cui parti philosophiae supponitur.* During the thirteenth century a new type of "extrinsic" prologue came into vogue that discussed some aspect of the hierarchy of the sciences and/or the processes of human understanding, Aristotelian epistemology and notions of scientific procedure providing the conceptualization (Minnis, *Author-*

163

ship 15–25, 30–33). Many forms of this prologue were possible: sometimes vestiges of the twelfth-century *intrinsecus* schema appear in these initial prologues; sometimes the four major causes as identified by Aristotle provide their structure; sometimes it is crucial terms such as *scientia* and *sapientia* which are at the center of attention. The "intrinsic" prologue changed also during this period, the older *accessus* paradigm being supplanted by, or used in some combination with, a schema based on the Aristotelian four causes. Thus the author was the work's efficient cause; the material he had used its material cause; the form of his writing (considered in terms of both style and structure) its formal cause; his ultimate objective in writing its final cause. Sometimes there was a distinct and discrete "extrinsic" prologue, formally cut off from the "intrinsic" prologue that followed it; on other occasions a single prologue could begin with an extrinsic discussion of some notion relating to science, wisdom, and knowledge and move into an "intrinsic" analysis of the text itself.

Finally, the "sermon-type" prologue may be defined (Minnis, *Authorship* 64). In prologues to twelfth-century Biblical commentaries there was a formal development whereby a technique that for generations had been used in sermons was applied in textual exposition (Smalley 109–10). At the very beginning an *auctoritas*, i.e., an extract from an *auctor*, would be quoted and divided up and discussed in the course of the prologue, at some stage (though not necessarily at the outset) being applied to the text. Originally the *auctoritas* was a Biblical one—hardly surprising, given the origins of this technique in the sermon and the fact that the prologues were introducing Bible commentaries. But in the thirteenth century secular *auctoritates* could be cited and used in the same way, Aristotle being a great source of pithy sayings (Minnis and Scott 319–20). By the end of the thirteenth century any kind of *auctoritas*, whether secular or sacred, could appear at the beginning of a commentary on any type of *auctor*, whether theological, philosophical, poetical, or whatever.

Dante's *Convivio* begins with one of the most sophisticated of the original "extrinsic" prologues in any vernacular language, which takes its point of departure from Aristotle's dictum that every man naturally longs for knowledge or sapience and proceeds to discuss the causes which inhibit this desire (1.1). With good reason Dante employed this kind of introduction. The initiated would instantly recognize its antecedents and would be well-disposed towards the learned treatise (for so it would be identified) that followed; one can therefore imagine the mixture of surprise and admiration (or perhaps antipathy, in some cases?) with which the *Convivio*'s first readers would have then encountered the actual objects of the commentary's analysis, Dante's own *canzoni*. Never before had vernacular poems been treated to such erudite exegesis, been taken with such scholarly seriousness.

But let us begin with "new" commentary and/or "self-commentary" of a more fundamental and representative kind, the attempts of two remarkable vernacular poets, the Spaniard Juan Ruiz and the Englishman John Gower, to follow in the footsteps of Ovid—and part and parcel of this enterprise was their appropriation of aspects of the academic literary criticism that circulated in manuscript with Ovid's poetry.

The "clerke Ovide," Ovid as interpreted as a scientific and moral *auctor*, offered a corpus of highly erotic and potentially subversive poetic fiction (Minnis, "Moral Gower" 54–57). He therefore supplied medieval love-poets with a sort of role model, while the established conventions of Ovid criticism provided them with the vocabulary and the formulae with which they could describe and justify their own writings. It must be added (to bring out the full complexity of the situation) that the contrasts and apparent contradictions in Ovid—the way he seemed to move from the sublime to the ridiculous, from creation myths to creative courtship, from the emotional heights and depths of wronged women to the hyperbolically elaborate strategies of seduction—encouraged in some of them a vein of parodic humor (including self-parody), thus producing a tone that sat rather uneasily with the self-enhancing seriousness necessary in one who wished to claim or solicit the accolade of *auctor*-ship. One such writer, it could be argued, was Juan Ruiz.[3]

The Libro de Buen Amor *and the Academic Prologues to Ovid*

The varieties of academic prologue which we have just described may be found in exegesis of Ovid. Pierre Bersuire's *Ovidius moralizatus* (the second redaction of which dates from the 1350s) seems to have been influenced by the sermon-type prologue, for it begins with a quotation from II Timothy (4:4): "they will turn away from listening to the truth and will turn to fables." St. Paul's dictum is ingeniously interpreted—if not twisted—to mean that one may find truth in the fables of the poets, the moral exposition of Ovid on a grand scale thereby being rationalized (Minnis and Scott 366–67). The commentary on the *Metamorphoses* that Dante's friend and correspondent Giovanni del Virgilio wrote c.1322–23 begins its "Aristotelian Prologue" with a Biblical quotation, in this case Ecclesiasticus 47:16, "You were filled as a river with wisdom and your soul covered the earth, and you multiplied riddles in parables and your name is spread abroad even unto the islands." "Although [here] the words are applied to something quite different from the matter at present under discussion," he declares, "yet they can be marvellously well adapted to our purpose, just as if they had here spoken in praise of Ovid" (Minnis and Scott 360–61). Giovanni manages to extract from them the four Aristotelian causes. The efficient cause, for example, is found in the first portion of this quotation:[4]

> So I say the efficient cause is referred to in the words "you were filled,"
> as may be spoken of Ovid, who was "filled with the river of wisdom,"
> something which is quite obvious from all the works he wrote. This could
> be made clearer, if it were the appropriate moment, by comparing him to
> a river. But I pass over that. (Minnis and Scott 361)

The efficient cause, he continues, may be identified as being twofold—Ovid and God! This notion had first, as one would expect, been applied in commentary on the Bible, being used in discussion of the relationship between divine inspiration, and hence ultimate authorship, of the Bible and the literary roles of the honored human writers. Giovanni's use of it indicates the degree of respect with which he believes Ovid should be treated. He proceeds to offer a life of the poet and a review of all his works.

In the Salamanca manuscript (dated 1343) of the *Libro de Buen Amor* appears a Spanish prose introduction to the work, the work of either Juan Ruiz himself (as seems highly likely) or some redactor who wished to exploit the conventions of Ovid-commentary in the service of his author. It may be identified as a sermon-type prologue, which offers both "extrinsic" and "intrinsic" material. Psalm 31:10 is cited and interpreted in terms of what "some schooled in philosophy" have identified as particularly pertaining to the human soul, namely understanding, will, and memory (Ruiz, *Book* 23–27). The central theme is that by true understanding man knows the good and consequently knows the bad. The Biblical text is divided and discussed in the traditional manner. Finally, an "intrinsic" treatment of the *Libro* itself is provided. Ruiz (assuming that this is by his own hand) declares that his intention is a good one; he has written "in mindfulness of the good"; a man or woman with true understanding will choose and act upon it—which presumably means that such a person will understand what is good and what is evil as described in the book and behave accordingly (*Book* 27). However, this does not mean, Ruiz continues, that the book is dangerous for those of little understanding. In fact they will be educated by it, for

> through reading and by realizing the evil that is done or is intended to be done by those who persist in their evil arts, and in discovering that their most clever, deceitful practices, which they use to sin and to deceive women, are made public, they will arouse their memory and not despise their reputation. . . . And they will cast off and abhor the ways and evil arts of heedless love (*loco amor*), which makes them lose their souls and fall under the wrath of God. . . .

These passages contain more explicitly Christian elaborations of notions which occur regularly in the *accessus Ovidiani*, particularly the introductions to the *Heroides* and the *Remedium amoris*. The introductions to the *Remedium amoris* explain that, in order to make amends for the offensive *Ars amatoria*, on account of which he had been exiled, Ovid "set out to write this book [the *Remedium*] in which he advises both young men and girls trapped in the snares of love as to how they may arm themselves against unlawful love." The poet's *intentio*, therefore, was to give "certain precepts" by which "unlawful love" may be removed (Minnis and Scott 25).[5] Similarly, introductions to the *Heroides* argue that in this text Ovid has supplied positive examples of good behavior and negative examples of evil behavior, thereby illustrating what should be done and what should be shunned:

> His intention (*intentio*) is to commend lawful marriage and love. . . . The work pertains to ethics (*ethice supponitur*), because he is teaching good morality and eradicating evil behaviour. The ultimate end (*finalis causa*) of the work is this, that, having seen the advantage (*utilitas*) gained from lawful love, and the misfortunes which arise from foolish and unlawful love, we may shun both of these and may adhere to chaste love.
>
> (Minnis and Scott 21)

In a similar vein, Ruiz declares that

> my intention (*intençión*) was not to write this in order to give models for
> sinning or for speaking evil. But it was to guide every person back to the
> true memory of doing good, and to give an example of good behaviour
> and admonitions for salvation, so that all might be warned and thus be
> better able to guard against such mastery as some use in the service of
> worldly love. (*Book* 27)

St. Gregory, he continues, says that arrows which are seen beforehand
wound a man less, and we can protect ourselves better from what we
have seen beforehand—here Ruiz is enlisting saintly support for a
notion that had for generations been a cliché of Ovid criticism. Indeed, notions gleaned from his reading of the glossed Ovid could well
have given Ruiz the idea of beginning his prologue with a discussion
of how knowledge of both the good and the evil are necessary for true
understanding.

And this brings us to consider the central crux of the Ruiz introduction, the point at which, at the very center of the "intrinsic" prologue, there is what appears to be, on the face of it, an astounding
volte-face. So sudden, indeed, is the transition that some have taken it
as evidence that Ruiz was in some way parodying the techniques of
the sermon. For, having warned against love, Ruiz proceeds to recom-
mend his book as being a guide to it:

> However, inasmuch as it is human to sin, if anyone should wish (which I
> do not advise) to have a taste of this worldly love, here they will find
> some models for doing so. (*Book* 27)

So, this book can be said to give understanding (here Ruiz returns to
his opening *auctoritas*) in two ways: those who would understand the
good and do good works in the love of God will take it in one way,

while those who desire "foolish worldly love" will understand it in another way. This ambivalence is not without precedent, however; it reflects tensions within the medieval understanding of Ovid, that ambivalent *auctor* who could write as a moral philosopher in the *Metamorphoses* and the *Heroides* (so that Giovanni del Virgilio could suggest that God Himself was in a specific sense the ultimate efficient cause of the former) and yet be responsible for such a morally offensive work as the *Ars amatoria*. Ovid's purpose in the *Art of Love*, declares a typical commentator, "is to instruct young men in the art of love, and how they should behave towards girls when having a love-affair. . . . The way he proceeds in this work is to show how a girl may be picked up (*possit inveniri*), how when picked up she may be won over, and, once won over, how her love may be retained" (Minnis and Scott 24). Later, of course, Ovid retracted and wrote a remedy for such love. In other words, the art of love and its remedy are interrelated; the one presupposes the other. The ambivalence we are discussing could even enter into the analysis of a work that was relatively easy to justify, the *Heroides*. The intention of this work could be the identification of unchaste or foolish forms of love, declares one scrupulous and comprehensive commentator, "or else to show how some women may be courted by letter, or how the results of living chastely may benefit us" (Minnis and Scott 23). In other words, some readers will find in the work models for love-letters, others will take it as an awful warning, and it may put some people off human love entirely! The transitions in the Ruiz prologue would have seemed far less surprising to those readers who knew the "Medieval Ovid" who was his source—i.e., Ovid as interpreted in the Middle Ages, entailing systematic moralization together with an ultimate harmonizing of discords by appeal to the poet's eventual repentance, as recorded in the *Remedium*, and indeed (for those who were prepared to take the *De Vetula* on trust) to his conversion to Christianity.

170

Having said all that, one may wonder if there is something intentionally amusing about the way in which this Spanish *accessus* puts the *remedium* before the *ars* (or, more accurately, the *ars* in the middle of the *remedium*), thereby disrupting rather than duplicating the standard *vita Ovidii*. This putative wit may confirm us in the belief that the Spanish prose introduction to the *Libro* was the work of Ruiz himself, though of course this is not proof positive. Had Ruiz kept to the traditional pattern, his obvious and direct appropriation of Ovidian criticism would have placed his *Libro* in a direct line of succession, as it were, from the Roman *magister amoris*. But Ruiz, it could then be argued, was not content to be simply conventional.

On the other hand, one should note the structural impossibility of moving straight from a Biblical quotation (as required by the sermon-type prologue) into a recommendation of an *ars amatoria*. Inevitably the emphasis on the remedial aspects would come first. Moreover, Ruiz ends the prologue by emphasizing the moral utility of his book, assuring us of his good *intençión* (in the passage quoted above) and reiterating his earlier claim that he wished "to guide every person back to the true memory of doing good." *Ethice supponitur. . . .*

Auctor *and* Persona aliorum *in Gower's Self-Commentary*

Turning now to John Gower's *Confessio amantis*, it may be argued that this work begins with a twofold introduction that is probably indebted to the stock combination of "extrinsic" and "intrinsic" prologues. Moreover, early manuscripts of the poem contain Latin glosses, which are probably the work of Gower himself. There are several reasons for this hypothesis, the most weighty being that when the Middle English text was revised (three versions were produced in the 1390s), the gloss was revised to match. Moreover, Gower's authorship of the Latin links designed to bring together his trilingual *oeuvre* into a single corpus has never seriously been doubted—so why should he not have written the Latin glosses on the *Confessio* as well, especially as the links and the glosses have the common objective of decking the vernacular texts in their finest colors, treating them to the kind of layout that was commonplace in manuscripts containing Latin works of unimpeachable authority? The main argument against Gower's authorship of the glosses seems to be that they appear to diverge from the text, sometimes taking a more staunchly moral line than the poem. My point is that this is an utterly commonplace phenomenon in academic commentary on *auctores*, and hence there is no reason to be surprised by its occurrence in the *Confessio amantis* glosses; indeed, this divergence can be taken as evidence of Gower's careful cultivation of the stance of the learned and moralizing scholastic commentator.

The source of the form of Gower's long English verse *Prologus* was probably the "sapiential" type (i.e., the type that focused on wisdom, *sapientia*) of "extrinsic" prologue that in the later Middle Ages introduced many a late-medieval commentary or philosophical treatise (Minnis, *Authorship* 177–82). A good example is afforded by the beginning of St. Thomas Aquinas's *Summa contra gentiles* (1259–64). In its "extrinsic" prologue Aristotle's statement that "it is the function of the wise man to order" (*sapientis est ordinare*) is taken as the point of departure for a discussion of the intention of the divine *auctor* and the general order of His universe, these being the "highest causes" which the wise man (*sapiens*) should investigate. "Truth must be the last end of the whole universe; and the consideration thereof must be the chief occupation of wisdom." All this is followed by an "intrinsic" prologue wherein Aquinas explains his intention in this work and the manner in which he has ordered it. The relationship between the two prologues is too obvious to miss (Minnis, "Moral Gower" 67–68).

Returning to the *Confessio amantis*, it may be observed that the beginning of this poem resembles a scholastic preface that first treats of the "extrinsic" aspects of the text in the context of a discussion of wisdom in general, and then proceeds to discuss the text itself. Gower's *Prologus* is an "extrinsic" prologue about wisdom (see *Prologus* 66 ff.), while the treatise that follows it is about love (Minnis, *Authorship* 177–83). *Sapientia* and *amor* are linked through the donnish joke that love has "put under" many a wise man. Hence, it seems fitting that a *Prologus* on wisdom should be followed by a treatise about love. Gower's declared intention is "in some part" to advise "the wyse man" (lines 64–65), and so the *Prologus* warns of the ways in which the temporal rulers, the Church, and the commons have ceased to follow wisdom. At two points it is emphasized that God alone has the wisdom necessary for full understanding of worldly fortune (*Prologus* 66–72, 1086–88). Then, in his "intrinsic" prologue (1.1–92) Gower proceeds to explain precisely what is within his compass. He cannot stretch his hand up to heaven and set the world to rights; instead he will change the style of his writings and speak of a matter with which all the world has to do, namely Love.

The formal significance of this transition is made absolutely clear by the opening gloss of the Latin commentary. It is structured in accordance with the traditional *accessus* headings, namely *intentio auctoris*, *nomen libelli* (a variant on *titulus/nomen libri*), and *materia*:

> Since in the *Prologus* the way in which the divisiveness of our current state has overcome the love of Charity has already been treated, the author intends (*intendit auctor*) presently to compose his book, the name (*nomen*) of which is called "The Lover's Confession," about that love by which not only human kind but also all living things naturally are made subject. And because not a few lovers frequently are enticed by the passions of desire beyond what is fitting, the subject-matter (*materia*) of the book is spread out more specially on these topics throughout its length. (*English Works* 1:35–36)

This stance is maintained throughout the commentary; these very sentiments are echoed in the very last gloss on the poem:

> Here at the end he recapitulates concerning that which at the beginning of the first book he promised he would treat more specially, in the case of love (*in amoris causa*). Truly, he concludes that the pleasure of all love apart from charity is nothing. For whoever abides in charity, abides in God. (*English Works* 2:475)

The Middle English poem gradually reveals all the problems and preoccupations of a typical "courtly lover," Amans, thereby instructing its audience in love-doctrine, in the then-fashionable way of conducting an affair. Such is the perspective offered by the text. But a far wider perspective is offered by the commentary: here we are taken beyond "the case of love" to a larger world of ethical verities and moral absolutes. Writing in English, Gower identifies himself as an example of the committed lover: this character is sometimes ridiculous but always sympathetic; he has the power to move and amuse by turns. Writing in Latin, Gower assures us that this is all a fiction. He is only pretending to be an Amans; what this *persona* actually exemplifies are the fatuous and perhaps reprehensible passions and excesses of human love.

> Here as it were in the person of those other people (*in persona aliorum*) whom love constrains, the author, feigning himself to be a lover (*fingens se auctor esse Amantem* . . .) proposes to write of their various passions one by one in the various distinctions of this book. (*English Works* 1:37)

John Gower, as (would-be) *auctor*, has of course not been fooled; he knows that love is eminently resistible, that the *sapiens* can rule fortune. Love may have subjugated many a wise man (*Prologus* 76), but in the very nature of things love is subject to wisdom, and reason can —and should—control the promptings of will.

To speak of the Latin glosses as "summaries" or "side notes" to the poem, as some have done, is therefore misleading, inasmuch as those terms imply a relationship of semantic parity and equivalence. For the relationship between text and gloss is actually an interpretive one: the gloss is not simply explaining the text but is consistently interpreting it—and the single most important aspect of this interpretation is moralization. Thus, when Genius, the priest of Venus, recommends *fin' amors* as a secure and proper channel for the desires of "every gentil herte" (4.1451–58), we find in the margin a Latin comment to the effect that this is not true in itself, but is rather what lovers believe: "Non quia sic se habet veritas, set opinio Amantum." This has been dismissed as the remark of a "literal-minded copyist who misunderstood part or all of the passage" (Bennett 116n1).[6] What is more likely is that Gower (assuming, as is probable, that he wrote the Latin commentary) was guarding against possible misunderstanding of this part of the story of Rosiphelee by a literal-minded reader who might leap to the conclusion that promiscuity was being condoned. After all, in his *De amore* (1184–86) Andreas Capellanus had alleged that all men and women are obliged to love, while not to love is a defect of nature—opinions which are very close to several of the erroneous propositions condemned by Stephen Tempier, Bishop of Paris, in 1277 (see Denomy, and Hissette 294–99, 304, 315). Similarly, the final gloss on the poem (as quoted above), in declaring that the pleasure of all love apart from charity is nothing, goes far beyond the corresponding portion of text that, while recognizing many of the limitations of human love, certainly does not condemn it outright. The point that Gower's English makes is that to all things there is a season and for the aged lover (as he is now revealed to be) the age of love has passed; "elde" functions as a natural *remedium amoris*. There is, therefore, a necessary distance between Gower's "text" and "glose," a distance that is explicable by reference to the value-laden strategies of medieval exegesis.

But it would be simplistic, and quite inaccurate, to suggest that the text of the *Confessio amantis* offers "lust" while its commentary offers "lore." For there is an abundance of lore in the text itself. The *Prologus*, as already noted, is an "extrinsic" prologue that is concerned with social wisdom, a concern shared by the epilogue, while Book 7 constitutes a little "Regiment of Princes." Then there is the didactic function of Genius, who constantly interprets his love-stories in a way reminiscent of, and sometimes dependent upon, the moralizing glosses on Ovid, and whose expertise and authority sometimes excel those of a "clerke" of Venus in a strict view of that role (as, for example, when he provides *exempla* of virtuous kings, or recommends to his charge now chastity and now "honeste" love in marriage). Moreover, on occasion the commentary is anticipating ethical views which will subsequently be made abundantly clear in the text—a good example being the controversial gloss on 4.1451–58. At that point the text's own (perfectly respectable) attitude has not as yet been indicated; all will be revealed a few lines later, when Genius draws attention to the many misfortunes which accompany the love of paramours and encourages every maiden to hurry to the feast of "honeste" married love and childbearing (4.1467–1501). The eventual fate of Rosiphelee, who decides to stop being slothful in love, is never specified, but the reader is left in no doubt that she should have opted for marriage. In sum, the Latin commentary may be said to link up with, and consolidate, the moral highlights of the English text, and on occasion to go beyond what the text is recommending. There is *interpretive distance* (to coin a phrase) between text and gloss, and on occasion they are quite far apart, but certainly they are not at opposite poles.

Alastair J. Minnis

Glossing the Game of Love:
The Commentary on Les Echecs Amoureux

Remarkably similar things can be said about what appears to be the first major French commentary on an original poem written in that language, the commentary on *Les Echecs Amoureux* (both of which seem to date from the late fourteenth century). This poem has a less direct link with Ovid than Gower's *Confessio amantis*, which drew on him as the main source for its love-stories: it was clearly inspired and heavily influenced by the *Roman de la Rose*, and Jean de Meun, responsible for the greater part of that work, was very much regarded as a "Medieval Ovidian."[7] And the commentator's initial defense of the *Echecs Amoureux* is certainly reminiscent of a particular kind of *accessus Ovidiani*: "the principal intention (*entente*) of the author in question and the end (*fin*) of his book," it declares, "is to concentrate on virtue and good works and to flee from all evil and all foolish idleness." With this ethical end in view, the commentator is anxious to put some distance between the poet and the *personae* which he employs, including the *persona* of the amorous young man who plays the chess of love with his lady. "We should know first of all," he explains,

> that the author of this poem . . . feigns (*faint*) and says many things that are not to be taken according to the letter (*a la lettre*), although they may be lifelike (*formablement*), and that there may be some truth secretly hidden beneath the letter and the fiction. . . . And because of this he feigns and introduces several characters (*personnes*), each of whom speaks in his turn as is appropriate to his nature, in the manner of feigning used in *The Romance of the Rose*. (Jones 31)[8]

177

One recalls the Gower-commentary's statement that the author of the *Confessio amantis* is feigning himself to be a lover and speaking *in persona aliorum.*

At the end of the commentary the large fictional element in the poem is once again emphasized, the commentator being anxious to warn that what the text says should not be taken as a simple record of the writer's own experience. "What he says about having mated," we are assured,

> should not be understood according to the letter in such a way as to mean
> that he was maddened and overcome by love. But he feigns this, to take
> the occasion for speaking of love better, more pleasantly, and more beauti-
> fully. For in this way this subject is made pleasant and agreeable to many
> people, as it was [said] at the beginning of this present book [i.e., the
> commentary]. (Jones 1291)

The commentator is quite consistent, then, in his desire to sunder the author from his *personae*. The moral note is then struck, as the commentator adds another justification:

> This was also to show better the error and deception that exist in mad,
> delectable love and the great, immutable dangers in which those who are
> too bemused by it place themselves. It is the principal intention of this
> author and the end of his book to reprove and blame their folly as a thing
> contrary to reason, as can clearly appear by the progress of his poem.

We are back in the world of the *accessus Ovidiani.*

Love is against reason, the argument declares; the fact that the author presents himself as having mated in the garden of mirth in the *left* corner of the chessboard is highly significant, for this signifies sensuality (whereas the right signifies reason). The poet's recognition of this, we are assured, is obvious from the end of the poem. The God of Love, on seeing that he has won the young man, joyfully presents him with the commandments of love—the direct source is Ovid's *Ars amatoria*. Apparently, though the commentator does not put it in these words, this should be understood as the victory of unreason. But this victory is only temporary, for the *ars* is followed by the *remedium amoris*. Pallas (wisdom, prudence, reason) is given the last word. She comes, the commentator explains, "fully to reprove and blame his folly" and to show him that "the delectable life" is in fact "a deceptive and perilous life" (Jones 1293). Then he offers a rapid summary of a major part of the poem.

> And here the lady Pallas told and showed him many beautiful lessons and fine things profitable to ethics and to honest life, and which it would be good to explain. But for certain reasons I shall be quiet at this [point] for the moment. Amen. (Jones 1294)

The main reason for this silence is surely that the text, by becoming explicitly moral itself, has rendered the gloss redundant. And so the commentator can in this final stretch take his leave of his author, having helped him over the earlier hurdles. As with the *Confessio amantis* commentary, there is interpretive distance between text and gloss, yet their goals are the same—and so, when the text becomes morally self-sufficient, it can be allowed to speak for itself. Thus, *amor* is harmonized (to some extent!) with *auctoritas*, and the poem as a whole can be professed to pertain to ethics.

The tension between Ovidian love and textual authority was far more marked, and the subject of heated debate, in the *querelle de la Rose* (c.1401–c.1403). Both sides conceived of Jean de Meun as a "New Ovid," and the arguments used for and against his part of the poem often draw upon and manipulate the conventions of Ovid criticism. But I have discussed those matters elsewhere;[9] here I wish to concentrate on one particularly interesting move within this debate, a move beyond the parameters of Ovid criticism and away from the quest for secular *auctoritas* towards more elevated role-models and a higher *auctoritas*.

Beyond Ovid: Towards a Higher Auctoritas

In one of the letters which he wrote in defense of Jean de Meun, Pierre Col appeals to the precedent of Biblical lovers. Jean Gerson had, in his *Traité contre le Roman de la Rose*, attacked the poem on the grounds that "he who made it was a foolish lover." Why, then, Pierre Col asks, does Lady Eloquence—a personification in Gerson's work—not first draw such conclusions "against Solomon, David, and other foolish lovers, who were long before Meun, whose books are made a part of holy Scripture and their words a part of the holy mystery of the Mass"?

> Who caused Uriah the good knight to be killed by treachery in order to commit adultery with his wife? A foolish lover. Who caused the temples with the idols to be built for the love of strange women? A foolish lover. . . . Do we not read that St. Peter and St. Paul were firmer in the faith after they had sinned, and many others similarly? I say that the Master Jean de Meun, because he had been a foolish lover, was very firm in reason; for the better he knew the folly which is in foolish love by experience, the better was he able to scorn it and to praise reason. And when he made this book of the *Rose*, he was no longer a foolish lover (and had repented of being one), as is clear from his speaking so well of Reason. (Hicks 94; Baird and Kane 97–98)

Here Col is drawing on a controversy in Scriptural exegesis, over how the sins of major Scriptural *auctores* could be reconciled with their undeniable *auctoritas*. Theologians had for generations attempted to

180

cope with the unpalatable historical facts that King David, saint and supreme prophet, had committed adultery with Bathsheba and engineered the situation in which her husband Uriah was killed, and that King Solomon, the son of that mutual pair, had been led astray by his excessive love of women, even to the extent of worshipping strange gods. Twelfth-century Biblical commentators had allegorized David as Christ, Bathsheba as the Church, and Uriah as the devil. Their successors, some of whom seem to have been worried by the obvious clash between the literal and spiritual meanings here, were willing to accept that David and Solomon (and, in a very different capacity, St. Paul) had indeed sinned, but translated them into *exempla* of what to do and what to avoid (Minnis, *Authorship* 103–10). St. Bonaventure, commenting on Ecclesiastes (c.1254–57), affirmed that this work was written not by a sinner but by a penitent man who regretted his sins (Minnis, *Authorship* 110–11). Similarly, the English Dominican Thomas Waleys, commenting on the Psalter in the early fourteenth century, described David and St. Paul as having passed through a state of sin; they were writing not as sinners but as men who had once been sinners, and hence one can have confidence in their books (Minnis, *Authorship* 105–06). Arguments such as this were obviously in Col's mind when he wrote the above passage. A writer's amatory experience, then, does not necessarily invalidate his work—providing that he has put his *amours* behind him. An *auctor* may not be *in* love; he has to be *out* of love to be utterly acceptable.

But what if a writer does *not* leave his love behind? This causes considerable problems for his commentator, as is well illustrated by a passage in Boccaccio's short treatise in praise of Dante, the *Trattatello* (first version c.1351–35). Here he suggests that Dante's persistent "lust" (*lussuria*) did not seriously damage his status as a writer. Having shifted some of the blame onto the irresistible female sex (with the aid of ideas from Walter Map), he proceeds with a familiar argument about the sins of the *auctores* of Scripture:

> Amid such virtue, amid such learning as we have noted there to have been in this magnificent poet, lust (*lussuria*) found most ample space; and not just in his youthful years, but also in maturity. Although this vice may be natural, common, and to some extent necessary, it cannot in truth be decently commended, much less excused. But who among mortals can play the just judge in condemning it? Not I. O feeble resolve! O bestial appetite of men! What thing can women not work in us, if they wish, since they can achieve such great things without even trying? They have charm, beauty, and natural sexual instinct and many other things working continually on their behalf within the hearts of men. And that this be true, let us pass over what Jove did for Europa, or what Hercules did for Iole, or what Paris did for Helen, since as these things are poetic fictions many people of little understanding would dismiss them as fables; but let this be illustrated by things that nobody can rightly deny. Was there more than one woman in the world when our first father, having abandoned the commandment given him by the very mouth of God, succumbed to her persuasions? Of course not. And David, even though he had many wives, only needed to see Bathsheba to forget, on her account, God, his kingdom, himself, and his integrity, becoming first an adulterer and then a murderer. . . . And Solomon, to whose wisdom nobody, excepting the Son of God, has ever attained: did he not abandon Him who had made him wise and, to please a woman, kneel and adore Baalim? What did Herod do? What about those many others, drawn along by nothing but their pleasure? Among so many men of such calibre, then, our poet may pass, not excused but accused with his head hanging not so low as it would otherwise have done had he alone been at fault. (Minnis and Scott 502–03)

The initial point here is that Boccaccio cannot blame the poet's sins on his youth, in which age a man was believed to be physiologically prone to physical passion. To be of mature age and be in love was much harder to defend (and to be an aged lover was to run the risk of

182

being regarded as utterly ridiculous—witness the many medieval caricatures of the *senex amans*). Neither, apparently, can he point to a change of heart, which would enable a close parallel to be drawn between Dante and David. Or, indeed, between Dante and Ovid, who (according to the *vitae Ovidii* exemplified earlier) was supposed to have put his interest in love-poetry behind him. What Boccaccio can, and does, do is use the analogy to suggest that, while Dante may not be excused, at least he is in good company, and certainly not unworthy to be numbered amongst some of the greatest *auctores*.

In his *Decameron* (Fourth day, Introduction) Boccaccio had used the same sort of argument in defense of his own liking for women and wish to please them in his writing. Feminine beauty, he points out, was "much admired" by "Guido Cavalcanti and Dante Alighieri in their old age, and by Cino da Pistoia in his dotage." Then Boccaccio moves from the moderns to the ancients. He could pursue his case still further by citing history-books which are "filled with examples from antiquity of outstanding men, who, in their declining years, strove with might and main to give pleasure to the ladies" (Segre 258–59; McWilliam 329). The point seems to be that if such distinguished men (who are—as if to lend further emphasis—in their old age, when age might well have chilled their blood and wisdom taught them to know better) were still susceptible to female charm, then he, Boccaccio, can hardly be accused with utter severity. The form in which the argument figures in the *Trattatello* passage quoted above is significantly different, of course, for in the later work it helps make the case that Dante's *lussuria* does not automatically cancel his claim to *auctor*-ship. In the *Trattatello*, and more fully in his *Exposizioni sopra la Comedia di Dante* (1373–74), Boccaccio adopted the methods of academic commentary—and hence he took on board some of the problems endemic to that type of textual interpretation, the issue of whether *amor* can be reconciled with *auctoritas* being a good

183

example. It is as if in this instance Boccaccio was more occupied with a crux of medieval criticism than with his author, for he ignores Dante's own self-justifying strategies in the *Convivio*, not to mention the complexities of Dante's authorial view of love in the *Comedia*.

This is not to say that Dante himself sought to ignore the standards and style of medieval criticism—because nothing could be further from the truth. Dante-commentary begins with Dante, and so we may turn to the *Convivio* to investigate the ways in which he *did* exploit the traditions of exegesis. Our main interest is in the fact that, in the most problematic stretch of this superb self-commentary, he uses the method with which twelfth-century Scriptural exegetes had resolved the problem of apparently sinful *auctores*, namely, allegorical interpretation.

After his "extrinsic" prologue, Dante claims that two motives lie behind his self-commentary: the fear of infamy and the wish to give instruction. The reader of his *canzoni* may have formed the impression that he had pursued a great passion of love. But in fact virtue was the "moving cause," as, he promises, the subsequent expositions will make clear (1.2; Cordati 12; Wicksteed 12). In fact, no real problem is presented by the second and third *canzoni* analyzed in the *Convivio*, for their moral sense and intention seem quite obvious. The *Voi che' ntendendo* is a very different matter, however, for its ostensible subject is the compassionate *donna gentile* who, according to the *Vita nuova*, had comforted Dante for a short time after the death of Beatrice. Literally the poem (which had been written much earlier, between late 1293 and Spring of 1294) refers to that love-affair. Allegorically, according to Dante's self-commentary, it describes the consolation of philosophy.

While the editors of Dante's lyrics, Kenelm Foster and Patrick Boyde, admit that there is nothing in the text "to compel an allegorical interpretation" of this *canzone*, they conclude that there is "no cogent reason why we should take this [i.e., the meaning as explained in the *Convivio*] as an afterthought and suppose that he did not originally write the poem with that intention" (2:160–62, 341–62). However, I see no reason to rule out the possibility that Dante retrospectively allegorized a poem that originally had referred to a real love-affair, this being done not as an "afterthought"—to cite Foster and Boyde's demeaning term—but as part of a calculated attempt to elevate vernacular poetry through the appropriation (and adaptation, of course) of scholastic literary theory. This suggestion takes account of the moral, and moralizing, bias of the medieval commentary-tradition that Dante was drawing on in *Il Convivio*. The crucial point to grasp here, as in the cases of Gower's self-commentary and the *Echecs Amoureux* commentary, is that interpretive distance exists between text and gloss: their relationship is not one of semantic parity and equivalence, as most Dante scholars have assumed. The strategies of commentary, far from being neutral methods for extracting the single definitive meaning of a text, are themselves suffused with definite values which define the commentator's reference and render his moral conclusion inevitable, whether he is expounding an "ancient" or a "modern" text, someone else's work or his own. This is not, of course, to imply that Dante is trapped within the interpretive system he has adopted: rather, he is exploiting it with impressive awareness of its swings and roundabouts.[10]

In the allegorical exposition of *Voi che'ntendendo* the human love-object is *replaced* by an edifying personification, as the *donna gentile* becomes Dame Philosophy. In the *Divine Comedy*, however, the human love-object is *equated* with the edifying personification, as Beatrice leads the narrator through paradise, even unto the Empyrean Heaven. Human love, according to our previous argument, had to be a thing of the past in order to be wholly acceptable in an *auctor*. Here is a new twist—the limiting, transient, and earthly elements of the

185

love are left in the past, while in the present what exists is the love of soul for soul. This form of love, a *translatio* of the purest possible element in human love to the level of *caritas*, is quite compatible with literary authority. Here in the *Comedy*, it may be said, is Dante's ultimate reconciliation of the matter of vernacular poetry with the method of late-medieval literary theory. Vernacular poetry, born out of human love (as Dante suggested in the *Vita nuova*), has come of age and attained maturity; it has been accepted into the canon.

But, of course, the tensions remain. At the end of the *Comedy*, Beatrice must give place to St. Bernard of Clairvaux, the ultimate *magister amoris* for Christians. Going beyond Ovid did not enable a poet to escape utterly from those problems regularly encountered by those medieval Ovidians who sought to share that somewhat paradoxical respectability enjoyed by the writer who was the great expert on not only human love but also its rejection.

Can one, then, be an author and be in love? The official medieval answers seem to have been that past passion may be accommodated but contemporary involvement is highly suspect; that it is preferable to remember love than to make it; that distant and/or dead beloveds are better than living ones. The circle is irrevocably a circle and cannot be squared—at least, for the time being, until culture itself changes, as of course it has done. The very attempts of medieval love-poets (and critics of love-poems) to square that circle are, however, in themselves of considerable cultural significance. No literary criticism is value-free, as we often hear nowadays from the advocates of the "New New Criticism." The most self-aware of the self-exegetes of the later Middle Ages knew that fact full well. And here they sought a means of valorizing their own poetry.

Alastair J. Minnis

NOTES

1. This title is designed to cover aspects of the academic-style commentary that certain writers provided for *their own* vernacular works, and which was produced by people *other* than the original authors.

2. It should perhaps be emphasized that I am not implying that this was the *only* worthwhile process of validation available to late-medieval love-poets; such a view would be critically reductive in the extreme, and historically inaccurate. Within the tradition of the poetry of "courtly love," for example, the appeal to high quality of sentiment was often made, *fin'amors* being at once the condition and the justification for fine poetry. Here I am solely concerned with those poets who found in the scholastic commentary tradition a means of "canonizing" certain vernacular works. This is, it should be recognized, a very narrow band of writers, from different countries and cultures; the extent to which they are representative of their time and place is a subject for debate. But what they have in common, and what makes them quite remarkable from our point of view, is the degree of consistency with which they exploited the forms and techniques of clerkly criticism. One can therefore postulate certain shared goals and objectives, to the extent that a major cultural movement may be identified. Literary authority is moving from Latin into the European vernaculars.

3. Another was, of course, Geoffrey Chaucer. The *Troilus* epilogue reveals him edging his vernacular tragedy into the line of succession from the great classical *poetae*, yet the richly ironic *House of Fame* (followed up by the challenging Legend of Good Women, which includes a depiction of Dido very different from Virgil's) seem to shake the very foundation of literary *auctoritas*, trust in the superior veracity of past masters. This matter is discussed in my article, "*De Vulgari auctoritate:* Chaucer, Gower and the Men of Great Authority," *Chaucer and Gower: Difference, Mutuality, Exchange,* ed. R. F. Yeager, English Literary Studies Monograph Ser., 51 (U of Victoria, 1991): 36–74.

187

4. Such dividing up of the initial text (a version of what was called *divisio textus*) in order to provide the framework of the prologue means that Giovanni's introduction corresponds more closely to the "sermon-type prologue" as defined above than does Bersuire's effort. The *Libro de Buen Amor* prologue also conforms to that paradigm in its *divisio textus*.

5. This discussion may be compared with John Dagenais' important article, "A Further Source for the Literary Ideas in Juan Ruiz's Prologue," *Journal of Hispanic Studies* 11 (1960): 23–52.

6. G. C. Macaulay's note (Gower, *English Works* 1: 506) is far more perceptive: "The author dissociates himself personally from the extreme doctrines enunciated in the text, as at first he took care to remind his readers that the character of a lover was for him only an assumed one (i.63 ff. margin)." Clearly, Macaulay recognized the consistency of the commentary.

7. These matters are discussed in my article, "Theorizing the Rose: Commentary Tradition in the *Querelle de la Rose*," *Poetics: Theory and Practice in Medieval English Literature*, ed. P. Boitani and A. Torti, J. A. W. Bennett Memorial Lectures, Seventh Ser. (Cambridge: Brewer, 1991): 13–36.

8. These translations from the *Echecs Amoureux* commentary follow Jones, but I have made numerous personal alterations in the light of the French manuscript that is reproduced in her dissertation. Since writing this article, I have learned from Bruno Roy that the *Echecs Amoureux* commentator is to be identified with Evrart de Conty (c.1330–1405), physician to Charles V and also to Blanche of Navarre, widow of Philippe VI. The evidence is admirably laid out by Françoise Guichard-Tesson, "Evrart de Conty, auteur de la 'Glose des echecs amoureux'," *Le Moyen français* 8–9 (1981): 111–48. An edition of this text by Bruno Roy and Guichard-Tesson is to be published in 1992. I myself discuss the *Echecs Amoureux* commentary at more length in my article, "Late-Medieval Vernacular Literature and Latin Exegetical Traditions," forthcoming in the proceedings of the University of Heidelberg symposium *Archäo-*

Alastair J. Minnis

logie der Literarischen Kommunikation IV: Text und Kommentar (30th May–2nd June 1991), which is being edited by Professor Jan Assmann.

9. For discussion see Minnis, "Theorizing the Rose."

10. Compare my article "*Amor* and *Auctoritas* in the Self-Commentary of Dante and Francesco da Barberino" *Poetica* 32 (1990): 25–42.

WORKS CITED

Baird, Joseph L., and John R. Kane, eds. *La Querelle de la Rose: Letters and Documents*. Chapel Hill: North Carolina UP, 1978.

Bennett, J. A. W. "Gower's 'Honeste Love'." *Patterns of Love and Courtesy*. Ed. John Lawlor. London: Arnold, 1966. 107–21.

Boccaccio, Giovanni. *Decameron*. Trans. G. H. McWilliam. Harmondsworth: Penguin, 1972.

———. *Opere*. Ed. C. Segre. 4th ed. Milan: Mursia, 1967.

Dante Alighieri. *Il Convivio*. Ed. Bruna Cordati. Turin: Loescher, 1968.

———. *The Convivio*. Trans. Philip H. Wicksteed. London: Dent, 1931.

———. *Lyric Poetry*. Ed. Kenelm Foster and Patrick Boyde. 2 vols. Oxford: Clarendon, 1967.

———. *Opere*. Ed. E. Moore and Paget Toynbee. Oxford: Clarendon, 1924.

———. *Vita nuova*. Trans. Barbara Reynolds. Harmondsworth: Penguin, 1969.

Denomy, A. J. "The *De Amore* of Andreas Capellanus and the Condemnation of 1277." *Mediaeval Studies* 8 (1946): 107–49.

Gower, John. *English Works*. Ed. G. C. Macaulay, 2 vols. EETS e.s. 81, 82. London: Oxford UP, 1900–01.

Hicks, Eric, ed. *Le Débat sur Le Roman de la Rose*. Paris: Champion, 1977.

Hissette, R. *Enquête sur les 219 articles condamnés a Paris le 7 Mars 1277*. Philosophes médiévaux 22. Louvain and Paris: Publications Universitaires, 1977.

Alastair J. Minnis

Jones, Joan Morton. *The Chess of Love [Old French Text with Translation and Commentary]*. Diss. U. Nebraska, 1968. Ann Arbor: UMI.

Minnis, A. J. *Medieval Theory of Authorship: Scholastic Literary Attitudes in the Later Middle Ages*. London: Scolar, 1984; 2nd ed. Aldershot: Scolar, 1988.

———. "'Moral Gower' and Medieval Literary Theory." *Gower's Confessio amantis: Responses and Reassessments*. Ed. A. J. Minnis. Cambridge: Brewer, 1983. 50–78.

Minnis, A. J., and A. B. Scott, eds. *Medieval Literary Theory and Criticism c. 1100–c.1375: The Commentary Tradition*. Oxford: Clarendon, 1988.

Ruiz, Juan. *The Book of True Love*. Ed. S. R. Daly and A. N. Zahareas. University Park, PA and London: Pennsylvania State UP, 1978.

Smalley, Beryl. "Peter Comestor on the Gospels and his Sources." *Recherches de théologie ancienne et médiévale* 46 (1979): 84–129.

Nimrod, the Commentaries on Genesis, and Chaucer

John M. Fyler

Judson Allen, to whose memory this volume is dedicated, made his most significant contribution to Chaucer studies by grounding his criticism in the rich medieval commentarial tradition. He used manuscripts, that is to say, not so much for their palaeographical interest as to highlight a number of texts that survive only in manuscript form, bringing them to bear on the largest issues of structure and meaning in Chaucer's poetry. Along with Malcolm Parkes and Alastair Minnis, and largely anticipating them, Judson Allen introduced many Chaucerians to the distinguished work of the Oxford historical school, in particular, of Beryl Smalley and Richard W. Hunt. Smalley and Hunt were both concerned with two interconnected but separable types of medieval commentaries: interpretations of the Bible and interpretations of the classics (the second being in some measure influenced by the first). Much of Allen's work fell within the area described by Hunt's studies of medieval grammatical theory and Smalley's book on *English Friars and Antiquity in the Fourteenth Century*; my remarks in this essay pay homage to the other major strand in their work, the tradition of Biblical commentary examined by Smalley's *Study of the Bible in the Middle Ages* and Hunt's D. Phil. dissertation on Alexander Nequam (ed. Gibson).

I have been interested for some time in the patristic and medieval commentaries on the opening chapters of Genesis, especially as they discuss the origin and nature of language and its quick decline from an original purity—first as part of Adam's fall, most decisively with the confusion of tongues at Babel. Searching for comments on language and signification makes even more obvious what is already self-evident: the massive influence of Augustine on later Biblical commentary. For Augustine's exceptional interest in such issues is manifest in his shorter philosophical treatises *On the Teacher* and *On Order*, in his several commentaries on Genesis, and in the *City of God*; and his remarks are repeated, often verbatim, in Biblical commentaries throughout the Middle Ages. Later commentaries do add flashes of original insight to the Augustinian substratum, especially in writers of such power as Bede and Abelard. But for my purposes here the most significant additions to Augustine are from the Jewish and Christian apocryphal materials, which embellish the Genesis text with stories such as the one about Lamech's killing Cain and his own son Tubal-cain. Most medieval commentators derive their small knowledge of Hebrew directly from St. Jerome (though they also obtain information, at first or second hand, from Josephus), and Jerome's etymologies of Hebrew names and reference to the Jewish tradition of commentary are of abiding influence. But as Beryl Smalley above all has shown, especially in her study of Andrew of St. Victor, there was an independent interest in rabbinical exegesis—notably in the twelfth century and particularly in the person of Rashi—and a remarkable dependence on Jewish tradition, the "Hebraica veritas," to explain the literal meaning of the Old Testament. These various strands—Augustine, Josephus, the apocrypha and pseudepigrapha, rabbinical tradition—all come together very interestingly in later medieval accounts of the Tower of Babel; and I think that they illuminate Chaucer's poetry, even as they flesh out the narrative of Genesis 10–11.

Though not in so thoroughgoing a fashion as Dante, Chaucer is frequently interested in issues of language and signification. His interest is most conspicuous in *The House of Fame*, where he gives a comic account of significant sound in its context of babble and mean-ingless noise. But he also makes such issues central in the sequence of tales from the Second Nun's to the Parson's, a sequence that forms a coda to the *Canterbury Tales* as a whole. The end of the *Canterbury Tales*, as I have argued previously, "transcends words and a delight in poetic artifice by moving beyond them—first by an ironic disinte-gration, then with utter seriousness—to the absolute simplicity of supernatural truth, where no words are necessary and human language cannot follow" (155). The details of this ironic disintegration are most fully described by James Dean, in his essay "Dismantling the Canter-bury Book"; Donald Howard had previously sketched out its contours. In Howard's words, "The movement of this sequence, like that of Fragment I, is degenerative"; The Manciple's Tale "lets language itself fall beneath corrupt human nature. The rest, or at least the end, is silence" (304). This process of degeneration, defined with a specifically linguistic reference, in fact begins in Fragment VIII. Chaucer uses the tales of the Second Nun and Canon's Yeoman to recapitulate the history of human language, and this recapitulation serves as a meton-ymy for the larger issues of our history on earth and our salvation. After the Manciple has shown that stories and proverbs apparently teach us nothing, after the Canon's Yeoman has shown the degradation of our speech, the only recourse is to brush away the web of words altogether.

In these tales we see language in extremes, as it nears its ter-mination. For its beginnings, we must turn to the Biblical account, where the first appearance of language in human history is of course Adam's naming of the birds and animals, in Genesis 2. In Eden there is a meaningful correspondence of name and reality, of sign and thing; and this correspondence is threatened, if not entirely destroyed, by the Fall. Original sin has other linguistic effects, even on children's initial attempts to speak. Dante argues that Adam's first word must have been

"El," the name of God: "for just as after the transgression of the human race, anyone's first venture in speech is a cry of woe, it is reasonable that whoever existed before this transgression would have started out in joy" (7). And Augustine, when he remembers his childhood in the *Confessions*, remembers that a child learns to speak primarily because he comes to realize that cries and gestures are less effective ways of communicating the demands of his corrupted will (1.8; p. 9). But the decisive event for language in later history, in effect a second Fall, was the building of the Tower of Babel. Before, "the earth was of one tongue, and of the same speech" (Gen. 11:9 [Douay-Rheims trans]); afterwards, God punishes human pride by deciding: "let us . . . there confound their tongue, that they may not understand one another's speech" (11:7). If the evanescence of speech explains the origins of written language, Augustine argues, Babel explains its divisions: "A sign of this pride is that tower erected in the heavens where impious men deserved that not only their minds but also their voices should be dissonant" (*On Christian Doctrine* 2.4; p. 36). Dante punishes the builder of the tower, Nimrod, with utter isolation: in *Inferno* 31 he speaks an unintelligible language and is unable to understand anyone else's speech. For the rest of us, the after-effects of Babel are more mundane: it is simply true, as Augustine says, that

> if two men meet, and are forced by some compelling reason not to pass on but to stay in company, then if neither knows the other's language, it is easier for dumb animals, even of different kinds, to associate together than these men, although both are human beings. For when men cannot communicate their thoughts to each other, simply because of difference of language, all the similarity of their common human nature is of no avail to unite them in fellowship. So true is this that a man would be more cheerful with his dog for company than with a foreigner. (*City of God* 19.7; p. 861)

These responses suggest Babel's vivid place in the Western

196

imagination, which it owes in part, no doubt, to its potential for visual representation: like the Ark and Abraham's sacrifice of Isaac, it lends itself to such striking visual images as Brueghel's painting or the illumination in BL MS. Egerton 1894. The prominence of the story is also in part due to the identification of Babel and Babylon in Biblical geography. In the famous map of the world in Hereford Cathedral, the symmetrical design makes Eden, Babylon, Jerusalem, Rome, and Gibraltar equidistant from each other, as points marking the major events, as well as geographical landmarks, in the history of humankind. More important still is the typological symmetry, for Babel is the symbolic type of Pentecost (Acts 2:1–12); and in the *Speculum Humanae Salvationis*, the two scenes are represented side by side (chap. XXXIV). In this typological view, the hellish extremes of linguistic division are countered by heavenly possibilities. The confusion of tongues, like Adam's Fall, has its ordained place in the history of redemption. According to the *Glossa Ordinaria*, which copies Isidore of Seville's exegesis of the story (PL 83.237–38), Babel has symbolic meaning as "mundi superbia, vel haereticorum dogmata" (pride of the world, or the doctrines of heretics), which will give way at last to "unitas confessionis et fidei" (unity of confession and faith) (PL 113.114).

Although Babel is the type of Pentecost, which promises the redemption of human speech, the more common emphasis is on its continuing degeneration, in step with everything else in the declining world. In Fragment VIII Chaucer in effect presents the extremes of language before and after Babel. We move from the Golden Age to the Iron, from the heavenly suffusion and clarity of outline in the primitive Church to a demonic present, from the sweet odor of sanctity in St. Cecilia's tale to the Canon's Yeoman's world, in which man must indeed eat bread in the sweat of his face. (Four of the thirteen Chaucerian instances of the word "sweat," which almost invariably has overtones of crass comedy in his poetry, are in this tale; and sweating is precisely what St. Cecilia does *not* do in her fiery torture [SNT 522 in *The Riverside Chaucer*].) The ballade "The Former Age" in effect comments on the Yeoman's vocation:

> But cursed was the tyme, I dare wel seye,
> That men first dide hir swety bysinesse
> To grobbe up metal, lurkinge in derknesse,
> And in the riveres first gemmes soghte. (27–30)

In The Second Nun's Tale words are translucent: etymologies reveal a meaningful correspondence between sign and thing, language is unambiguous, rhetorical embellishment unnecessary. Augustine's *On Christian Doctrine* recommends rhetorical training, so that the Christian teacher may compete on an equal footing with the teachers of evil (4.2; pp. 118–19). Cecilia is obviously in no need of his concern. She persuades her husband to live in a celibate marriage (152–61) and her jailer to become a Christian (372–78) with the righteous assurance of plain speech. St. Paul appears in a vision, with "a book with lettre of gold in honde" (202), to reinforce her message; her own words are as luminous as the apostle's, which, as the narrator repeats, "al with gold ywriten were" (210). She need say little more than "Believe," and her word is sufficient. Indeed, the verbal abruptness of both the saint and her tormentor—"Whoso wol nat sacrifise,/ Swape of his heed; this my sentence heer" (365–66)—captures perfectly the predominant tone in the *Acta Martyrum*.

Her world, then, has the fresh clarity of a spring morning, with the savor of invisible roses and lilies, and an awakening to the humble simplicity of the Truth:

> Tiburce answerde, "Seistow this to me
> In soothnesse, or in dreem I herkne this?"

"In dremes," quod Valerian, "han we be
Unto this tyme, brother myn, ywis.
But now at erst in trouthe oure dwellyng is." (260–64)

In The Canon's Yeoman's Tale, on the other hand, the Golden Age has
given way to grubbers for gold, the golden letters of St. Paul's book to
the Yeoman's crass boast that his Canon could pave the road to
Canterbury with precious metals (625–26). Chaucer's use of alchemy
to point his moral adds a further irony: if by an Ovidian paradigm flux
replaces the original stability of the cosmos, the alchemist in effect
tries to metamorphose things backwards, to find the gold beneath the
superficies of baser metals in the decaying world. But the fact of the
world's decline is apparent in the alchemist's method; the quest for the
singular through "multiplying" requires the deception of borrowing
gold in the attempt to find it:

To muchel folk we doon illusioun,
And borwe gold, be it a pound or two,
Or ten, or twelve, or manye sommes mo,
And make hem wenen, at the leeste weye,
That of a pound we koude make tweye. (673–77)

Yet multiplication is most likely to lead not to the singular but to
nothing: "A man may lightly lerne, if he have aught,/ To multiplie, and
brynge his good to naught!" (1400–01). In this process the Second
Nun's urge to defeat idleness, "the ministre and the norice unto vices"
(1), by "leveful bisynesse" (5) turns into the frenzy of the Canon and
Yeoman, sweaty and driven by their obsession to hectic activity (576).
In an alchemist's version of the Tower of Babel, a broken pot provokes
hellish dissension (906–31, esp. 916–17); and gold in the fallen world
is, paradoxically, consumed by the very process of searching for it:

> Considereth, sires, how that, in ech estaat,
> Bitwixe men and gold ther is debaat
> So ferforth that unnethes is ther noon.
> This multiplying blent so many oon
> That in good feith I trowe that it bee
> The cause grettest of swich scarsetee. (1388–93)

But the obsessive search goes on, in part simply because misery loves company (747), and the adepts of multiplying search for converts as much as for gulls. One can hardly forget, in this context, Cecilia's scornful charge that the pagans take a stone and call it a god (500–01): the alchemist does the same thing with his "philosophres stoon" (862, 1452–63), indeed, with the object of his quest: "The idols of the Gentiles are silver and gold ("Simulacra gentium argentum et aurum"), the works of the hands of men" (Ps. 113B: 4).

The fogginess of the Yeoman's mind, and of the world he describes, is summed up by Chaucer's jokes on the word "multiplying." Its primary meaning in The Canon's Yeoman's Tale is "to practice alchemy." But words also "multiply," as one of the entries for *multiplien* in the Middle English Dictionary indicates; and the Eagle in the *House of Fame* explains how

> Everych ayr another stereth
> More and more, and speche up bereth,
> Or voys, or noyse, or word, or soun,
> Ay through multiplicacioun,
> Til hyt be atte Hous of Fame. (817–21)

"Multiplicacioun," whether of metals or of words, exemplifies the fragmentation and confusion of human experience. In the *House of Fame*, rapidly multiplying words seek their proper resting place in the turbulent air. In The Canon's Yeoman's Tale the proliferation of words and of alchemy are analogous if not related processes; the great jokes of this tale are primarily linguistic ones. For if words in The Second Nun's Tale are translucent, in the Yeoman's world they are opaque. Jargon and technical vocabulary are self-consciously and deliberately obfuscatory—counters in a shell game. The false canon of the tale can "so wynde" (980) himself in his jargon that he can fool anyone; and the Yeoman describes the practice of his master and himself in much the same fashion:

> Whan we been there as we shul exercise
> Oure elvysshe craft, we semen wonder wise,
> Oure termes been so clergial and so queynte. (750–52)

Here as always in Chaucer's poetry, the word "termes" implies a specialist's argot; and the General Prologue offers several examples of how "termes" can be used for self-promotion and the deception of others.

Yet in The Canon's Yeoman's Tale, the confidence man himself becomes the gull. The opacity of jargon prevents even its users from achieving any clear sight:

> Philosophres speken so mystily
> In this craft that men kan nat come therby,
> For any wit that men han now-a-dayes.
> They mowe wel chiteren as doon jayes,
> And in hir termes sette hir lust and peyne,
> But to hir purpos shul they nevere atteyne. (1394–99)

Just as Chaucer in the General Prologue describes the Physician by a list of names, the authors of his medical textbooks, so the Canon's Yeoman gives us a hilarious list of terms, out of order, "as they come to mynde," and not set "in hir kynde" (788–89). His case of logorrhea lasts for forty lines before it abates. But then, having returned to his narration, the Yeoman interrupts himself once again: "Yet forgat I to maken rehersaille" (852) of another seven terms, also out of order and incoherently presented.

The final joke in the tale epitomizes Chaucer's perception of language in the fallen world. In The Second Nun's Tale the word "name" appears five times, twice to emphasize the virtuous power of the name "Christian" (454, 456), three times in the etymology of Cecilia's own name (85, 91, 102), in which the name itself points us to the realities it signifies. In The Canon's Yeoman's Tale the memorable occurrences of the word come at the end, when it becomes apparent that the philosopher's stone is, by God's decree (1468–74), beyond the reach either of alchemists or of the signifying power of words. No one, we are told, should become an alchemist "But if that he th'entencioun and speche/ Of philosophres understonde kan" (1443–44); but we discover immediately, when Plato refuses to tell what he knows, that such understanding is not attainable:

"Telle me the name of the privee stoon."
　And Plato answerde unto hym anoon,
"Take the stoon that Titanos men name."
　"Which is that?" quod he. "Magnasia is the same,"
Seyde Plato. "Ye, sire, and is it thus?
This is *ignotum per ignocius*.
What is Magnasia, good sire, I yow preye?"
　"It is a water that is maad, I seye,
Of elementes foure," quod Plato.
　"Telle me the roote, good sire," quod he tho,
"Of that water, if it be youre wil."
　"Nay, nay," quod Plato, "certein, that I nyl.
The philosophres sworn were everychoon
That they sholden discovere it unto noon,
Ne in no book it write in no manere." (1452–66)

202

John M. Fyler

The confusion of the alchemist punishes his presumption, his effort to find gold beneath the *superficies* of baser metals in the decaying world: as Jean de Meun says, the alchemist takes metals and "reduces them to their primordial matter" ("les ramene/ A lor matire premerene") (16069–70). Such presumption is exactly what God punishes at Babel. This pride is especially associated with Nimrod; for although Genesis offers no suggestion that Nimrod is the builder of the tower, other than that Babylon is named as "the beginning of his kingdom" (Gen. 10:10), he is universally so identified in the commentaries. The one time that Chaucer names him, in his lyric "The Former Age," he does so in the same breath with "Jupiter the likerous" (56–59), conflating classical mythology and the Genesis narrative. Chaucer here follows a long-standing tradition: the ninth-century *Ecloga Theoduli* corrects Pseustis' fable of the giants' rebellion against Jove with Alithia's true account of the Tower of Babel (85–92), and the association of Nimrod with the pagan giants takes on added force from the mention in Genesis 6:4 of the giants "upon the earth in those days" (see Dronke 136n48). (Moreover, in the Septuagint and Vetus Latina versions of the Bible, Nimrod is called "giant"—at the points where Jerome substitutes "potens" and "robustus" [Menner 122]). Dante follows this tradition in *Inferno* 31, where Nimrod appears with the giants Ephialtes and Antaeus.

Nimrod's presumption and pride define his character as "potens in terra" (mighty on the earth) and "robustus venator coram Domino" (a stout hunter before the Lord) (Gen. 10:8–9). His name itself, St. Jerome says, means "tyrannus, vel profugus, aut transgressor" (tyrant, or fugitive, or transgressor) (PL 23.782); and his hunting and his tyranny are related to his pride. According to Rupert of Deutz, Nimrod is called a "mighty hunter" because he "laid hold of an unaccustomed tyranny as if by hunting" (PL 167.366). And although the beginnings of warfare are usually attributed to Nimrod's descendant Ninus

(Isidore, *Etymologiae* 18.1.1; Hugh of St. Victor, *Didascalicon* 85), the two of them are sometimes confused. Philippe de Mézières, in his *Letter to King Richard II*, describes Nimrod's "jardin horrible et perilleux," in which there is no "justice, amour, regle ne policie," whose inhabitants are heretics, magicians, and astrologers, and which figures forth "les effusions du sanc humain des le commencement du monde" (all the instances of the shedding of human blood since the beginning of the world).

The connection here between bloodshed, magic, and astrology becomes more explicable when we know that Nimrod, in a tradition deriving from the apocryphal literature, is associated with astronomy and arcane knowledge. According to the *Revelations* of pseudo-Methodius, which were translated into Latin in the eighth century and into English by John Trevisa in the fourteenth, Noah had a fourth son named Ionitus, who was expert in astronomy and became Nimrod's teacher (*Sibyllinische Texte* 63–65, Trevisa 97–99; see Livesey and Rouse 213–24, Dronke 112–17, and Smithers 155–56). Peter Comestor copies this story (PL 198.1088), and his account is widely diffused in the later Middle Ages. It appears in the text that accompanies the illustrations of BL MS. Egerton 1894 (James 7–8, 31), and also in Robert Holkot's commentary on the Book of Wisdom (lectio 126). Hugh of St. Victor, in his catalogue of the founders of all the arts, notes that "Nemroth the Giant was the greatest astrologer, and to his name astronomy too is ascribed" (84); and John Gower describes Nimrod as one of the first writers about astronomy (*Confessio Amantis* 2: 272). His building of the Tower of Babel, in part to further his expertise in star-lore, characterizes his presumptuous quest of forbidden knowledge (*Glossa Ordinaria*, PL 113.113; Peter Riga, *Aurora* 689–706). Indeed, the *Bible Moralisée* comments on Babel as the vainglory of "astronomers and philosophers" "reduced to nothing" (MS. Bodl. 270b, fol. 11ᵛ).

In these accretions to the Biblical narrative of Babel, there are certainly themes that Chaucer makes prominent in The Canon's Yeoman's Tale. But Nimrod's final exploit brings us still closer to the world of the alchemists. Remigius of Auxerre names him as the first fire-worshipper (PL 131.80), following such apocryphal accounts as the one in the *Book of the Cave of Treasures* (142–43). And in the pseudo-Clementine *Recognitions* (PG 1.1224–25), he is identified as the first worshipper of idols, specifically as the tyrant who compelled the Chaldaeans to worship fire. (Many medieval accounts describe this version of Nimrod's tyranny, among them Peter Comestor [PL 198. 1088]; Vincent of Beauvais' *Speculum Historiale* 1.100 [p. 37]; Brunetto Latini's *Livres dou Tresor* [35]; Higden's *Polychronicon* [trans. Trevisa, 251]; and Gower's *Confessio Amantis* [marginal note, 1: 423]. BL MS. Egerton 1894, printed in facsimile by M. R. James, illustrates Nimrod's tyrannizing over other men, and shows an act of fire-worship [fol. 5ʳ].) As Hugh of St. Victor sums up Nimrod's achievements:

> he began to exercise power over others through violence, and led them into idolatry, so that they might worship fire as God, because he saw the very great uses by the benefit of the sun, which is fiery, affecting the earth. Which error the Chaldaeans followed afterwards (PL 175.49).

The Canon and his Yeoman are, as fire-worshippers, lineal descendants of Nimrod's Chaldaeans. Their connection with their ancestors is, I think, yet more startling, in the context of one last addition to the Biblical narrative of Genesis. Peter Comestor habitually interrupts his textbook history of the Bible with what his manuscripts term "additiones," "incidentia," or "glose," and what Stephen Langton calls Peter's "glosa extrinseca." These "additions" are in effect footnotes or expansions of material corollary to Old Testament history. In Peter's rewriting of Genesis, when he describes Nimrod's tyranny, idolatry, and fire-worship, he adds this little story:

> Chaldaei ignem adorabant, et cogebant alios idem facere, comburentes alia idola. Sacerdotes vero Canopi hoc audientes, quod magnum idolum in honore Beli formaverant, removentes coronam auream apposuerunt vas fictile ad modum coronae perforatum foraminibus cera obturatis. Venientes Chaldaei opposuerunt ignem, et liquefacta cera aqua defluens, quae erat in corona exstinxit ignem, et praevaluerunt Canopi idola. (PL 198.1088–89)

> The Chaldaeans worshipped fire, and compelled others to do the same, burning up other idols. The priests of Canopus, having heard this, fashioned a great idol in honor of Bel, and after they removed its golden crown, they attached an earthen vessel in the manner of a crown, perforated by holes stopped up with wax. When the Chaldaeans arrived they set a fire against it, and after the wax liquefied, the water that was in the crown, flowing down, put out the fire, and the idols of Canopus prevailed.

I have been unable to discover an earlier version of this story, which may come from rabbinical tradition or, perhaps more likely, from chronicle accounts of ancient history. But Peter's retelling of it gives it a wide currency. Although, like the other *additiones*, it does not appear in every copy of the *Historia Scholastica*, Chaucer would almost certainly have seen it when he read the work. Of the sixteen manuscripts of Peter Comestor in the British Library dating from the fourteenth century or before, nine include the story. (These include: Royal 7 F.III, fol. 3 [dated 1191–92]; two fourteenth-century manuscripts, Harley 4132, fol. 7ᵛ and Add. 21985, fol. 9ᵛ; and six thirteenth-century ones: Stowe 4, fol. 16ᵛ; Egerton 2833, fol. 14; Royal 2 C.I, fol. 10; 3 A.XI, fol. 10ᵛ; 4 D.VII, fol. 19 [from St. Albans]; and 7 B.VI, fol. 8ᵛ. Most of the others include none of the *additiones* at all.) Like all the *additiones*, this one is especially conspicuous—highlighted by being set off from the text, either as an inset or as a gloss in the margin—and would catch the eye of any reader of Peter Comestor's standard work.

It certainly caught the eye of Peter's imitators, who often move the story from the margin to the body of the text. In the 1290s Guyart Desmoulins made a French translation of the *Historia Scholastica*. The story of the Chaldaeans and the priests of Canopus appears in each of the nine copies of this work in the British Library. (The most interesting of these, for extra-literary reasons, is no doubt Royal 19 D.II, captured at the battle of Poitiers [fol. 16, "glose incidens"]. The other fourteenth-century manuscripts include Royal 19 D.IV, fol. 18–18ᵛ [where the story is titled "Incidens," included in the text but underlined in red]; Royal 17 E.VII, fol. 14ᵛ; Royal 19 D.VI, fol. 15ᵛ, and 15 D.III, fol. 15 ["glose," incorporated in the text]. The remaining four are fifteenth-century manuscripts: Harley 4381, fol. 15, and Add. 18856, fol. 17 ["glose"]; Royal 19 D.III, fol. 15ᵛ ["Incident"]; and Royal 18 D.IX, fol. 36ᵛ ["Incidens"] [the Bible of Edward IV, dated 1479].) Moreover, Guido da Pisa quotes this story—citing Peter Comestor—in his commentary on canto 31 of the *Inferno* (639); indeed, he makes it an integral part of his account of Nimrod and the tower of Babel. Nimrod compelled men to worship fire; the Chaldaeans followed his example and got their comeuppance with the wax trick; Nimrod gathered together all the sons of Noah, that is to say, the whole human race, and they began to build the Tower of Babel.[1]

Now this trick of the priests of Canopus is of course precisely the trick the alchemist uses twice to gull his victim, with silver instead of water behind the wax seal (1159–64; 1266–69); and the source of this part of The Canon's Yeoman's Tale has never been identified. There are other more indirect indications that when Chaucer wrote The Canon's Yeoman's Tale, he had in mind the story of Babel—describing as it does the fall of language and the origins of idolatry. But it seems quite plausible to me that his rumination on Peter Comestor's narrative, including this "addition," provoked his thinking. Indeed, although I cannot prove it, I like to think that this little narrative gave Chaucer the idea for his own particular version of idolatry confounded.

NOTE

1. The text of Guido da Pisa reads as follows:

Istoria vero ipsius scribit Moyses in libro *Genesis*, que a magistro Petro Manducatore taliter compilatur. Nembroth fuit filius Chus, filii Cham, qui fuit filius Noe. Hic itaque Nembroth cepit primus esse in terra potens, et robustus venator in terra hominum coram domino, idest extinctor et oppressor, amore dominandi. Et cogebat homines ignem adorare. Hunc secuti, Caldei ignem adorabant et ad idem alios cogebant, alia ydola comburentes. Sacerdotes vero Canopey hoc audientes, eo quod magnum ydolum in honorem Beli formaverant, removentes coronam auream, apposuerunt vas fictile ad modum corone factum, undique perforatum, plenum aqua, foraminibus cera obturatis. Caldei vero apposuerunt ignem; sed liquefacta cera, aqua defluens que erat in corona ignem extinxit. Nembroth itaque, amore dominandi succensus, omnes filios Noe, hoc est universum genus humanum, in campo Sennaar congregavit in unum, et ceperunt edificare turrim que pertingeret usque ad celos, habentes lateres pro saxis et bitumen pro cemento. Descendit autem Dominus ut videret turrim, idest animadvertit ut puniret, et ait ad angelos: "Venite, confundamus linguam eorum, ut non intelligat unusquisque vocem proximi sui." (638–39)

John M. Fyler

WORKS CITED

Augustine. *The City of God*. Trans. Henry Bettenson. Harmondsworth: Penguin, 1972.

———. *Confessions*. Trans. F. J. Sheed. London: Sheed & Ward, 1943.

———. *On Christian Doctrine*. Trans. D. W. Robertson, Jr. Indianapolis: Bobbs-Merrill, 1958.

Bible. Douay-Rheims trans. London: Catholic Truth Society, 1955.

The Book of the Cave of Treasures. Trans. Sir E. A. Wallis Budge. London: The Religious Tract Society, 1927.

Brunetto Latini. *Li Livres dou Tresor*. Ed. Francis J. Carmody. University of California Pubs. in Modern Philology 22. Berkeley and Los Angeles: U of California P, 1948.

Chaucer, Geoffrey. *The Riverside Chaucer*. General ed. Larry D. Benson. 3rd ed. Boston: Houghton-Mifflin, 1987.

Dante Alighieri. *Inferno*. Ed. and trans., with commentary, Charles Singleton. Princeton: Princeton UP, 1970.

———. *Literary Criticism of Dante Alighieri*. Trans. Robert S. Haller. Lincoln: U of Nebraska P, 1973.

Dean, James. "Dismantling the Canterbury Book." *PMLA* 100 (1985): 746–62.

Dronke, Peter. *Dante and Medieval Latin Traditions*. Cambridge: Cambridge UP, 1986.

Ecloga Theoduli. Ed. J. Osternacher. Urfahr: Collegium Petrinum, 1902.

Fyler, John M. *Chaucer and Ovid*. New Haven: Yale UP, 1979.

Gower, John. *Confessio Amantis*. Ed. G. C. Macaulay. 2 vols. London: EETS, 1900–01.

Guido da Pisa. *Expositiones et Glose super Comediam Dantis; or, Commentary on Dante's Inferno*. Ed. Vincenzo Cioffari. Albany, NY: SUNY P, 1974.

Higden, Ranulf. *Polychronicon*. Trans. John Trevisa. Ed. Churchill Babington. Rolls Series 41. London, 1869.

Holkot, Robert. *Super Librum Sapientie*. Basel: Johann Amerbach, 1489.

Howard, Donald R. *The Idea of the Canterbury Tales*. Berkeley: U of California P, 1976.

Hugh of St. Victor. *Didascalicon*. Trans. Jerome Taylor. New York: Columbia UP, 1961.

Hunt, Richard W. *The History of Grammar in the Middle Ages: Collected Papers*. Ed. G. L. Bursill-Hall. Amsterdam: Benjamins, 1980.

———. *The Schools and the Cloister: The Life and Writings of Alexander Nequam (1157–1217)*. Ed. Margaret Gibson. Oxford: Clarendon, 1984.

Isidore of Seville. *Etymologiae*. Ed. W. M. Lindsay. 2 vols. Oxford: Clarendon, 1911.

James, M. R. *Illustrations of the Book of Genesis*. Oxford: Roxburghe Club, 1921.

Jean de Meun and Guillaume de Lorris. *Le Roman de la Rose*. Ed. Daniel Poirion. Paris: Garnier-Flammarion, 1974.

Livesey, Steven J., and Richard H. Rouse. "Nimrod the Astronomer." *Traditio* 37 (1981): 203–66.

Menner, Robert J., ed. *The Poetical Dialogues of Solomon and Saturn*. New York: MLA, 1941.

210

Peter Riga. *Aurora.* Ed. Paul E. Beichner C.S.C. 2 vols. Univ. of Notre Dame Publications in Medieval Studies 19. Notre Dame: U of Notre Dame P, 1965.

Philippe de Mézières. *Letter to King Richard II.* Ed. G. W. Coopland. Liverpool: Liverpool UP, 1975.

Sibyllinische Texte und Forschungen. Ed. Ernst Sackur. Halle a. S.: Max Niemeyer, 1898.

Smalley, Beryl. "Andrew of St. Victor, Abbot of Wigmore: A Twelfth-Century Hebraist." *Recherches de Théologie Ancienne et Médiévale* 10 (1938): 358–73.

―――. *English Friars and Antiquity in the Early Fourteenth Century.* Oxford: Blackwell, 1960.

―――. *The Study of the Bible in the Middle Ages.* 2nd ed. Oxford: Blackwell, 1952.

Smithers, G. V., ed. *Kyng Alisaunder.* EETS o.s. 237. Oxford: Oxford UP, 1957.

Speculum Humanae Salvationis. Ed. M. R. James and Bernhard Berenson. Oxford: Oxford UP, 1926.

Trevisa, John. *Dialogus . . . , Methodius' 'þe Bygynnyng of þe World and þe Ende of Worldes'.* Ed. A. J. Perry. EETS o.s. 167. Oxford: Oxford UP, 1925.

Vincent of Beauvais. *Speculum Historiale.* Douai, 1624; rpt. Graz: Akademische Druck-u. Verlagsanstalt, 1965.

John of Cornwall's Innovations and Their Possible Effects on Chaucer

Cynthia Renee Bland

During the 1340s John of Cornwall, an Oxford grammar master, began to use English instead of the customary French to teach Latin.[1] According to an oft-quoted comment by John Trevisa, Richard Pencrych and "oþere men of Pencriche"[2] learned John's teaching methods and spread them so that by 1385 English had become the usual language of instruction in grammar schools all over England. The date of John of Cornwall's summa, *Speculum gramaticale*, 1346,[3] and its occasional use of English paradigms and example sentences, corroborate Trevisa's claim that he was teaching Latin in English around the time of the Black Death. Chaucer, who must have been educated during the early 1350s, may well have learned his Latin grammar through the medium of English (Howard 24). A schoolroom in which the master explained the Latin grammatical figure *synecdoche* in English and used English sentences as examples may account for a syntactically puzzling phrase in Chaucer's *House of Fame*, where an adjective, *conservatyf*, appears to take an object, *soun* (*The Riverside Chaucer* II: 847).

John of Cornwall's life, at least during the 1340s, can be reconstructed from various records. The colophon to *Speculum gramaticale* in MS. Auct. F.3.9 proves that he was teaching Latin grammar in 1346[4] and its contents, to be discussed below, show that he was doing so in English. The Merton College Records for the years 1347

213

and 1348 account for payments to Master John of Cornwall and his assistant for teaching grammar to boys living in Nunne Hall, preparing to enter Merton. Since John was also paid for the rent of his school, the boys must have been sent to him, rather than his being brought to Merton.[5] Oxford city records provide evidence that John of Cornwall was a householder living in the neighborhood of Cattestreet, and that his school was there also, probably close to what is presently the Scholæ Gramaticæ et Historiæ in the Bodleian Library Quadrangle. He witnessed documents in 1341 and 1349 whereby residences in Cattestreet changed hands[6]; and in 1344 his name appeared in the list of the many householders of the northeast ward of Oxford fined by the Assize of Bread and Ale.[7]

Finally, John of Cornwall's will, dated 8 June 1349, is preserved in Brian Twyne's extracts from Oxford City Records. It provides that John's school in Cattestreet be sold at his death, the proceeds to go toward paying his debts; if any money should be left over, John directs his executors to spend it for some charitable purpose for the sake of his soul and that of his wife, Agnes.[8] No records mention John as alive after 1349, though, admittedly, the Merton College Records for 1349–67 are lost; and so we do not know whether they would have mentioned him again (Stevenson 427). Given that the Black Death was rampant in 1349 and his will is dated that year, it seems logical to assume that John was afraid he might die of the plague, and that he may well have done so.

John of Cornwall may have been a master of arts (Hunt 141), but he was more likely a master of grammar, one who had not gone through the whole university program for the seven liberal arts but who was licensed by the Chancellor to teach Latin grammar.[9] In order to receive his license, John, like all candidates, had to appear before a board composed of a group of representatives from several branches of the liberal arts faculty and pass examinations in four areas: Latin verse composition, *dictamen*, the authors, and the parts of speech.

According to the Oxford statutes regulating the grammar faculty,[10] John of Cornwall was supposed to teach the boys how to compose verses and letters in Latin and how to parse. The Oxford statute regarding the teaching of composition specifies that every two weeks grammar masters must assign verses and letters to be written over the next holiday. The compositions were to be written using appropriate diction, concise sentences, and clear metaphors, and they were supposed to be meaningful (not just *pro forma*). The verses and the letter were to be written on parchment, and the day after the students came back to school they were supposed to show the master what they had written and recite it to him by heart.[11]

Another statute urged grammar masters to take special care to teach the more elementary students how to parse, and specified the method: after asking the student to name a part of speech of a word under consideration, they should then ask him to list its accidents.[12]

The focus of John's *Speculum gramaticale* on the parts of speech and on construction fulfills the intent of this statute. One passage in particular exemplifies how English was used in parsing Latin sentences. John of Cornwall begins his discussion of the noun as a part of speech as follows:

"*Nomen*, quid est?"
"Pars orationis."
"Construe *nomen quid est*."
"O magister, 'quid,' *what*; 'nomen,' a *noun*; 'est,' *is*."[13]

This is a short interlude in the midst of more complex questions on whether there are eight, one, or maybe even eleven parts of speech (before), and whether 'scamnum' is a noun (after). In actual classroom usage, John of Cornwall would probably have proceeded to ask, of *nomen*, "quot accidunt," and may well have expected an answer in English, such as, "VI. Qualite, comparyson, gendyr, nowmbyr, figur, and case."[14]

The technique just exemplified, of having students "construe" or translate Latin sentences into English before parsing them, became firmly entrenched quickly. By the late fourteenth century it was thought necessary to write a statute requiring the grammar masters to have their students construe in both English and French, lest French be entirely ignored.[15]

John of Cornwall's *Summa, Speculum gramaticale,* is significant mainly because it uses English—albeit sparsely, in paradigms, example sentences, and translation exercises. Its occasional use of English terminology to describe both Latin and English grammar anticipates the approach of the fifteenth-century Middle English grammar texts as well as some aspects of modern English traditional grammar. In one passage, for example, John illustrates the tenses of the verb *doceo* with the corresponding forms of *teche,* and defines in English the Latin names for the tenses:

> Item, querendum est quot sunt tempora in verbo. Dicendum est quod quinque: præsens, þe tyme þat is now, ut *doceo,* 'I teche'; preteritum inperfectum, þe tyme þat is fulli agon, ut *docui,* 'I have tauȝte'; preteritum plusquam perfectum, þe tyme þat is longe agon, ut *docueram,* 'I hadde itau?te'; ffuturum, þe tyme þat is to come, ut *docebo,* 'I schal teche'. Iste est modus informandi pueros per omnes coniugaciones.[16]

This passage is significant not only for its English definitions of tenses, but also for the statement "This is the way to teach boys all the conjugations," which may serve as evidence that John's treatise is intended as a reference book for grammar masters to use. In fact, MS. Auct. F.3.9, judging from its contents as well as its original owner-

216

ship by an institution with a school, was probably compiled for this purpose.[17] Also, as David Thomson has shown, the Oxford Grammar faculty served as much to train masters outside of Oxford as to regulate them in Oxford ("Oxford Grammar Masters" 299).

The *Speculum* is a summa in the form of a question commentary. Both elementary and advanced grammatical topics are discussed, with each topic presented as a debatable point, as can be seen from the outset. Perhaps the very first example would be as good as any to demonstrate the approach: "Primo querendo quid sit constructio siue oratio constructa."[18] In order to define *constructio* the author poses several questions: whether *constructio* and *oratio constructa* are the same thing, whether every *oratio* is a *congrua dictionum ordinacio*, and whether *constructio*, being an equivocal term, may be defined.

Since both *constructio* and *oratio constructa* mean "congrua dictionum ordinacio congruum intellectum in animo auditoris faciens,"[19] they appear to be the same. John proves that they differ because *constructio* means the component parts of a sentence whereas *oratio* means the sentence itself. "Filius Petri legit Virgilium" is a single *oratio* composed of three *constructiones: filius Petri, filius Petri legit,* and *legit Virgilium.*

The problem with the statement that every *oratio* is a *congrua dictionum ordinacio* is that one word, such as *honestas*, is an *oratio perfecta* but not a *congrua dictionum ordinacio* because it is only one word.[20] The problem is resolved by ruling, "Quedam est oratio que tantum secundum intellectum et non secundum vocem est congrua dictionum ordinacio."

The reason why *constructio* may not be defined is that according to Petrus Helias nouns ending in -tio, which are derived from verbs, mean four things. In this case, *constructio* might be 'constructe rei passio' or 'construentis vel instruentis actio,' or 'modus construendi' or 'ipsum constructum.'[21] John of Cornwall's solution to this problem is admirable: he removes the "equivocacio" by declaring that what he means is "modo construendi," not "re constructa"; therefore "constructio egregie poterit diffinire."

The reader can ascertain from this cumbersome approach to the first question that, even though the opening sentence of the text says that the treatise is "ad instructionem rudium et nouorum"—for the instruction of the ignorant and the unskilled—it is really not for beginners. A student must have mastered at least his Donatus before he could even begin to learn what the *Speculum* has to teach. That John of Cornwall expected such knowledge is clear from the passage following the extract of classroom dialogue quoted above, "*Nomen*, quid est?" The next question is "*Scamnum* que pars?" If one were to answer "Nomen," the argument to the contrary would be, "Nomen est pars orationis sed *scamnum* non est pars orationis cum in oratione non ponatur, igitur non est nomen." In the *Ars Minor*, *scamnum* is given as the example of a neuter noun (Holtz 587).

The main sign that the *Speculum* is intended for advanced students is its disputacious character, which was exemplified above with respect to the treatise's "primo querendo." Several contemporary records show that disputations were commonly carried on in grammar schools. One of the Oxford statutes regulating the grammar faculty bound the masters supervising the grammar schools to hold a disputation on grammatical topics on Fridays.[22] The same Merton College account for the year 1347–48 that mentions payment to John of Cornwall also accounts for two and one half shillings paid out for tablets for the grammarians to report the arguments.[23] A regulation from the St. Albans school statutes of 1309 requires a student who wants to achieve the status of bachelor "to take a proverb from the master and compose verses, model letters and a *rithmus* on the subject, as well as carrying on a disputation in the school."[24] According to John Stow's *Survey of London*, schoolboys in that city engaged in contests involving disputation on "the principles of grammar" from the twelfth century through the early sixteenth century (Chase 17).

That dialectic had invaded the province of grammar by the twelfth century is a well-established fact. Indeed, two major systems of grammatical analysis, *regimen* and modistic grammar, developed from the scrutiny of language by logicians. The *Speculum gramaticale*, while espousing neither of these systems, incorporates terminology from both.[25] Even though not intended for beginners, it is clearly a grammar-school text, so the methods of the *modistæ* when they occur are watered down.

When regarded in the light of the best medieval Latin grammatical texts, the *Speculum* does not shine. When we remember that the *Speculum* is the first treatise to record some teaching techniques which appear again in the fifteenth century in the Middle English grammatical texts,[26] and some which may have influenced Chaucer's style, we see the *Speculum* as a mirror worth looking through. Its most important contributions to the teaching of grammar are its systematic use of *latinitates*, sentences in Latin given to exemplify certain points of grammar, and, in connection with this, its use of English sentences to elucidate the Latin. As far as we know the *Speculum* is the first grammatical text of British provenance "to include both example sentences in Latin alone and ones in Latin and English together."[27]

The following extract from his section on verbs which are active in form but passive in meaning shows how John of Cornwall occasionally uses English translations of Latin phrases and sentences given to exemplify grammatical rules:

Verba vero neutrapassiva sunt ista: *Exulo, vapulo, veneo, fio, liceo*, et *nubo*, et significant passionem per modum actionis et habent construi cum ablatiuis interposita præpositione, ut *Vapulo a te*, anglice 'I am bete of

219

þe,' *qui venis a me*, 'þe which art sold of me,' *qui exulo ab anglia*, 'þe which am banished or flemed out of ingelond.'[28]

John of Cornwall sometimes gives the English sentences first in *latinitates* in the *Speculum*. In the example that follows, the reason is to show how some passive constructions in English must be translated into impersonal ones in Latin because the corresponding Latin verbs (namely *obvio* and *servio*) may not be made passive:[29]

> Nota quod quandocumque aliqui locucio per unam illorum facienda profer-
> atur fieri debet per eius impersonale: *I am wel imett*, 'mihi bene obuiatur,'
> id est 'mihi bene obuiacio sit.' Item, *ʒif I go to þe carfocus of misdoars I
> mai be mett* 'Si vadam ad quadriuium a malefactoribus, possit mihi obui-
> ari,' id est, 'obuiacio mihi potest fieri.' Si dicatur anglice, *I am wel served
> of a man todai of þe whiche I was ʒistirdai wel y ansuerid*, sic fiat latin-
> um: 'Mihi bene seruitur hodie ab uno homine a quo mihi heri bene respon-
> debatur,' id est 'responsum fiebat.'[30]

In a number of other instances in the *Speculum*, John bases a definition or a rule "on the practicalities of translation" or "on vernacular syntactic patterns"[31] and in this way he departs from the *auctoritates*. We may also note with regard to the above extract that John gives alternative Latin translations to the English sentences. If other contemporary schoolmasters did the same, then all over England in the fourteenth century students were learning that style is flexible, that sentences may be styled in different ways to achieve different effects. Chaucer, as we know, was an enthusiastic experimenter with style, and one wonders if his enthusiasm was fostered in his grammar school classroom.

Now we must examine the question, "How quickly did John of Cornwall's innovations spread?" in order to begin to consider whether Chaucer may have been educated in English. We know that Higden thought that the standard method of teaching Latin in England was by way of French.[32] Trevisa's comment begins "Þys mannere was moche y-used to fore þe firste moreyn," and thereby leaves open the possibility that people taught Latin in English before John of Cornwall. John himself was teaching in English by 1346. Because of his position on the grammar faculty at Oxford, the center of grammatical instruction at this time, his methods were more likely to be propagated than those of an innovator living elsewhere. The "first moreyn" killed off many educated people who were fluent in French and Latin, including schoolmasters. Their replacements were less well prepared and must have turned gratefully to the new teaching method, which made it easier for them to instruct students in a language that they were not entirely comfortable with themselves, as well as making it easier for students to learn.[33]

Evidence exists from the late 1300s to show that grammatical terminology in English had already become standardized by that time. Langland, in some famous grammatical metaphors in the C-text of *Piers Plowman*, a Wycliffite writer, in the General Prologue to the second version of the translation of the Bible, and John Trevisa, in his translation of Bartholomeus Anglicus' *De Rerum Natura*, all use English grammatical terms which are found in Middle English grammars of Latin in the fifteenth century.[34]

To sum up the known sequence of events in the spread of English instruction in Latin grammar: Higden was unaware of it in the 1340s, though some schools may have already begun practicing it; John of Cornwall, who was an Oxford resident by 1341, was teaching in English by 1346, to judge from the contents of his *Speculum*; Richard Pencrych, who may have taught under John in the 1340s, was living near Merton College in 1367 and had established a hall, probably for grammatical instruction, before 1380; John Trevisa knew about the turn of events because he lived in Oxford from 1361–79; and in the 1370s and

80s Langland, a Wycliffite, and Trevisa used the same English grammatical terminology that reappears in fifteenth-century grammatical texts, indicating that such terminology was widely used by then.

Could Chaucer have learned his Latin grammar in English? Since London was less than a day's journey from Oxford, the new way of teaching grammar must have spread there quickly. Chaucer was probably born nearer to 1345 than to 1340.[35] If we estimate his date of birth as 1343 at the earliest, then, if he went to grammar school, he would have done so in the early 1350s. The first specific reference to Geoffrey Chaucer is from the household accounts of Elizabeth, Countess of Ulster, from 1357, which show that he had entered her service by then, probably at around the age of fourteen.

Although "no direct evidence as to Chaucer's schooling has come to light" (Crow and Olson 12), "scholars favor the Almonry School at St. Paul's as the one Chaucer attended, deciding the matter from its proximity (it was about a three-minute walk from the Chaucer home), its prominence as the cathedral school, and its books" (Howard 25). Indeed, as Edith Rickert showed in a seminal article, the library at St. Paul's school contained the classical works which Chaucer used as sources, which were not widely available elsewhere in London, and which the St. Paul's alumni could borrow after they left school. The works on grammar in the library included several copies of Priscian's *Institutiones*, several of the *Doctrinale* of Alexander de Villa Dei, a gloss on the *Doctrinale* bound with a treatise *de regiminibus*, the *Absoluta* of Petrus Hispanus, works by Isidore, Bede, John of Garland, and numerous short anonymous texts on topics such as difficult points of grammar, principles of accenting, ambiguous words, and versification.[36] At least some of these texts, as well as Donatus' *Ars grammatica*, would have been available in almost any grammar school of the time.

Chaucer probably started school after the Black Death, when education was in "disarray" as a result of the deaths of many experienced teachers. If so, he would have construed his lessons in English. His fluency in French would have come from his upbringing (Howard 24).

In his article "Grammatical Theory and the *House of Fame*," Martin Irvine argues convincingly that Chaucer's work reflects his knowledge of the "middle range of *grammatica*" from such texts as Priscian's *Institutiones* and the commentaries on it by William of Conches and Petrus Helias (852–53). However, he does not see "teaching grammars" such as Donatus' *Ars Minor*, the *Doctrinale* of Alexander de Villa Dei, or the *Grecismus* of Eberhard of Bethune as "directly relevant to the *House of Fame*" (852). I would argue, on the contrary, that these "teaching grammars," especially if they were explained in English, shed light on a grammatical crux in the poem that I happened upon while preparing a definition of the word *soun* (n.) for *The Middle English Dictionary*.

The word *soun* is used in a strange construction where it appears to be the object of an adjective, *conservatyf*. The sentence reads:

And this place of which I telle
Ther as Fame lyst to duelle
Ys set amyddys of these three,
Heven, erthe, and eke the see,
As most conservatyf the soun. (*HF* II: 843–47).

The modern reader is inclined to stop short here and ask, "Shouldn't this be 'conservatyf of' or 'for the soun'?" The explanatory note to this line in *The Riverside Chaucer* repeats Robinson's statement "that this construction in which the adjective takes an object, like a participle, is most peculiar."[37] If one looks up the Old French etymon 'conservative,' one finds that it always occurs with *des* or *du*. Neither

Visser nor Mustanoja records a Middle English construction in which an adjective takes an object.

The closest syntactic parallels to the phrase *conservatyf the soun* are found in the Middle English grammatical texts from the fifteenth century, in discussions of the grammatical figure *synecdoche*. As the following example will demonstrate, sometimes the term applied to the figure of speech in which a part stands for the whole or the whole for a part; sometimes it referred to a figure of speech in which an adjective governs the accusative case, and which modern Latin grammarians call "accusative of respect" (see Gildersleeve and Lodge 215). The Middle English text labelled *EE* by Thomson states the rule clearly and gives several examples of the figure with the English version first and the Latin second:

> How knowest *synodoche*? A syngnyng of the party to al or a signyng of al to the party. In how many maners schal he be made? By foure. By whych foure? Whenne that at is the hole is delyueryd in to the party wythoute gouernynge of an accusatyf case, as 'Thys maide is clere the kynde,' *Ista virga est clara genus*. How in the secunde manere? As whenne that at is of the party is delyueryd to the hole wyth gouernyng of the accusatif case, as 'This man is whyte the face,' *Iste homo est albus faciem*. In the thrydde manere is whenne that at is of the hole is delyueryd to the party wythoute gouerning of the accusatyf case, as 'A goode soule is weddyd to my brother,' *Bonus animus est nuptus fatri meo*. In the furthe manere whenne that at is of party is delyueryd into the hole wyth gouernyng of the accusatyf case, as 'Ion is cryps the hede,' *Iohannes est crippus caput*. Thys be the principal reulys that Precian putteth in the furst bokis of construccion.[38] (Thomson, *An Edition* 182)

The figure *synecdoche* is discussed in several elementary grammars which might have been used in Chaucer's grammar school: Donatus' *De Schematibus*, Alexander de Villa Dei's *Doctrinale*, and Eberhard of Bethune's *Græcismus*. Though the first Middle English grammars of Latin date from the fifteenth century, we know from the use of English grammatical terms by Langland, Trevisa, and the Wycliffites that these were pretty well standardized by the 1380s. In explaining *synecdoche* Chaucer's grammar master may well have exemplified the construction in much the same way as do the fifteenth-century texts. Indeed, John of Cornwall, although he does not use English examples of synecdoche, illustrates the construction with Latin sentences containing some of the same words as those occurring in *Text EE*: "Bonus animus mulieris est mihi nuptus . . . Homo albus pedem currit . . . hoc est albus caput."[39]

Although 'conservatyf the soun' is not precisely a literal translation of a phrase using the Latin figure *synecdoche*, because it does not involve a part standing for a whole or vice-versa, it sounds like the same construction. Regarding *synecdoche*, David Thomson comments, "There is a strong suspicion that the grammarians created an English expression in order to exemplify the Latin" (*An Edition* xx). He does not "find any convincing evidence for its use in Middle English" except possibly for *Piers Plowman* A 8.834, "'Blynde & bedrede & i-broken here membris,' where 'the' is recorded as a variant of 'here'" (*Texts* xxi). The only place where Chaucer was likely to hear a phrase constructed like 'conservatyf the soun' was in a grammar school classroom in which the master gave English sentences to exemplify the Latin.

I believe that Chaucer was taught his Latin grammar by way of English, and that this is one reason why he chose to write literature in English instead of French. John Gower, fifteen or twenty years Chaucer's senior, wrote literature in Latin, French, and English, all with about the same facility. His English works, however, are not regarded as highly as Chaucer's, and for good reason. Dominica Legge once commented that Chaucer could just as easily have chosen to write in

Anglo-Norman as in English; that Chaucer's name could have "stood beside" Gower's "on the roll of Anglo-Norman writers" of which Gower's is the last, but instead he "sounded the death-knell of Anglo-Norman literature, and cast off the tradition which Gower was intended to foster" (360). If "Chaucer had not flung his cap over the windmill and plunged into the English language," his French poetry could have been as good as Gower's (Legge 357). If John of Cornwall's teaching methods had not caught on, and if Chaucer had not been exposed to the new methodology, he might have decided to write in French, and the history of the English language and its literature would have been quite different.

NOTES

1. Ranulf Higden gives the following as one reason for the "apayrynge of þe burþe tunge," the sad state of contemporary English: "Children in scole aʒenst þe vsage and manere of alle oþer naciouns beeþ compelled for to leue hire owne langage, and for to construe hir lessouns and here þynges in Frensche, and so þey haveþ seþ þe Normans come first in to Engelond." At this point John Trevisa, translating the work in 1385, adds a famous comment:

> Þis manere was moche i-vsed to for firste deth and is siþþe sumdel i-chaunged; for Iohn Cornwaille, a maister of grammer, chaunged þe lore in gramer scole and construccioun of Frensche in to Englishe; and Richard Pencriche lerned þe manere of techynge of hym and oþere men of Pencrich; so þat now þe ʒere of oure Lorde a þowsand þre hundred and foure score and fyue . . . in alle þe gramere scoles of Engelond, children leueþ Frensche and construeþ and lerneþ an Englische; . . . here auauntage is, þat þey lerneþ her gramer in lasse tyme þan children were i-woned to doo; disauauntage is þat now children of gramer scole conneþ na more Frensche þan can hir left heele" (Babington 2: 158–59).

2. Richard Pencrych may well have been the anonymous assistant master mentioned in the Merton College records for 1347–48 as being paid along with John of Cornwall

to teach grammar to the boys living in Nunne Hall (See Leach, *Educational Charters* 300–03). His surname indicates a Cornish origin, so an association of some sort with a John of Cornwall in Oxford would have been natural.

3. This date is recorded by the scribe of the one copy of the *Speculum* which survives in Oxford, Bodleian Library MS. Auct. F.3.9, in the colophon, which is quoted below in note 4. The *Catalogue of the Library of Syon Monastery* records that another copy of the *Speculum* was there in manuscript A.17 (Bateson 3), now lost. Bursill-Hall's *Census* erroneously states that the *Speculum gramaticale* may be found in Paris, Bibliotheque Nationale Cod. Lat. 15462 and in Berlin (West) Staatsbibliothek Preussischer Kulturbesitz Cod Lat. Q.562.

4. The colophon reads, "Et sic finitur tractatus super donatum de congruetatibus gramatice qui intitulatur speculum gramaticale editus a magistro Johanne Brian dicto de Cornubia: Anno domini M°CCC°XL°vj° et cetera quod J.B." (and here ends the treatise on Donatus concerning syntactic relationships which is entitled "The Grammatical Mirror," by Master John Brian of Cornwall. A.D. 1346. [signed] J.B. [the scribe]).

5. Stevenson was the first to discuss this evidence. He quotes the relevant Merton Records (425–26). They are also available in Leach, *Educational Charters* 300–03.

6. In a document dated January 10, 1341, the name Iohanne de Cornubia is listed as a witness that Simon Faunt has granted a messuage to John Faunt (Salter, *Cart. St. John* 1: 440). A document dated December 3, 1349, whereby John of Oxenford grants three messuages to Henry of Malmesbury states that one of these messuages is in the parish of St. Peter in the East "inter tenementum abbatis & conuentus de Eynsham ex parte boriali & tenementum magistri Iohannes de Cornubia ex parte australi" (Salter, *Cart. Oseney* 2: 306).

7. Salter, *Medieval Archives* 2: 228. John was fined eight shillings, probably for charging someone too much for ale he had brewed. According to Salter, "so common was it to brew ale and to sell it that our rolls must contain more than half the householders of the town for the years they cover" (182).

8. Twyne quotes John's will as follows:

> Ego Johannes Bryan de Cornubia, compos mentis, hac die Domini in cras-
> tino Sancti Trinitatis, videlicet 8 die mensis Junii anno domini 1349, con-
> do testammentum in hunc modum. . . . Lego, volo et ordino scolas meas
> inter vicum Scholarum et Catstret, Oxon., situatus cum omnibus suis iur-
> ibus et pertinentibus executoribus meis, et vendens ipsas, et de precio
> earundem satisfiat creditoribus meis, et residuum, si quod fuerit, volo et
> ordino quod illud distribuat per communem assensum et visum executorum
> meorum in pios usus pro anima mea et anima Agnae uxoris meae (Oxford,
> Bodleian Library, MS. Twyne 23, pp. 335–36).

9. See Thomson, "Oxford Grammar Masters" for a thorough explanation of the M. Gram. degree.

10. An edition of the statutes regulating the grammar faculty is available in Anstey 436–45. The medieval statute-book in its entirety was edited by Strickland Gibson (*Statuta antiqua universitatis oxoniensis* [Oxford: Clarendon, 1931]); this edition is not widely available in the U.S. Several of the grammar statutes are quoted in Hunt, in Orme's *English Schools*, in Thomson's "Oxford Grammar Masters," and in Murphy's "Literary Implications." My summary comments below are based on Anstey's edition.

11. This statute reads:

> *Item*, tenentur singulus quindenis versus dare, et literas compositas verbis
> decentibus non ampullosis aut sesquipedalibus, et clausulis succintis,
> decoris, metaphoris manifestis, et, quantum possint, sententia refertis, quos
> versus et quas literas debent recipientes in proximo die feriato vel ante in
> pergamento scribere, et inde sequente die, cum Scholas venerint, Magistro
> suo corde tenus reddere et scripturam suam offere (Anstey 2: 437–38).

12. "Ut primo, quæsito et responso sub qua parte orationis contineatur dictio de qua quæritur, tunc statim quæritur parti illi quot accidunt, et tunc per ordinem de accidentibus interrogetur, ut sic addiscant per seipsos partes suas repetere" (Anstey 2: 438).

13. MS. Auct. F.3.9, p. 13; also printed in Thomson, *A Descriptive Catalogue* 40.

14. Thomson, *An Edition* 1. This answer from one of the Middle English *Accedence* texts may be taken as a typical English version of the response from Donatus' *Ars minor*. For a full discussion of *Accendence* texts see Bland 47–59.

15. "Tenentur etiam construere necnon construendi significaciones dictionum docere in Anglico et vicissim in Gallico, ne illa lingua Gallica penitus sit omissa" (Anstey 2: 438). Also quoted in Thomson, "Oxford Grammar Masters" 309.

16. MS. Auct. F.3.9, p. 9, col. 2. For more examples of John's use of English see Bland 95–96.

17. Besides the *Speculum,* MS. Auct. F.3.9 contains the *Memoriale iuniorum* of Thomas of Hanney, a poem of 3500 hexameters on Latin grammar, Donatus' *Ars Minor,* two treatises on dictamen, a set of extracts from classical authors, and a treatise on versification (Madan 2: 689). MS. Auct. F.3.9 first belonged to the Benedictine cathedral priory of St. Mary in Coventry, which, according to Leach's *History,* had a school that later became Warwick School. The lost Syon manuscript that contained the *Speculum* was also full of *grammaticalia* (Bateson 3).

18. The following summary is based directly on the *Speculum* in MS. Auct. F.3.9, p. 1. Quotations in the summary are taken from there unless otherwise noted.

19. Priscian defines *oratio* as "ordinacio dictionum congrua, sententiam perfectam demonstans" (Keil 2: 53). According to Petrus Helias, *constructio* is "congrua dictionum ordinatio" (Tolson 1). A list of definitions of grammatical terms from Oxford, Lincoln College MS. Lat. 129, from the early fifteenth century, says, "Quid est constructio? Est congrua dictionum ordinacio congruum intellectum in anima auditoris faciens," and "Quid est oratio? Est congrua dictionum ordinacio congruam et perfectam sentenciam demonstrans" (fol. 91ʳ).

20. This example is taken from Priscian's explanation of *oratio,* the beginning of which is quoted in note 24 (Keil 2: 53).

21. Petrus Helias (fl. 1140) was the most influential of the premodistic grammarians, and was quoted *passim* by many grammarians throughout the Middle Ages. His *Sum-*

ma super Priscianum survives in some thirty manuscripts. The part on construction, Priscian's last two books, has been edited by Tolson. The rest of the treatise remains unedited, though large extracts were printed by Thurot.

22. "Item, statutum est quod Magistri scholarum grammaticalium teneantur die Veneris grammaticalia duntaxat disputare" (Anstey 2: 444).

23. "Item in diversis paribus tabellarum albarum pro gramaticis pro argumentis reportandis" (Leach, *Educational Charters* 300).

24. Orme, *English Schools* 101, from Leach, *Educational Charters* 244–45.

25. On its uses of modistic terminology see Hunt 181–83.

26. For a discussion of this point see Thomson, *A Descriptive Catalogue* 40.

27. Orme, "Latin and English Sentences" 49.

28. MS. Auct. F.3.9, p. 10.

29. The Middle English *Informacio* and *Formula* Texts include verses listing the verbs, such as *obvio* and *servio*, which are intransitive and therefore may not be made passive. See, for example, *Text AA* in Thomson, *An Edition* 144.

30. MS. Auct. F.3.9, p. 10

31. Thomson, *A Descriptive Catalogue* (40).

32. For Higden's exact words see note 1 above.

33. At the end of Trevisa's comment, he says that the advantage of the new method is that children learn grammar faster than they did before. See above, note 1.

34. Thomson, *An Edition* xiv and xxviinn15–17. The specific passages are cited there.

35. For the available evidence on his date of birth see Crow and Olson 372–74.

36. Rickert quotes inventories from two bequests to the library, William Tolleshunt's in 1328 (258) and William Ravenstone's (265–70).

37. *Riverside* also refers the reader to Grennan's article, which argues plausibly, though not entirely convincingly, that Chaucer is translating literally a phrase from Walter Burley's *Physics*, 'virtutem conseruatiuam locati existentis,' (Grennan 44).

38. The Middle English grammatical text entitled *Regemina secundum Magistrum Wacfilde* has a rule for *ex vi senoteges* (synecdoche) with nouns. See Bland 193n70.

39. MS. Auct. F. 3.9, p. 68.

MANUSCRIPTS CITED

Oxford, Bodleian Library MS. Auct. F.3.9.

Oxford, Bodleian Library MS. Twyne 23.

Oxford, Lincoln College MS. Lat. 129.

WORKS CITED

Anstey, Henry, ed. *Munimenta Academica*. London: Longmans, 1868.

Babington, C. and J. R. Lumby, eds. *Polychronicon Ranulphi Higden Monachi Cestrensis together with the English Translations of John of Trevisa and an unknown writer of the Fifteenth Century*. Rolls Series 41. 9 vols. London: Longman, 1865–86.

Bateson, Mary, ed. *Catalogue of Library of the Syon Monastery, Isleworth*. Cambridge: Cambridge UP, 1898.

Bland, Cynthia Renée. *The Teaching of Grammar in Late Medieval England*. East Lansing, MI: Colleagues P, 1991.

Bursill-Hall, G. L. *A Census of Medieval Latin Grammatical Manuscripts*. Stuttgart-Bad Cannstatt: Frommann-Holzboog, 1981.

Chase, Wayland Johnson. *The Ars Minor of Donatus*. University of Wisconsin Studies, 11. Madison: U of Wisconsin P, 1926.

Chaucer, Geoffrey. *The Riverside Chaucer*. 3rd. ed. General ed. Larry D. Benson. Boston: Houghton Mifflin, 1987.

Crow, Martin M. and Clair C. Olson, eds. *Chaucer Life Records*. Austin: U of Texas P, 1966.

Gildersleeve, B. L. and Gonzalez Lodge. *Gildersleeve's Latin Grammar*. 3rd ed. London: MacMillan, 1957.

Grennan, Joseph E. "Science and Poetry in Chaucer's *House of Fame*." *Annuale Medievale* 8 (1967): 38–45.

Holtz, Louis, ed. *Ars Donati Gramatici Vrbis Romæ* in *Donat et la Tradition de l'Enseignement Grammatical*. Paris: Centre National de la Recherche Scientifique, 1981.

Howard, Donald. *Chaucer: His Life, His Works, His World*. New York: Fawcett Columbine, 1987.

Hunt, R. W. *Collected Papers: The History of Grammar in the Middle Ages*, ed. G. L. Bursill-Hall. Amsterdam: John Benjamins, 1980.

Irvine, Martin. "Medieval Grammatical Theory and Chaucer's *House of Fame*." *Speculum* 60 (1985): 859–76.

Keil, Heinrich, ed. *Grammatici Latini*. 8 vols. Leipzig: Teubner, 1855–1923.

Leach, A. F. *Educational Charters and Documents, 598–1909*. Cambridge: Cambridge UP, 1911.

———. *History of Warwick School*. London: Archibald Constable, 1906.

Legge, M. Dominica. *Anglo-Norman Literature and Its Background*. Oxford: Clarendon, 1963.

Madan, F. et al., eds. *A Summary Catalogue of Western Manuscripts in the Bodleian Library at Oxford*. 7 vols. in 8. Oxford: Clarendon, 1895–1953.

Murphy, James J. "Literary Implications of Instruction in the Verbal Arts in Fourteenth-Century England." *Leeds Studies in English* n.s. 1 (1967): 199–35.

Mustanoja, Tauno F. *A Middle English Syntax, Part I: Parts of Speech*, Mémoires de la Societé Neophilologique de Helsinki, 23 (1960).

Orme, Nicholas. *English Schools in the Middle Ages*. London: Methuen, 1973.

———. "Latin and English Sentences in Fifteenth-Century Schoolbooks." *Yale University Library Gazette* 60 (1985): 47–57.

Rickert, Edith. "Chaucer at School." *Modern Philology* 29 (1932): 257–74.

Salter, H. E., ed. *A Cartulary of the Hospital of St. John the Baptist.* 3 vols. Oxford Historical Society 66, 68–69. Oxford: Clarendon, 1914–17.

———. *Cartulary of Oseney Abbey.* 6 vols. Oxford Historical Society 89–91, 97–98, 101. Oxford: Clarendon, 1929–36.

———. *Medieval Archives of the University of Oxford.* 2 vols. Oxford Historical Society 70, 73. Oxford: Clarendon, 1920–21.

Stevenson, W. A. "The Introduction of English as the Vehicle of Instruction in English Schools." *An English Miscellany Presented to Dr. Furnivall in Honour of His Seventy-Fifth Birthday* (Oxford: Clarendon, 1901): 421–29.

Taylor, John. *The Universal Chronicle of Ranulf Higden*. Oxford: Clarendon, 1966.

Thomson, David. *A Descriptive Catalogue of Middle English Grammatical Texts*, New York: Garland, 1979.

———. *An Edition of the Middle English Grammatical Texts.* New York: Garland, 1984.

———. "The Oxford Grammar Masters Revisited." *Medieval Studies* 45 (1983): 298–310.

Cynthia Renee Bland

Thurot, Charles. *Notices et Extraits de divers manuscits latins pour servir à l'histoire des doctrines grammaticales au moyen age. Notices et extraits des manuscits de la Bibliotheque Imperiale* 22: 2 (1868); rpt. Frankfurt: Minerva, 1967.

Tolson, J. E., ed. *Petrus Helias, Summa in Priscianum Minorem.* Université de Copenhague, Cahiers de l'Institut du Moyen-age Grec et Latin, 27–28 (1978).

Visser, F. Th. *An Historical Syntax of the English Language,* 3 Parts in 4 Vols. Leiden: Brill, 1963.

Langland's Reading: Some Evidence from MSS. Containing Religious Prophecy

Kathryn Kerby-Fulton

Students of *Piers Plowman* have rarely had the luxury, so often afforded to Chaucer scholars, of knowing precisely what Langland had read. In spite of the assiduous work of scholars over the years on quotations, allusions, and possible sources, Langland is never usually thought of as having had a personal bookshelf in the way Chaucer is.[1] But as J. B. Allen said in his short piece, "Reading and Looking Things Up in Chaucer's England," "When [a medieval poet] used books, he had to use specific books. He could not quote the Zeitgeist" ("Langland's Reading" 1). Langland, too, must have used specific books (whether his own or someone else's), and Allen's notion that we ought to be investigating not just what a poet had read but how and in what context he found what he read, still has infinite applications in Langland studies.

What follows is an application of this approach to my own area of interest, Langland's knowledge of medieval Latin religious prophecy. While it is impossible, given the current state of knowledge, to suggest even particular works, let alone particular MSS., as sources for the poem, a study of the kinds of books in which he would have had to have read prophecies can be illuminating. After looking at the descriptions, and in most cases the MSS. themselves, of about sixty medieval books of English provenance containing Latin prophecy,[2] I feel able to make the following educated guesses: (1) that Langland probably

237

came by his knowledge of religious prophecy while perusing such collections, initially, in search of other kinds of literature; (2) that, allowing for the differences in purpose and character between vernacular and Latin MS. collections, the kind of company which religious prophecy keeps in MS. is similar to the kind of company which *Piers Plowman* itself often keeps; (3) that medieval religious miscellanies are not necessarily as miscellaneous as they sometimes appear. In many cases there seem to be principles of selection at work, that is, apparently unrelated works may have been copied into the same MS. because of some association in the mind of the copyist. Obviously these points cannot be adequately investigated in a short paper, and given the state of our knowledge about Langland's sources, about the rationale behind medieval miscellanies, and about the production of religious prophecy itself, much of what follows is, of necessity, going to be tentative.[3] I am consoled here by Judson Boyce Allen's rueful comment: "In my work on Langland, I have looked at dozens of medieval MSS. that turned out to be books that Langland never saw" ("Reading" 1). Whether Langland ever saw any of the MSS. that I will be discussing is not the point: he must have seen MSS. similar to these, and so, I think, they have something to teach us.

Unfortunately, I cannot restate here the detailed case I have made elsewhere for the relevance of medieval Latin religious prophecy to *Piers Plowman*.[4] Briefly, however, such prophecies are characterized by the kind of reformist zeal and apocalyptic foreboding which one also sees in the prophetic passages in *Piers Plowman*. Anxiety about the fate of the Church in a period of rampant clerical corruption, and the role of individual orders, especially the friars, in this crisis are paramount to medieval religious prophets just as they are to Langland. Rumors of Antichrist, anxieties about the conversion of the non-Christian peoples, threats from within Christendom and without, disasters, portents, and constant fear of divine chastisement all figure largely in such prophecies. These writers, like Langland, are looking for the signs of the times in each recent and current event and, at the same time, are looking to the Bible for typological precedents. The discovery that Langland quotes a religious prophecy in his own prediction of a reforming king who will chastise the monasteries was what, for me, finally settled the question of this indebtedness.[5] But I knew that medieval Latin religious prophecy was not native to England and its dissemination there is less obvious than it is in Europe. How much prophecy would have been available to a Latin-literate fourteenth-century Englishman is the question that first interested me in the MS. tradition of apocalyptic thought.

There are two immediate ways to answer such a question: first, by surveying the contents of surviving MSS. which are known to be of English provenance and, second, by surveying the contents of medieval library catalogues. The pitfalls of such a study are many: for example, it can be difficult to establish English provenance or ownership,[6] and because many prophecies are short works they are often added to MSS. on flyleaves or blank pages, and it can be difficult to say precisely when this was done. Medieval library catalogues are notoriously summary, rarely listing the contents of miscellanies in any great detail. Prophecies often do not appear in the descriptions of even relatively modern catalogues.[7] After working with medieval catalogue descriptions and tables of contents for a while, I began to wonder whether Langland had had as hard a time finding such things as I was having. To add to the problem, I was not reassured by the fact that paleographers and specialists in library history tend to regard religious prophecies not exactly as rarities, but as unusual enough to be remarked upon in surveys of medieval libraries. "Slightly unusual" is the way that one such scholar describes the occurrence of a Latin prophecy in a personal library.[8] While I have turned up enough evidence to suggest that religious prophecy was available in some form

239

to medieval readers in most libraries of any size, the fact that it was considered something of an acquired taste in mid fourteenth-century England is itself instructive. We still know very little about who composed, read, and transmitted religious prophecy, i.e., who used it and how interested readers came upon it: by chance, by word of mouth, or by some more organized process.

I will return shortly to the question of how readers could have been directed to prophecies in medieval libraries, but I suspect that they may well have known what approximately sixty MS. descriptions and a lot of plodding through catalogues has recently taught me: Latin religious prophecies are most likely to occur in three types of miscellanies: (1) those containing historical, geographical (usually travel), and marvel literature, which I call "chronicle and *mirabilia*" collections; (2) those containing literature devoted to the ideals and practices of the ascetic life, often accompanied by condemnations of laxity: these I call "ascetic and reformist" collections; and (3) those containing the literature of clerical controversy and clerical satire (e.g., antimendicant literature, anti-Wycliffite literature, etc.).

Obviously, these categories are going to overlap with one another, and, given the miscellaneous nature of medieval miscellanies, there will be works which belong to none of these categories. But within the limits that one can categorize multi-purpose books, these are relatively usable groupings. For this paper, I have chosen seven sample MSS. written before 1400 to illustrate these three different miscellany types. Of these, category one, chronicle and *mirabilia* literature, seems to be the most common of the three types (by my rough count just under half of the MSS. surveyed fall into this category). For this reason, and because of the variety of material these MSS. present, I will dwell on this type of MS. a little longer than on the others.

The reason for its association with historical literature in medieval miscellanies has to do with the nature of religious prophecy. The major prophetic writers, such as Joachim of Fiore and Hildegard of Bingen, who are primarily responsible for the genre of the late medieval religious prophecy in many respects, were concerned to understand current Church problems and abuses within the larger perspective of Salvation History. Their prophecies for the future were based largely on extrapolations of historical, usually biblical, patterns of the past. All history for them was, as the German scholars say, *Kirchengeschichte*, Church History (see Rauh). Speculations on the course of history, then, are the essence of religious prophecy.

Along with historical material one often finds medieval geographical works, usually in the form of travel literature, and accounts of marvels or *mirabilia*. The association of prophecies with marvels probably needs no further explanation, but their relationship, more broadly, with travel literature perhaps does: medieval travel literature frequently deals with travels to the Holy Land or the Orient and as such fits in well with the concerns of religious prophets for whom the fate of the heathen was a key factor in apocalyptic history. Perhaps the best way to illustrate this is to quote from a very popular Latin prophecy, the Tripoli prophecy, which Robert Lerner has recently made the subject of a book-length study:

> The High Cedar of Lebanon will be felled, and Tripoli will soon be destroyed. . . . Within fifteen years there will be one god and one faith. The other god has vanished. The sons of Israel will be liberated from captivity. . . . Woe then to the clergy. . . . The mendicant orders and many other sects will be annihilated. . . . Then there will be peace in the whole world . . . and the city of Jerusalem will be glorified. . . . And in such tranquillity news will be heard of Antichrist and of all marvels. . . . Be vigilant! (43; 204 for Latin text)

This version of the prophecy was done just after the fall of Tripoli in 1289. It underlines not only the anxieties of pious Christians for the fate of the Holy Land, the ultimate future of the non-Christian peoples, and Christendom itself, but, closer to home, their concerns with the state of the Church and clergy. Many of these concerns, of course, are reflected in Langland.

My first example of the kind of chronicle and *mirabilia* collection in which one finds prophecies illustrates well the notion that makers of miscellanies copied prophecies into collections containing works which expressed similar concerns. Trinity College, Dublin MS. 496 is an early fourteenth-century book, possibly of Norwich provenance, and probably produced by or for members of the secular clergy, judging by its various items on ecclesiastical organization (see Appendix). It contains various chronicles, some *mirabilia* literature, and two items which deal with the Holy Land. It is made up of a number of booklets in various contemporary hands, but in the opinion of its most recent and thorough cataloguer, Marvin Colker, the booklets were bound together "at an early date."[9] The description given in the Appendix is from the seventeenth-century catalogue by Bernard, and I am using it here because it is like a medieval one in the summary and haphazard style of its cataloguing (although one must say that Abbot's attempt in 1900 is little better). Prophecies, like other short works, were generally ignored in early catalogues, and while they sometimes occur in medieval tables of contents, this MS. does not have one. However, just preceding Bede on the Holy Land there is actually a religious prophecy, although how an earlier reader would have known this without reading the whole book is open to question. I suspect that the related concerns of other non-apocalyptic items in the MS. were the key to the organization for both copyist and reader.

The prophecy advertises itself as having been "found" after the fall of Damietta to the Turks in 1250, an event that was devastating to the Christian West.[10] It pretends to predict the fall of Damietta, among other harrowing and portentous events, which it claims were

242

heralded by a comet. The author, we are assured, is learned in astronomy and has long studied and kept vigil—in other words he has all the credentials of a prophet. Like most short prophecies the setting and the assurances are probably fictitious, but the concerns are real. Before copying the prophecy, and the Bede, *De locis sancta*, the same scribe copied a letter concerning conditions after the fall of Damietta and various short chronicles. In fact the entire booklet is written in this hand and shows a strong interest in the course of history, the fate of the Holy land, and the non-Christian peoples.

Early cataloguers, however, did not always leave readers to fend for themselves. A similar MS. to TCD 496 is Bodleian Library, Oxford MS. Douce 88, a fourteenth-century description of which, happily, occurs in the medieval catalogue of the library of St. Augustine's, Canterbury, as number 870.[11] It begins with a bestiary, but among items dealing with the orient, *mirabilia*, and a variety of religious pieces there appears a reference to "prophetia paparum," which refers to a copy of the series of illustrated predictions concerning future popes usually attributed in medieval MSS. to Joachim of Fiore.[12] As interesting as its MS. context is the way the medieval cataloguer treats the entry. Even though he does not name Joachim here, in his description of #879, which contains the prophecy of Hildegard of Bingen, he adds that a prophecy of Abbot Joachim's can be found "supra in Bestiar' Henr' de Burgham," which suggests that the medieval cataloguer associated the two works together, and wanted to ensure that an interested reader would be aware of both. To a modern scholar of medieval apocalypticism, this is a reassuring and instructive point. It suggests that in spite of the fact that prophecies were "slightly uncommon," the medieval habit of comparing different prophets, as attested in prophetic treatises, was well understood by librarians.[13]

A third and final example of the kind of MS. which carries prophecies amid historical, travel, and portent literature is British Library MS. Royal 13 E.IX.[14] This one brings us even closer to Langland's interests and to the kind of context into which *Piers Plowman* itself was often copied. Described as "one of the finest St. Albans manuscripts," it was copied at the end of the fourteenth century under the supervision of Thomas Walsingham, whose chronicle it also contains (Galbraith 16). The MS. includes various Latin prophecies, political and religious, among which is the Tripoli prophecy and a prophetic letter written in 1356 by John of Rupescissa, one of the best known of fourteenth-century religious prophets.[15] Constantly imprisoned for his radical Franciscan leanings, John poured out prophecies from various convent and papal prisons, warning, just as he does in this frequently copied letter, that wealthy clergy will soon be forcefully despoiled of their temporalities, a prediction that readers of Langland will recognize (see *Piers* V.168–79; XV.207–32).

The prophecy, which is introduced by the scribe as containing *mirabilia*, appears in a now familiar context of literature of marvels and the East, among which is a Latin version of the guidebook for pilgrims travelling to the Holy Land, known as *Mandeville's Travels* to Middle English scholars, and here described as *Itinerarium Iohannis Maundeville de mirabilibus mundi* (item 12, fol. 40). Shortly afterwards there occurs a work called the *Anti-Alcoran Machometi* (item 14, fol. 78), written by a Dominican missionary to the East early in the fourteenth century. Following this is a life of Mahomet (item 15), which gives an account of the supposed sign of the dove, also mentioned in *Piers Plowman* (XVII.165–86). This type of literature sets the stage nicely in the collection for the anti-Saracenism of John's prophecy: he predicts that although in the coming events the Jews and Tartars will be converted, the Saracens will be destroyed. The prophecy is followed by Richard Rolle's *De Emendatione Vitae* (fol. 95), which might seem like appropriate reading for any monk who has just waded through the imminent threats against the clergy described in the previous item. Whether or not such a thought was in this copyist's mind, there can be little doubt that religious prophecies were often inserted in ascetic and devotional miscellanies specifically for the purposes of reproving license and arousing vigilance (see Lerner 106–08, passim). And given Langland's concern for the conversion of the heathen, and the reform of the religious, one can imagine him consulting this type of MS. and coming upon such a prophecy with interest.

In fact, as Ann Middleton notes, the kind of chronicle and *mirabilia* miscellany we have been discussing is just the kind of MS. in which *Piers Plowman* itself can frequently be found. More specifically, she mentions that the work that occurs most often in MSS. with *Piers* is, rather surprisingly, *Mandeville's Travels*. They occur together in no less than five MSS., one of which, Cambridge U. L. MS. Dd 1.17, contains a collection of "Latin works of biblical, British, 'Saracen,' and oriental history."[16]

What immediately strikes a scholar of medieval apocalypticism upon looking at the contents of this MS. is the similarity between it and the kind of MS. which often carries Latin religious prophecy. Middleton observes "Whoever caused the book to be assembled . . . , his conception of world history is Olympian," which would be a good description of the religious prophet's point of view. His concern for the fate of the East, she notes, is largely for "the prophecies and prospects of its conversion" (106). In this, Langland's sympathies are similar to those of Joachite-influenced Franciscans (see Daniel). Langland, too, was greatly exercised about the fate of the non-Christian peoples, and in this he reflects this same mentality. Although, as we shall see in the next MS., pre fourteenth-century prophets often viewed non-Christians as a military threat as well, the conversion of the heathen is traditionally a central theme in apocalyptic thought.

245

This association of prophecies with chronicles illuminates a comment that Langland makes at the end of his prophecy of Church renewal under a reforming king in Passus V of the C-Text. He says, "Ac ar þat kyng come, as cronicles me tolde,/ Clerkes and holy churche shal be clothed newe" (178–79). It is important to note that chronicles themselves often contained prophecies and this is perhaps another reason why they became associated in miscellanies. Clearly, Langland had consulted chronicles himself on the fate of the clergy and prospects for Church reform, no doubt in the kind of MS. at which we have been looking.

That prophecies occur in MSS. containing largely ascetic and devotional literature will come as a surprise to no one, although the conservative nature of such collections sometimes makes them seem like odd homes for such material. However, the need for reform, both personal and corporate, is probably the connection, and in this sense they represent well the kinds of tensions between individual and Church reform with which readers of *Piers Plowman* are so familiar. A good example of such a MS. is Corpus Christi College, Cambridge 288, formerly in the medieval library of the Benedictine Cathedral Priory, Christ Church, Canterbury (described by James, *Descriptive Catalogue*). The description of this thirteenth-century MS. in the Appendix comes from the fourteenth-century catalogue made by Henry of Eastry, where it appears as #1389.[17] Once again, shorter texts have fallen through the cracks. Just before the (Pseudo-) Methodius tract occurs a poem on the corruption of the Church (with a space left for music!). The *Liber Methodii* (ed. Sackur) is the popular pseudonymous apocalyptic text written while Christendom witnessed the rise of Islam; it particularly emphasizes the threat of the sons of Ishmael or the Islamic peoples (see also Emmerson). This same concern is echoed in the last item recorded in the medieval catalogue (*Libellus qualiter Tartari inuaserunt regna Christianorum*), although it is promptly

246

followed by an item concerning Franciscan missions to the infidels. This juxtaposition illustrates well the mixture of fear of invasion and hope of conversion with which the infidels were regarded in the thirteenth century (see Lerner, 9–24, passim). Sandwiched in between Methodius and the piece on the Tartars are two prophecies of Hildegard of Bingen which deal with apocalyptic issues closer to home, notably, the rise of a group of pseudo-prophets (who by Langland's time were identified as the friars), and the prediction that the nobility will soon forcefully despoil the decadent clergy of their wealth. All these pieces are copied in the same hand (fols. 98^v–109^v), and they obviously formed a coherent group for whoever collected them.[18]

A sense of the pressing need for Church reform coupled with apocalyptic expectation also expresses itself in Trinity College, Dublin MS. (Abbot) 347, a miscellany of the late thirteenth-century/early fourteenth-century that belonged to the Irish Franciscan House of Multifarnham.[19] Reformist interests are apparent everywhere in the MS.; here, however, they are motivated by the evangelical optimism of the friars rather than the worldweariness of the older Benedictine tradition.[20] The MS. is written in various hands, but the same ones recur throughout, and despite some early fourteenth-century additions, it has the look of a collection co-operatively compiled by contemporaries in the late thirteenth century. Among sermons and sermon aids are various pieces which show eschatological interest (e.g., fols. 165^r–166^r) and many which show concern with clerical reform and controversy (e.g., fols. 9^r, 337^r–338^r, and 225^v–226^v). Alongside the practical items which would draw any friar or priest to the MS. (and it was later owned by a priest)[21] are two prophecies attributed to Joachim of Fiore. The first predicts, among other apocalyptic events, a papal schism and the coming of Antichrist; the second, more truly Joachite in ideology, prophesies two new orders of spiritual leaders who will bring renewal to a decaying Church.[22] As Langland would later, the author condemns the evils of false brethren, scholastic philosophy, and all manner of laxity. There can be little doubt, both from the look of the MS. and its contents, of the university background of the copyist of the prophecies; with its heavy use of abbreviation and its small size the book resembles other MSS. of the fraternal "vade mecum" type.[23] Certainly, and more generally, it resembles the kind of book in which one would expect to find someone with Langland's interests and educational background browsing.

The last important category of English MSS. containing Latin religious prophecy includes those which also contain current clerical controversies. The literature of antimendicant controversies in particular seems often to have been associated with religious prophecies, perhaps because William of St. Amour had couched his own attacks on the friars in prophetic language.[24] The threats of clerical chastisement which are so common a feature of all religious prophecy were easily associated with antimendicant feuding. Since we know that Langland had a particularly detailed knowledge of antimendicant issues, it seems likely that he came by some of his knowledge of religious prophecy in this way.[25]

A good example of the kind of collection that would have attracted his interest is MS. Balliol College, Oxford 149, a fourteenth-century MS. of Oxford provenance that contains, among sermons and other items of ecclesiastical interest, both religious prophecy and antimendicant material. The book is made up of two booklets, the second of which is written "at least a generation earlier" than the first; however, a shared system of decoration throughout suggests that both originated in the same house or scriptorium.[26] The second, and earlier (mid fourteenth century), booklet contains "The Columbinus Prophecy" (fol. 205ᵛ), which predicts the appearance of Antichrist, a reign of terror during which clerics will be forced to hide their tonsures, and the destruction of papal power. It is followed by William of St. Amour's polemical treatise against the friars, which disguised itself as a warning of pseudo-apostles who will afflict the Church during the last days. These two pieces form an interesting prelude to some letters of complaint against papal decisions which follow (fols. 218ᵛ ff.). Whoever copied these pieces, probably a member of the secular clergy, clearly saw them as related and probably felt that the papacy had much for which to answer.

Also in the MS., in a booklet copied during the last quarter of the fourteenth century and attached to the earlier one, there occurs another antimendicant piece, this time by Uthred de Boldon, one which, it has been argued, Langland knew (Marcett). Following this there is an interesting series of notes referring to the dates of portentous events: the famous windstorm of 1362, to which Langland also ominously refers (V.116), the death of the Archbishop of Canterbury during the Peasant's Revolt of 1381, and the date of the plague. It looks as if the scribe, impressed by their importance (or else asleep at the switch!), copied them verbatim from his exemplar (he even copied a reference in the first person to the previous copyist's birthday). However, for the copyist of his exemplar, at least, if not for him, too, these were clearly portentous signs of the times, a theme echoed in the William of St. Amour piece and in "The Columbinus Prophecy" in the earlier booklet.[27] Taken as a whole, the two booklets which make up the miscellany, even though they were copied a generation apart, make a less miscellaneous book than one might think.

One frequently comes upon literature that we know Langland used or knew when looking up prophecies.[28] Can this be entirely coincidental? I think not. A more detailed study of these MSS. containing religious prophecy would, I think, tell us more about the kinds of books he read, and a study of their makers, owners, and readers would tell us more about him. What we need is more detailed analysis of the kind of MS. that J. B. Allen so appropriately called the "utility grade" medieval book, the kind of book that has for too long been taken for granted ("Reading," 1).

NOTES

1. It has been known for some time that Langland made his revisions for the C-text from a corrupt scribal copy of the B-text, that is, that he did not have his own copy from which to work. Whether this would have been because he was destitute or whether this had more to do with medieval methods of publication, or even some accident, has been the subject of speculation. See Kane and Donaldson, 121–23 especially, and Bennett 177–78. In any case, it seems prudent to doubt whether Langland had the privilege of a large personal bookshelf; he may have done his reading in convent, cathedral, or, indeed, college libraries. On Langland's learning, and the question of his having had a university education, see the recent study by Quick. On the other hand, borrowing books was possible: Ker 326 gives a list of libraries of medieval religious houses which, according to surviving records, loaned books to seculars; see also Piper 245. One can easily believe that Langland had clerical connections which would have enabled him to have access to books somehow.

2. I am currently engaged in a study of medieval MSS. of English provenance containing religious prophecy, which will provide more detailed evidence than can be presented here.

3. For an introduction to the medieval miscellany (principles of selection, etc.) see Rigg 24–35. On the religious collections more specifically see Pantin, chs. 9, 10, and Appendix 2. For a stimulating study of a collection of religious prophecies, Corpus Christi College, Cambridge MS. 404, see Lerner 93–101. Little is known at the moment about the production and transmission of these prophecies, but, along with Lerner, see Reeves, *Influence*.

4. Kerby-Fulton, *Reformist Apocalypticism and Piers Plowman*.

5. Langland uses the phrase "ad pristinum statum ire" in his reformer-king prophecy (V.171) that occurs in certain contemporary prophecies. See n. 4 above. All citations to *Piers Plowman* refer to the edition of the C-text by Derek Pearsall.

6. It can be difficult to establish exactly when MSS. of foreign origin actually arrived in England, as, for example, the important Joachite MS. (now Corpus Christi College, Oxford 255A), which may have come from the continent much earlier than the first record of its appearance in Oxford (see Tondelli et al. 2: 15–20). A similar problem exists with Merton College, Oxford, MS. L.2.9 (Coxe 160), an early thirteenth-century MS. that contains the visions of Hildegard of Bingen; Powicke believes it to have been in the college in medieval times, although the date of acquisition is unknown (36). English clergy frequently brought back MSS. from their travels (for example, Balliol College MS. 274, a Rhenish MS. which contains religious prophecies and was brought back in 1444 by William Gray, bishop of Ely, who had been on a trip to Cologne). All these factors have to be considered in any assessment of the availability of religious prophecy to medieval English readers.

7. Instances of this will be cited below; even a catalogue as recent as the *Summary Catalogue of Western Manuscripts in the Bodleian Library* does not always list incipits; the description of Bodl. 452 (S. C. 2402), fol. 89^r–^{v}, is typical: "Some latin prophecies . . ."; on the problems facing scholars of medieval prophecy, see Lerner 6–7.

8. Humphries 116. Humphries actually uses the phrase to describe the prophecies of John of Bridlington, which are in fact political rather than religious, but these are, if anything, somewhat more common than the religious type. Humphries' article establishes that Erghome's library was unusual in containing a large amount of prophecy of both types.

9. I am grateful to Trinity College Library for permission to see the MS. and for permission to quote Marvin Colker's splendid catalogue from typescript; the description discussed below and given in the Appendix is no. 454 in Bernard. The latter

suggests that the booklets were indeed together in the seventeenth century, although in a slightly different order: (using Colker's lettering of the booklets) booklet C was inserted into booklet G. The booklet containing the prophecy and the items discussed below (F in Colker) is entirely written in one early fourteenth-century hand.

10. Fols. 213ᵛ–215ʳ, incipit "Capta Damiata legatus de maxima machumeta"; explicit ". . . angustia nouiter geniti." On the fall of Damietta see Runciman 268 ff.

11. James, *Ancient Libraries* 290. See Appendix below.

12. On the pope prophecies see Reeves, "Some Popular Prophecies."

13. See, for example, the evidence in notes made by Henry of Kirkstede (in Corpus Christi College, Cambridge MS. 404, fols. 65ᵛ–66ʳ) that he is comparing prophecies (discussed in Lerner 95–96). For another instance see the comments made by Arnold of Villanova on the prophecy "Veh mundo in centum annis," ed. in Pou y Marti 55.

14. Described in Warner and Gilson, vol. 2. See Appendix for a summary of this description.

15. The letter is printed in Brown 2:496–507. On John of Rupescissa, see Bignami-Odier.

16. Middleton 105; see the Appendix below for her summary of the contents. Middleton's article expands on ideas initially put forward in Burrow. The MS. itself is described in *A Catalogue of the Manuscripts preserved in the Library of the University of Cambridge.*

17. James, *Ancient Libraries* 118; see also his description of MS. 288, *A Descriptive Catalogue* 58.

18. The excerpt, which begins at fol. 101ʳ, is from Hildegard's letter to the clergy of Cologne. On this letter and its associations with antimendicant propaganda, see Kerby-Fulton, "Hildegard."

19. See Appendix. I am grateful, once again, for permission to cite Colker's catalogue.

20. On the difference in attitudes between the old and new orders, see Constable.

21. On the ownership of MS. 347, see Colker's catalogue, and see also his "America Rediscovered."

22. On the Joachite concept of the two new orders, see Reeves, *Influence* 72 ff. The first prophecy, which begins "Corruent nobiles . . . ," is transcribed on p. 50. The second, which begins "Dixit Joachim," is unedited.

23. On portable "vade mecum" books, see D'Avray 61.

24. On William's use of eschatology, see Szittya.

25. On Langland's knowledge of antifraternal issues, see Adams.

26. The MS. is described in Mynors 130–35.

27. E. Randolph Daniel and I have published an edition of "The Columbinus Prophecy" in "English Joachimism 1300–1500: The Columbanus Prophecy," *Il profetismo ioachimita tra Quattrocento e Cinquecento*, ed. Gian Luca Potestà (Fiore: Centro Internazionale di Studi Gioachimiti, 1991).

28. For example, counting the copy of the papal bull "Exiit qui seminat" (fol. 75ʳ), which Gradon has recently suggested that Langland used in his portrait of Need, there are three pieces of literature in Balliol 149 alone which we can be fairly certain Langland knew. See Gradon 203.

APPENDIX

I. Trinity College, Dublin MS. 496, as described in Bernard's catalogue:
  1. Galfridi Monumeth. Historia, cum Merlini Prophetia & Expositione; & Proph. Aquilae & Sibyllae.
  2. Chronicon quoddam a nato Christo.
  3. Descriptiones quaedam de Sitibus Civitatum & locorum circa Hierosolymas, V. Beda Auctore.
  4. Nomina quaedam diversa Virorum.
  5. De miraculis regionum quarundam, 8vo. membr.
  Interseruntur vero quaedam de Edwardi Gestis, & Chronica nonulla, rhythmice; & de miraculo quodam Edw. Conf. H.67.

II. From fifteenth-century Catalogue of St. Augustine's, Canterbury, #870, ed. James (now MS. Bodl. Library Douce 88):
  Bestiarum et in eodem libro / pronosticationes / Quedam mirabilia Indie / Quedam de rege Alexandro / Expediciones eiusdem in Indica (?) / versus sibille de die iudicii / Narracio qualiter [Ihesus] fuit sacerdos in templo / de xii abusionibus seculi / sermo augustini in quo describit que sit vera penitencia / ymago mundi / Epistola Alex' ad Aristotelem de situ Indie / Epistola bragmanorum ad Alexandrum / versus de Roma / versus de proprietatibus arborum / versus de proprietatibus herbarum / de Mirabilibus Anglie et / alia quedam prophetia paparum / Nominale et verbale et / versus de Susanna   Henr' d Burgham.

III. British Library MS. Royal 13 E.IX (summarized from Warner and Gilson):
  1.   Nomina Romanorum pontificum
  2.   Nomina Imperatorum
  3.–5. Various pieces concerning English history
  6.   *De situ mundi et eius mirabilibus*
  7.   *Ymago Mundi* (attrib. to Honorius of Autun)
  8.–11. Mirabilia and various prophecies, Becket's Vision
  12.   *Itinerarium Iohannis Maundeville de mirabilibus mundi*
  13.   *De spiritu Willelmi* (a "demonological experience")
  14.   *Anti alcoron Machometi*

254

15. Life of Mahomet
16. Becket's Vision (another version)
17. Prophecy of a friar [John of Rupescissa] to Innocent VI
18. *Libellus de emendacione vite Ricardi heremite*
19.–25. Various chronicles, including Hidgen's, Walsingham's, and material relating to St. Albans abbey.

IV. Middleton's summary of Contents of Cambridge University Library Dd 1.17: "It includes, besides British histories and chronicles—Gildas, Henry of Huntington, Simeon of Durham, Florence of Worcester, Higden, and the 'history' of Geoffrey of Monmouth—and other histories of romance 'matters'—Turpin's *Life of Charlemagne*, Guido della Colonna's *Historia Troiana*—several works concerning eastern travels, crusades, and geographical and religious surveys: Jacques de Vitry's *Historia Hierosolimitana*, William of Tripoli, *De Statu Saracenorum*, Hayton's *Flos ystoriarum terrae orientis*, Marco Polo, *De Statu et Consuetudinibus Orientalium Regionum*, and three works on the Saracen faith and its foundations: *De Fide Saracenorum, Gesta Machometi*, and the *Ortus et processus Machometi*. These Latin works comprise the first two-thirds of the book, and give an impressively monumental setting to the English narratives that follow: *Piers*, a short work on visiting the sick, *Mandeville*, and the *Seven Sages of Rome*, which is then followed by Clement of Llanthony's *Concordia Evangelistarum*."

V. From fourteenth-century *Catalogue of Christ Church, Canterbury*, #1389, ed. James (now Corpus Christi College, Cambridge 288): Liber officiorum ecclesiasticorum. In hoc uol. cont.: Glose super Osee / Infancia saluatoris / Euangelium Nazareorum / Asseneth / Methodius / Prophetia Hildegardi / Epistole Frederici Imperatoris / Libellus qualiter Tartari inuaserunt regna Christianorum.

VI. Trinity College, Dublin MS. 347, from Abbot's catalogue: Tractatus Geographicus. Tract. de Sacramentis, de honestate clericorum. . . . Sermones.

255

Tract. de Vitiis et Virtutibus.

B. Augustini Regula.

F. Brecham. Merarium cum glossa.

Epist. B. Francisci . . . cum officio ejus et testamento.

Joachim (Ordo Praedicat.) [!]. Prophetiae.

Epistola Abgari.

Wyenne (Propheta). Prophetiae.

Annales Angliae et Hiberniae.

VII. Balliol College, Oxford MS. 149, summarized from Mynors' catalogue:
1. Late fourteenth-century booklet:
   - (a)–(o) Sermons
   - (p) *Periculis in falsis fratribus* (Uthred de Boldon), followed by various items of interest to a priest and notes of important dates in recent English history
   - (q)–(r) Sermons
   - (s) *Exiit qui seminat*
   - (t)–(x) Sermons

2. Mid fourteenth-century booklet:
   A commentary on the Apocalypse, the "Columbinus" prophecy (fol. 205ʳ), William of St. Amour's "De Periculis," various letters (two complaining to the Pope), and a sermon.

WORKS CITED

Abbot, T. K. *Catalogue of the Manuscripts in Trinity College, Dublin.* Dublin: Hodges, Figgis, 1900.

Adams, Robert. "The Nature of Need in *Piers Plowman* XX." *Traditio* 34 (1978): 266–84.

Allen, Judson Boyce. "Langland's Reading and Writing: *Detractor* and the Pardon Passus." *Speculum* 59.2 (1984): 342–66.

———. "Reading and Looking Things Up in Chaucer's England." *The Chaucer Newsletter* 7.1 (1985): 1–2.

Bennet, H. S. "The Production and Dissemination of Vernacular Manuscripts in the Fifteenth Century." *The Library,* 5th ser. 1 (1947): 167–78.

Bernard, Edward. *Catalogi librorum manuscriptorum Angliae et Hiberniae.* Oxford: Sheldonian Theatre, 1697.

Bignami-Odier, Jeanne. *Etudes sur Jean de Roquetaillade.* Paris: Vrin, 1952.

Brown, Edwardi, ed. *Fasciculus rerum expetendarum et fugiendarum.* 2 vols. London: R. Chiswell, 1690.

Burrow, J. A. "The Audience of *Piers Plowman.*" *Anglia* 75 (1957): 373–84; rpt. with a postscript in *Essays on Medieval Literature.* Oxford: Clarendon, 1984. 102–16.

A Catalogue of the Manuscripts preserved in the Library of the University of Cambridge. Cambridge: Cambridge UP, 1856.

Colker, Marvin. "America Rediscovered in the Thirteenth Century?" *Speculum* 54 (1979): 712–26.

————. *Catalogue of the Manuscripts in Trinity College Library, Dublin.* (Unpublished typescript held in the Library).

Constable, Giles. "Renewal and Reform in Religious Life: Concepts and Realities." *Renaissance and Renewal in the Twelfth Century.* Ed. Robert L. Benson and G. Constable. Cambridge, MA: Harvard UP, 1982. 37–67.

Coxe, H. O. *Catalogus Codicum MSS qui in Collegiis Aulisque Oxoniensibus. . . .* 2 vols. Oxford: Oxford UP, 1852.

Daniel, E. Randolph. *The Franciscan Concept of Mission in the High Middle Ages.* Lexington: U of Kentucky P, 1975.

D'Avray, D. L. "Portable Vade Mecum Books Containing Franciscan and Dominican Texts." *Manuscripts at Oxford: R. W. Hunt Memorial Exhibition.* Oxford: Bodleian Library, 1980. 51–53.

Edwards, A. S. G., and Derek Pearsall. "Literary Publication: The Manuscripts of the Major English Poetic Texts." *Book Production and Publishing, 1375–1475.* Ed. Jeremy Griffiths and Derek Pearsall. Cambridge: Cambridge UP, 1989. 257–78.

Emmerson, Richard K. *Antichrist in the Middle Ages.* Manchester, UK: Manchester UP, 1981.

Galbraith, V. H. "Thomas Walsingham and the St. Albans Chronicle, 1272–1422." *English Historical Review* 47 (1932): 12–29.

Gradon, Pamela. "Langland and the Ideology of Dissent." *Proceedings of the British Academy* 66 (1980): 179–205.

Humphries, K. W. "The Library of John Erghome and Personal Libraries of Fourteenth-century England." *A Medieval Miscellany in honour of Professor John Le Patourel.* Ed. R. L. Thomson. *Proceedings of the Leeds Philosophical and Literary Society* 18.1 (1982): 106–23.

James, M. R. *The Ancient Libraries of Canterbury and Dover*. Cambridge: Cambridge UP, 1903.

―――. *A Descriptive Catalogue of the Manuscripts in the Library of Corpus Christi College, Cambridge*. Cambridge: Cambridge UP, 1912.

Kane, George, and E. T. Donaldson, eds. *Piers Plowman: The B Version*. London: Athlone, 1975.

Ker, N. R. *Medieval Libraries of Great Britain*. 2nd ed. London: Royal Historical Society, 1964.

Kerby-Fulton, Kathryn. *Reformist Apocalypticism and Piers Plowman*. Cambridge: Cambridge UP, 1990.

―――. "Hildegard of Bingen and Antimendicant Propaganda." *Traditio* 43 (1987): 386–99.

Langland, William. *Piers Plowman: an edition of the C-text*. Ed. Derek Persall. London: Edward Arnold, 1978.

Lerner, Robert. *The Powers of Prophecy*. Berkeley and Los Angeles: U of California P, 1983.

Marcett, Mildred E. *Uthred of Boldon, Friar William Jordan and Piers Plowman*. New York: (privately published), 1938.

Middleton, Anne. "The Audience and Public of *Piers Plowman*." *Middle English Alliterative Poetry*. Ed. D. Lawton. Cambridge: Brewer, 1982. 101–23.

Mynors, R. A. B. *Catalogue of the Manuscripts of Balliol College, Oxford*. Oxford: Oxford UP, 1963.

Pantin, W. A. *The English Church in the Fourteenth Century*. Cambridge: Cambridge UP, 1955; rpt. Toronto: U of Toronto P, 1980.

259

Piper, A. J. "The Libraries of the Monks of Durham." *Medieval Scribes, Manuscripts and Libraries: Essays presented to N. R. Ker.* Ed. M. B. Parkes and A. G. Watson. London: Scholar P, 1978. 213–49.

Pou y Marti, José. *Visionarios, Beguinos y Fraticelos Catalanes.* Vich: Editorial Serafica, 1930.

Powicke, F. M. *Medieval Books of Merton College.* Oxford: Clarendon, 1931.

Quick, Anne Wenley. "Langland's Learning: The Direct Sources of Piers Plowman." Diss. U of Toronto, 1982.

Rauh, Horst D. *Das Bild des Antichrist im Mittelalter.* Beitrage zur Geschichte der Philosophie und Theologie des Mittelalters. ns 9. Munster: Aschendorff, 1973.

Reeves, Marjorie. *The Influence of Prophecy in the Later Middle Ages: A Study of Joachimism.* Oxford: Clarendon, 1969.

———. "Some Popular Prophecies from the Fourteenth to the Seventeenth Centuries." *Popular Belief and Practice.* Ed. G. J. Cuming and D. Baker. Studies in Church History, 8. Cambridge: Cambridge UP, 1972. 107–34.

Rigg, A. G. *A Glastonbury Miscellany of the Fifteenth Century.* Oxford: Oxford UP, 1968.

Runciman, Steven. *A History of the Crusades.* III. *The Kingdom of Acre and the Later Crusades.* Cambridge: Cambridge UP, 1955; rpt. New York: Harper, 1967.

Sackur, Ernst., ed. *Sibyllinische Texte und Forschungen.* Halle: Niemeyer, 1898.

A Summary Catalogue of Western Manuscripts in the Bodleian Library at Oxford. Ed. F. Madan, H. H. E. Craster, et al. 7 vols. in 8. Oxford: Clarendon, 1895–1953.

Szittya, Penn. *The Antifraternal Tradition in Medieval Literature.* Princeton, NJ: Princeton UP, 1986.

Kathryn Kerby-Fulton

Tondelli, L., Marjorie Reeves and B. Hirsch-Reich. *Il libro delle figure dell'abate Gioacchino da Fiore*. 2nd rev. ed. 2 vols. Turin: Societa Editrice Internazionale, 1953.

Warner, G. F., and J. G. Gilson. *Catalogue of the Western Manuscripts in the Old Royal and King's Collections*. 3 vols. London: Longman, 1921.

What to Call Petrarch's Griselda

Charlotte Cook Morse

Not long ago, beside a conference book exhibit, a colleague whom I respect claimed that the title of Petrarch's Griselda is *De obedientia ac fide uxoria mythologia*. I demurred. He insisted. Since that was not the point of the conversation, I noted to myself that he had no feel for manuscript culture, for the legacy of uncertainty that manuscript variation bequeaths us. Nor could he appreciate what the *ordinatio*, or apparatus of medieval manuscript texts, can tell us.

Variations in the *ordinatio* of manuscript texts, especially in introductory and closing rubrics that are not regarded as part of the text proper, can tell us about early interpretations (Parkes). Manuscript rubrics accompanying Petrarch's Griselda allow us to glimpse that early readers regarded the genre and significance of the story in differing ways. Although the presentation of some Petrarchan texts is authorial, none of the rubrics for the story of Griselda can confidently be ascribed to Petrarch.

No doubt many medievalists believe, with my colleague, that the phrase I have cited is Petrarch's title for the story of Griselda because it is the title attached to the story in the sixteenth-century printed editions of Petrarch's complete works, the Basle editions of 1554 and 1581. It is also the title attached to the English translation of Petrarch's Griselda most familiar to Chaucerians, who read Petrarch's tale because it is the source for Chaucer's Clerk's Tale. The phrase, probably not Petrarch's, is not exactly a title. Rather, it is part of a rubric that sometimes introduces the letter that contains the Griselda

(*Sen.* 17.3); much more rarely, it introduces the tale of Griselda within the letter. As Walter Ong explains in his book on Ramus, the modern idea of an authorial title arises in the later Renaissance, a belated effect of print culture (311–13). Earlier, headings or rubrics served to indicate the subject of a work. They were often scribal in origin, especially subject to variation, and too long to serve as titles in our modern sense, but for that reason more revealing as interpretations of the texts.[1] The standard way of citing Petrarch's letters is not by their rubrics, but by the first words of their texts, i.e., by incipits. Most of Petrarch's letters have no title in a modern sense.[2]

I am primarily concerned in this essay to explore what we can learn from rubrics that introduce and close the letter containing the Griselda. These rubrics lead me to focus ultimately on Griselda's virtues defined either as *obedientia* and *fides* or as *patientia* and *constantia*. But first I will review how the sixteenth-century Basle editions of Petrarch's works, treated as standard editions until well into the twentieth century, have led to undue favor for the *obedientia/fides* rubric and confusion about the epistolary context of the tale.

The title my colleague was citing, *De obedientia ac fide uxoria mythologia*, comes from the 1581 Basle edition, whence it passed to the Chaucer Society's presentation of the source of Chaucer's Clerk's Tale in 1875 and then to the most commonly consulted English translation, by R. D. French, first published in his *Chaucer Handbook* (1927, revised in 1947) and reprinted in Miller's collection of translated sources and backgrounds (1977), and in Kolve and Olson's Norton critical edition of the *Canterbury Tales* (1989). These editions render the title as "A Fable [*var.* Legend] of Wifely Obedience and Devotion." Barber (254) also uses as a title the *obedientia/fides* rubric from Severs; Kadish does not.

The Basle editions of 1554 and 1581 have led to other persistent confusions about the epistolary context of Petrarch's Griselda. It is widely accepted that Petrarch intended the four letters to Boccaccio written in 1373 and 1374 to form the seventeenth book of the letter collection of his old age, the *Rerum senilium libri*, commonly called the *Seniles*. In 1554 the Basle printer offered the third and fourth of these letters, run together, in volume one (600–07) of Petrarch's works, with no indication that they belong to the *Seniles*, which he printed in volume two (812–1070, continuous pagination). He does the same in the 1581 edition (1.540–47, 2.735–968). The heading for the letter containing the Griselda, "Librum tuum" (*Sen.* 17.3), indicates sender and recipient: "Franciscus Petrarcha/Ioan. Boccatio." The story "Est ad ytalie" is preceded by the rubric my colleague cited, as if it were a modern title, though in manuscripts the *obedientia/fides* rubric almost always precedes the letter "Librum tuum." In the Basle editions, "Ursit amor," the incipit of *Seniles* 17.4, occurs mid-page, mid-line, completely unremarked (1.606; 1.546).

Except in manuscripts containing the *Seniles*, it is rare for *Sen.* 17.4 to be copied with *Sen.* 17.3. I know of 188 manuscript copies of Petrarch's Latin Griselda; I have evidence for the rubrics accompanying 119 of these manuscript copies, i.e., the classifiable manuscripts (see Appendices I and IV). I have examined manuscripts in the British Library, in Cambridge University libraries, and in the Bodleian Library, Oxford, but in this essay I am citing the evidence of manuscript rubrics as it is reported in printed sources (see Bibliography I; for abbreviations used throughout this essay see Bibliography I and Appendix I).[3] Among the 115 classifiable manuscripts that are not copies of the *Seniles*, the two letters (*Sen.* 17.3–4) are copied one after the other only nine times, and in no instance are they completely run together. They are separated in the four manuscripts of the *Seniles* for which I have evidence of the rubrics. Nevertheless, the Basle editions have been so powerful an influence on modern perceptions that even the Italian translator of the *Seniles*, Giuseppe Fracassetti, doubted the separation of the two letters.[4]

Burke J. Severs, in *The Literary Relationships of Chaucer's Clerkes Tale*, recognized the separation of the two letters (*Sen.* 17.3 and 17.4), edited *Sen.* 17.3, and described the chronology of the four letters in book 17 (see also Wilkins 241–49, 265–66), as follows. In June 1373 Petrarch sent three letters to Boccaccio. The first of these is a letter of transmittal, now *Sen.* 17.1. It instructs Boccaccio to read first Petrarch's response to Boccaccio's advice to him to stop strenuous literary activity, now *Sen.* 17.2; and then to read the letter "Librum tuum" containing the translation of Boccaccio's Griselda (*Decameron* 10.10), now *Sen.* 17.3. The first three letters of *Sen.* 17 were actually composed in reverse order. Apparently as a result of the war between Padua and Venice, Boccaccio did not receive the letters, so in 1374 Petrarch again had *Sen.* 17.1–3 copied and he wrote another letter, "Ursit amor," now *Sen.* 17.4, describing the responses of two readers to the story of Griselda. The explicit in the *Seniles* for 17.4 seems designed to close the letter collection: Petrarch bids farewell to his friends and to his letters, and dates the letter 8 June 1374 ("Valete amici, valete epistole. Inter Colles Euganeos vj Idus Iunias 1374"; Laurenziana MS. 78.3, f. 228ᵛ, S2).[5] Petrarch died 18 July 1374. Months after his death, Boccaccio had still not received the two letters he had heard of (i.e., *Sen.* 17.2–3), as he indicates in a letter to Francesco da Brossano, Petrarch's son-in-law, dated November 1374 (Boccaccio 227).

Severs argued that the manuscripts he classified as family *d* descended from the 1373 version of Petrarch's letter containing the Griselda and that Petrarch revised the Griselda slightly in 1374; the evidence for revision is several omissions in his family *d* manuscripts (93–98), none of which is a *Seniles* manuscript and none of which includes *Sen.* 17.4. Vittorio Rossi, editor of the *Familiares*, did not doubt that some copies of the "Librum tuum" or of the Griselda may descend from the 1373 letter, but he suggested to Severs that his evidence for revision is consistent with scribal practice and need not imply that Petrarch revised the Griselda in 1374 (Severs 98n50).

No manuscript survives that shows signs of Petrarch's supervision. Fewer than six weeks separate the date on *Sen.* 17.4 and Petrarch's death. Martellotti (1179) says that Petrarch did not exercise the control over the *Seniles* that he exercised over the *Familiares* and says that manuscripts of the *Seniles*, which are not numerous, lead back to a single archetype, probably one in the care of the scholars of Padua and one certainly already tainted with error. Later Paduan humanists who supervised the text for the Venice edition of 1501, a text superior to the Basle editions, added the *Letter to Posterity* to the *Seniles* as the eighteenth book, a decision based on a final rubric in some manuscripts of the *Seniles* that claims to indicate Petrarch's intention: "*Rerum senilium liber* XVII explicit. Amen. In originali sequitur: incipit XVIII. Posteritati. De successibus studiorum suorum" (Wilkins 313; Ricci 5).[6] Wilkins regarded the farewells at the end of *Sen.* 17.4 as Petrarch's words and as not incompatible with the addition of the *Letter to Posterity* to the *Seniles*, since the *Letter* is a different sort of composition from the letters, written mainly to friends, that would precede the *Posteritati* (266). Rationalizing thus, Wilkins accepts both the seemingly final rubric for *Sen.* 17.4 and the addition of the *Letter to Posterity* to the *Seniles* (see also Bernardo).

Copies of *Sen.* 17.3 probably began to circulate in 1373. Petrarch remarks in the "Librum tuum" that "[the story] was praised and sought after by many" ("a multis et laudata et expetita fuerit," *Pref.* 46).[7] The letter or the story it contained was copied an enormous number of times: *Sen.* 17.3 fitted as comfortably into devotionally or morally oriented miscellanies as it did into humanist miscellanies. It was copied steadily through the fifteenth century and occasionally during the sixteenth; there are also several incunables of it.[8] Severs knew of sixty-five manuscripts, including the Vatican manuscripts listed by Vattasso (see Appendix II). Editors of the Censimento dei Codici Petrarcheschi (hereafter, Census), under the general editorship of Giuseppe Billanovich, have published censuses for Belgium (Ijsewijn), the British Isles (N. Mann), France (Pellegrin), Switzerland (Besomi), Trieste (Zamponi), the United States (Dutschke, and earlier Ullman), the Vatican (Pellegrin's supplement to Vattasso), and West Germany (Sottili; see Bibliography I).[9] The Census adds sixty-four manuscripts. In 1956 Vittore Branca listed manuscripts containing Petrarch's Griselda that he had come across in the course of research on Boccaccio; his list includes twenty-nine manuscripts not in Severs or the Census (226n7). Using Kristeller's *Iter Italicum*, Santoro's catalogue for the Biblioteca Trivulziana, and Jordan and Wool for the Ambrosiana, I have added a further thirty manuscripts containing Petrarch's Griselda, to make a comprehensive but certainly incomplete total of 188 known manuscripts (see Appendices I–IV).[10]

The title from the Basle edition that my colleague cited (*De obedientia ac fide uxoria mythologia*) derives from an early rubric, found both in manuscripts of the *Seniles* and in early copies of *Sen.* 17.3. In Laurenziana MS. 78.3, Florence (S2), a good fifteenth-century MS. (Severs 101n54), a rubric similar to the Basle title precedes the letter "Librum tuum": "Ad eundem insignis obedientia et fides uxoria" ("To the same [i.e., Boccaccio], remarkable obedience and wifely devotion"). The fourteenth-century Vatican MS. Lat. 1666 (V4) that Severs used as the base-text for his edition is not a manuscript of the *Seniles* but does contain *Sen.* 17.4 as well as *Sen.* 17.3. In this manuscript, the rubric preceding "Librum tuum" indicates the sender and the recipient of the letter, as many copies of individual letters do, with another version of the *obedientia/fides* rubric: "Francisci Petrarce poete leureati [*sic*] de insigni obedientia et fide uxoris ad Johannem

268

bocacium de certaldo" ("Francis Petrarch, poet laureate, on the remarkable obedience and devotion of a wife, to Giovanni Boccaccio of Certaldo"; Severs 42).

Two of four classifiable manuscripts of the *Seniles* do not exhibit what printed editions have led us to accept as standard *ordinatio*. A second Laurenziana manuscript of the *Seniles*, tentatively dated in the fifteenth century by Severs and identified by Rossi as having a good text, MS. Acquisti e Doni 266 (S3), has no introductory rubrics for the last letters, which it numbers continuously as letters 126 and 127. Paris, BN MS. Lat. 8571, also a manuscript of the *Seniles*, has no rubrics; it was copied in Bologna in 1410 (Golenistcheff-Koutouzoff 14, 248n1; P4.400). These manuscripts of the *Seniles* and others containing *Sen.* 17.3 that have no rubrics may reflect the earliest state of the *Seniles* collection.

The evidence of these four manuscripts offers in synopsis what a large number of manuscripts show. First, some manuscripts have no rubrics at all. Second, when rubrics exist, they usually indicate the sender and/or the recipient of the letter (some name Petrarch as the translator of Boccaccio's work). Third, in contrast to other types of extended introductory rubrics, versions of the *obedientia/fides* rubric do not usually offer a generic designation for the story, e.g., *mythologia*.

Of all manuscripts with introductory rubrics for the letter or the tale, a large number contain some term indicating genre. In the epistolary preface to the tale, "Librum tuum," and again in *Sen.* 17.4, "Ursit amor," Petrarch speculates on whether the Griselda is an *historia* or a *fabula*, a true story or a fiction, and in *Sen.* 17.4 favors *fabula* (see Middleton 133–35; Morse 60–64). In the manuscripts, however, scribes, and at least one artist,[11] favor *historia* in introductory and closing rubrics. In all, fifty-seven manuscripts designate the tale as an *historia*, e.g.: "Incipit historia Griseldis" [before the tale],

Berlin, Geheimes Statsarchiv MS. Lat. qu. 277 (AS230); "Ad eundem prefacio seu prologus in historiam Grisildis" [before the preface "Librum tuum"], Cambridge, Peterhouse MS. 81 (M19); "Incipit prologus in historiam Griseldis ad Iohannem Bocacium" [before the preface "Librum tuum"], London, BL MS. Harley 3081 (S5). Five call the tale a *fabula* (AS104, AS173, AS186, M85, P4.418), and three manuscripts written after 1475 echo Petrarch's preface in calling it *historia sive fabula* (AS236, M7, M131, the last with rubrics later than text). Two of these last manuscripts revert to *historia* in their explicits.

The most common phrase for designating the story as *historia* is *historia Griseldis*. This phrase stands alone or is embedded in longer rubrics in forty-one of the fifty-seven manuscripts, for example: "Incipit hystoria Griseldis de Ytalia," Brussels, Bib. Royale MS. II 1159 (Ij33); "Historia Griseldis translata de materno in latinum idioma per Petrarcam," Munich, Bayerische Staatsbib. MS. 6379 (AS128); "Descriptio historie Griseldis," Bern, Burgerbib. MS. Cod. 550 (B18); and many of the *patientia/constantia* rubrics, cited below (pp. 274–77). *Historia Griseldis* seems to be the strongest candidate for a late medieval *title* for the Griselda, if by title we mean only the common way of referring to this tale. In an additional eight manuscripts, the tale is described as an *historia* of Walter and his wife Griselda (AS224; B17; BG164; M7 explicit; M8; M33; M39; M131 explicit), and in yet another manuscript only Walter is named as the subject of the history (B33). Five other manuscripts also use the term *historia* (AS34, AS55, B11, M94, and PeL282). Three manuscripts identify the tale as an exemplum (BG115; AS218; AS59); the rubrics in the last manuscript suggestively use the terms *narracio, historia,* and *exemplum* to describe the tale. Two mid-fifteenth-century manuscripts call the tale a *vita* (M241; P6.285), and one of these calls it an *historia* in the explicit (P6.285). All of these terms are consistent with exemplary interpretations.

The choice of the term *fabula*, occurring occasionally in humanist manuscripts, may be a more self-conscious choice of generic term than *historia*. *Fabula* implies belief in the fictional status of the story; *historia* is ambiguous. In *Sen.* 17.4 Petrarch is irritated with the skeptical Veronese for treating the story as a fiction, i.e., untrue, and so refusing to make an exemplary interpretation (see Morse 60–61). Neither Petrarch, who favors *fabula*, nor the scribes who choose the term *fabula* imply a lesser commitment to an exemplary interpretation than those who choose *historia*. For example, one manuscript whose introductory rubric describes the letter as exemplary, as "de laudabili constancia unius mulieris Griseldis nomine" ("concerning the praiseworthy steadfastness of one woman by the name of Griselda"), sets the rubric "Explicit prohemium, incipit fabula" before the story itself (Trier, Stadtbib. MS. 1879/74 8° [AS186]).

The Venice editions of 1501 and 1503, each with the rubric "Ad eundem de insignis obedientia et fides uxoria," offer no generic designations, nor do most manuscripts that employ the *obedientia/fides* type of rubric. The theoretical implications of the term *mythologia*, used in the Basle editions, make it closer to *fabula* than to *historia*. I have, however, found no manuscript evidence at all for *mythologia*.

Historia, meaning "story" or "history," "narrative," is a term traditionally more compatible than *fabula* with an exemplary interpretation of a tale. As Judson Allen noted, the rhetoric of preaching had favored what were perceived to be true stories, or histories, for their persuasive value as exempla (46). For most late medieval readers, context governed whether they regarded a story as a true history or as a fiction (Allen 64–68). Though Petrarch treated the story as exemplary in *Sen.* 17.4 (see Morse 60–64), he favored the term *fabula* largely because he had found the story in the *Decameron*, a collection of *fabulae (Sen.* 17.4). Scattered use of the term *fabula* in manuscript rubrics where it seems to substitute for the scribes' more usual choice of *historia* never combines with other information in the rubrics to indicate an other-than-exemplary interpretation of the tale of Griselda.

The widespread use of the ambiguous term *historia* (i.e., narrative) apparently encouraged some fifteenth- and sixteenth-century readers to think of the story as a true history. Several scribes identify Walter with places better known than Saluzzo, which may imply that they consider him historical: he is once described as "Marchione Fferarie" (M39), once as "Marchione Pedemoncium" (B33), and once as "marchionem Montis Ferrati" (AS218). There is also clear evidence of the story of Griselda being accepted as history: for example, many editions and translations of Jacobus Philippus Foresti of Bergamo's *Supplementum chronicarum*, from as early as the 1485 Brescia edition, contain a lengthy redaction of the Petrarchan version of Griselda's story, added to the treatment of the Counts of Monferrato.[12] What seems to us an obviously fictional story was not so obviously fictional to its early audience.

Rubrics identifying Griselda's virtues, the most common kind of elaborated rubric, invite readers to appreciate her exemplary value, coincident with her historical value. Almost half of the classifiable manuscripts have such rubrics. These rubrics fall into two broad categories, the *obedientia/fides* rubrics and the *patientia/constantia* rubrics.

Almost one-half of the classifiable manuscripts (fifty-five MSS.) do not have any "title" in the sense my colleague intended the term. Of the 119 manuscripts that I can classify, thirty-three were written with no introductory rubric. Of these manuscripts, ten have explicits, or closing rubrics, and one has a brief rubric introducing the tale within the letter. Another nine manuscripts have introductory rubrics that describe or imply Petrarch as the translator of Boccaccio's story;

another eight manuscripts simply name the correspondents, and five others are miscellaneous. Longer manuscript rubrics often include the names of Petrarch and Boccaccio as correspondents or translators; I have classified them, however, by their explicit interpretation of the story of Griselda.

The rubric(s) describing Petrarch as translator of Boccaccio appear to be scribal. They are usually matter-of-fact and do not comment on Petrarch's style, for example: Munich, Bayerische Staatsbib. MS. 6379 (AS128), opens with "Historia Griseldis ultima in Decameron translata de vulgari in literalem sermonem per Petrarcham" ("The story of Griselda, the last in the Decameron, translated from the vulgate into Latin prose by Petrarch"), and closes with the story ". . . translata de materno in latinum idioma per Petrarcam" (". . . translated from the mother tongue into Latin by Petrarch"). Cambridge, Corpus Christi MS. 177 (M7) has an equally matter-of-fact statement about translation in its opening rubric. The closing rubric in Munich, Bayerische Staatsbib. MS. 5683 (AS126), draws upon the "Librum tuum" to explain the purpose of Petrarch's act of translation:

> Hystoria Griseldis posita prius a quodam in volgari lingua Italie quam postea Franciscus Petrarca poeta laureatus transtulit in hunc stilum ut eciam ab aliis nacionibus posset legi et intelligi et pluribus prodesse explicit feliciter.

> The story/history of Griselda formerly presented by someone in the vernacular language of Italy which afterward Francis Petrarch the poet laureate translated into this language so that it could also be read and understood by those of other nations and could be profitable to many, here happily ends.

The scribe of Milan, Ambros. MS. B 166 sup. (PeL277), makes an unusual value judgment in describing Petrarch's translation as ". . . mor-

273

alissima in latinum elegansque translatio" ("a most moral and elegant translation into Latin . . ."). The ultimate exemplar(s) behind manuscripts with rubrics on Petrarch's translating probably had no title.

Twenty-six, or perhaps twenty-seven,[13] manuscripts present the rubric "de insigni obedientia et fide uxoria" or variations of it, such as that in the Basle editions which lacks only the word *insignis*. Seventeen manuscripts contain all four words carrying semantic value: *insignis*, *obedientia*, *fides*, and *uxoria/uxoris*.[14] Six more, like the Basle editions, lack only the word *insignis* (AS238, M132, M210, PeL282, S10, S11). Two manuscripts contain only *de fide uxoris* (AS87, AS118); another has only *de insigni obediencia Griseldis* in its table of contents (AS20; the manuscript has lost its first folios on which the Griselda was copied).

A quite different set of rubrics that direct readers' attention to Griselda's virtues of *patientia* and/or *constantia*, i.e., steadfastness, occurs in variant forms as introductory rubrics in thirty manuscripts. Most of them are too long to mistake for titles. If they use any term for her female sex, they usually describe her as *mulier* (rarely as *puella*), a word that means either woman or wife, but is less insistent on Griselda's wifehood than the words *uxor/uxoria*. These rubrics vary in degree of elaboration. One of the least elaborate occurs early and may be unrelated to others that remark on Griselda's patience. Glasgow University Library MS. Hunter 480 (formerly V.7.7; M39), written by Italian hands and dated fourteenth–fifteenth century, has a rubric that emphasizes Griselda's patience and continues somewhat idiosyncratically: "Ff. P. de Paciencia Crisildis. Incipit Historia de Waltero Marchione Fferarie et sua Crisilde secundum eundem" (fol. 1ʳ). One other manuscript shares the brief title, "de paciencia Griseldis" (Vatican MS. Pal. Lat. 608; V84).

A more elaborate subset of *patientia* rubrics often found in fifteenth-century manuscripts gives a generic designation for the tale and

names Griselda's superlative virtues: ". . . de hystoria Griseldis, muli-
eris maxime patientie et constantie" ("with the story/history of Grisel-
da, a woman of the greatest steadfastness and patience"), in Bonn,
Univ. MS. 365 (AS10). Five manuscripts contain this rubric (also
AS18, AS29, AS75, AS120); it is added early to two more (Ij33,
Ij46). Two other manuscripts offer variants: one substitutes *pacis*
(BG114) and another substitutes *fide conjugalis* (CS162) for *patientie*.
Another manuscript abbreviates the virtues, leaving only *paciencie*
(AS5). Another nine manuscripts, plus Ulrich Zell's Cologne incunable, 1470?, reverse the order of the virtues to *constantia/patientia*,
substitute *constantia* for *hystoria* in two cases, and add the phrase "in
preconium omnium laudabilium mulierum" ("in celebration of all
praiseworthy women"), as in an early West Berlin Staatsarchiv manuscript, Lat. qu. 277 (AS230, dated C14–15).[15] In all, then, nineteen
manuscripts plus two variant manuscripts and Zell's print belong to
this set of rubrics.

Another subset of *patientia* rubrics celebrates Griselda as the
most patient woman: "Franciscus Petrarcha . . . de Grysilde pacientis-
sima muliere quandam laudabilem narracionem scripsit. . . ." ("F. P.
composed a certain praiseworthy narrative concerning the most patient
woman Griselda"), Oxford, Bodleian MS. Lat. Misc. d.34 (M225;
similarly M85). Three others combine a generic term with Griselda's
superlative patience: "Historia Grysildis mulieris pacientissime," London, BL MS. Add. 10094 (M49; also M9, Ij4). This rubric serves as
an explicit in four more manuscripts (V84, AS56, AS234, M96, the
last three of which have no introductory rubric). In a variant introductory rubric the scribe changed patience to steadfastness and fidelity,
and woman to girl: "Incipit historia Griseldis puelle constantissime et
fidelissime" ("Here begins the story/history of the most steadfast and
most faithful girl Griselda"), London, BL MS. Harley 3081 (S5; om.
M); in selecting *constantia* Harley 3081 chooses the virtue that Pet-

rarch specifically commends to his readers in his moral conclusion to the tale (6.72, 79). One manuscript describes Griselda as the "calmest (*pacatissime*) woman" (AS 14).

Five further manuscripts, whose rubrics never became standard ones, clearly belong with the manuscripts celebrating Griselda's patience and/or steadfastness and treating her virtue as exemplary. One describes her as "optima puella, pro exemplo pacience" ("the best girl, for the example of her patience"), Cologne, Hist. Archiv MS. GB 4° 214 (AS59; similarly AS126). Another calls the tale an "Exemplum patientie inaudite" ("An exemplum of unheard of patience"), Milan, Brera MS. AD XI 23 (BG115). In its explicit London, BL MS. Harley 2268 (M94) describes the tale as an "historia . . . patientie." A manuscript already cited (AS186) commends Griselda for her "praiseworthy steadfastness."

Manuscript rubrics for the Griselda rarely offer brief epitomes of her story, but those that do stress her patience. Two related English manuscripts identify Petrarch as the translator and summarize the story of Griselda in their introductory rubrics:

Dominus Franciscus Petrarcha transtulit de vulgari sermone Saluciarum in latinum sequentem historiam sive fabulam de nobili marchione Walterii domino terre Saluciarum quomodo duxit in uxorem Grisildem pauperculam et eius constanciam et paciamciam mirabiliter et acriter comprobavit.

Master Francis Petrarch translated from the vernacular language of Saluzzo into Latin the following history or fable of the noble marquis Walter lord of the land of Saluzzo, [telling] in what manner he took to wife Griselda, a poor little woman, and extraordinarily and harshly/shrewdly proved her steadfastness and patience.

> Cambridge, Corpus Christ MS. 177, f. 76ᵛ (M7);
> see also London, BL MS. Royal 8 B.vi (M131)

This rubric was copied in the Royal MS. by a hand later than that for its text, probably from the Corpus Christi MS., the source of other items in the Royal MS. It stresses not Griselda's wifehood but the virtues which she demonstrated in response to extraordinary testing. The unusual closing rubric of Glasgow University MS. Gen. 1125 (M33) also stresses Griselda's patience and perseverance in her tribulations: "Historia Galteri et Griseldis coniugum . . . de mirabili et virtuosa paciencia et perseverancia Griseldis in tribulationibus sibi illatis per Galterum eius virum" ("The story of Walter and Griselda his wife . . . concerning the admirable and virtuous patience and perseverance of Griselda in tribulations inflicted on her by her husband Walter").

Another brief epitome, apparently unique, occurs in the explicit of Cologne MS. Hist. Archiv. MS. GB 4° 214 (AS59):

> Explicit exemplum paciencie optime puelle Griseldis que primo electa est in comitissam, postea simulatione repudiata et cum in omnibus pacientissime se habuisset, iterum resumpta fuit.

> Here ends the exemplum of the patience of the excellent girl Griselda who first was chosen to be countess, afterward by pretense was repudiated and, since she had conducted herself most patiently in all things, was again taken back [as countess].

Griselda's patience (or steadfastness) is primary for these idiosyncratic scribes and very probably for their readers. Taking account of both beginning and closing rubrics, thirty-five manuscripts in all associate Griselda with patience or patience and/or steadfastness (*constantia*), three with steadfastness and fidelity or peace (BG114, CS162, S5), and one with calmness (AS14).

To conclude this survey of the rubrics to Petrarch's Griselda, I shall consider the implications of distinguishing Griselda's virtues as *obedientia/fides* or as *patientia/constantia*. It is significant that *obedi-*

entia/fides rubrics collocate with the term *uxor* for Griselda. These rubrics invite us to perceive Griselda's example as applicable to wives. Such an interpretation contradicts Petrarch's moral conclusion, which is the strongest reason for doubting that Petrarch composed or approved this rubric for the letter, *Sen.* 17.3, or for the tale within it. Petrarch took some trouble to redirect his story to its new readers of Latin, whom he assumed would be men. He says that he wrote the story not to encourage wives to be like Griselda, a feat scarcely imitable (*vix imitabilis*), but to encourage readers (i.e., men) to behave towards God as Griselda behaved towards her husband. The virtues Petrarch names in his moral conclusion are Griselda's *patientia* (*Sen.* 17.3.6.71, Severs 288; see also 6.80) and *constantia* (6.72; see also 6.79). In the story itself, a number of other virtues are ascribed to her, including *obedientia* and *fides*, but these are not what Petrarch chooses to emphasize in his conclusion. There is no question that male readers could easily deny the application of Griselda's example to themselves and treat the story as useful for encouraging their wives to be compliant. That is the response that Chaucer articulates through Harry Bailly (the Host stanza, 1212a–g). To limit the effect of the story in this way does not, however, seem to be Petrarch's intention, or Chaucer's either, for that matter.

No one has argued that Petrarch had any responsibility for rubrics commending Griselda's patience and steadfastness or has even paid attention to the frequency with which *patientia/constantia* rubrics occur in the manuscripts. Yet these rubrics are compatible with Petrarch's moral conclusion. The more elaborate of them usually acknowledge Griselda's femaleness through the use of the word *mulier*, a word that does not insist on her status as wife and thus does not restrict the application of her example to women, married or marriageable. More rarely, the terms *femina* or *puella* describe Griselda's femaleness in *patientia* rubrics.

278

The difference between the clusters *obedientia/fides* and *patientia/constantia* may not register as a very large one to us, since both sets of virtues tend to be read by us as suitable for passive subordinates, the condition in which we believe most women lived. In the Middle Ages both sets of virtues were interpreted more actively than they generally are now. The greatest difference between *obedientia* and *patientia* arises from the implied relationship of the virtuous person to the world beyond that person. For the religious, *obedientia* and *fides* involved conscious and active willed commitment, in relationship with another to whom one is obedient and devoted. When that "other" is God and the obedient and devoted are monks, these virtues carry little charge of gender. When the "other" is a husband, the charge of gender grows heavy on the obedient and devoted wife, whose dependence was so strongly reinforced by social and legal practice. Late medieval and early Renaissance courtesy literature strongly associates obedience and devotion with wives, as Diane Bornstein has shown (*Distaves* v–xx, *Lady* 46–121); Chaucer's Host uses the story of Griselda to encourage wifely obedience. In restricting the exemplary range of the story to wives who are urged to obedience, the Host diminishes the story. Nevertheless, his reading has been the most accessible one in the twentieth century, encouraged by modern use of the *obedientia/fides* rubric as a title. Modern readers who presume that Petrarch and Chaucer told this story to induce obedience in wives are usually hostile to the story.

The other set of virtues, patience and steadfastness, is associated with spiritual martyrdom (Morse 61–62, 81–83) and also has a distinguished history in ancient literature (on history and meaning, see Burnley and Hanna). They do not depend on the virtuous person's relationship to another for their practice. Patience involves suffering and endurance, which are individual activities, but *patientia*, etymologically related to the word "passive," has not been perceived as an attractive virtue in the twentieth century. In contrast, as Richard Kieckhefer has argued, patience is the most characteristic virtue of fourteenth-century saints. He explains the fashion for it as ultimately a response to the terrible times of famine, plague, and war, woes that were particularly intense in the fourteenth century (50–88). Caroline Walker Bynum argues against Kieckhefer's strongly reactive explanation of the late medieval embrace of suffering and also against the modern, popular tendency to interpret such bodily suffering as a denial of the body (*Holy Feast* 118–19, 211–18, 245–59; ". . . And Woman"). Rather, she maintains that the desire to imitate Christ was sufficient to move women and men to value suffering. Suffering with the suffering Christ offered a way to participate in Christ's redemption of the flesh (see also Kieckhefer 89–124). The excess of suffering—the surplus—that Griselda was willing to offer, which Jill Mann has explored, makes her like fourteenth-century saints as they are described by Bynum and Kieckhefer, though Kieckhefer points out how unlike saints' lives the happy ending of Griselda's story is (83–85).

Suffering makes the sufferer not directly subordinate to but, rather, analogous to Christ. It is a major element in what Weinstein and Bell call an androgynous model of sainthood (236). As they, Kieckhefer, and Bynum among others have shown, women were publicly acknowledged for their heroic suffering in the fourteenth century and helped to create the devotional climate that carried over to the fifteenth century. Women offered examples for admiration and for generalized imitation of their virtues (on the "imitation-wonderment topos," see Kieckhefer 12–14 and Bynum, *Holy Feast* 85 and 336n85). The scribe of Munich, Bayerische Staatsbib. MS. 5683 (AS126) implicitly applies the topos to Griselda when he describes her in his introductory rubric as "admirande paciencie" ("to be admired for her patience") and then in his explicit suggests that Petrarch translated her story to make it profitable to many (see above, p. 273).

Petrarch, in emphasizing Griselda's virtues of patience and steadfastness, implies a Christian subtext that Chaucer exploits by introducing Christian references and allusions (see Kellogg 284–91, Morse 80–81). The virtues of patience and steadfastness are as celebrated in the stoicism of Cicero and Seneca, two of Petrarch's favorite ancient writers, as they are in late medieval interpretations of Christ and the Virgin. Through these virtues, people might achieve governance over themselves, equal to the heroism of conquerors.[16] So, Petrarch implicitly argues, did Griselda achieve heroism, a heroism appropriately presented in a classicized style (Morse 77–81; Bernardo 57, 68–69). Petrarch combined a classicized style and a Christian subtext.

Petrarch's desire to link men—and implicitly himself—with Griselda follows the medieval pattern of male use of the female gender that Bynum describes, where men reverse their sexual role, losing power, authority, and status, in order to share in "the great reversal at the heart of the gospel: that fact that it is the contemptible who *are redeemed*" (*Holy Feast* 284). For Petrarch, there was no serious conflict between his religious life and his love for the ancients when he saw the human role as that of the *patiens*, the suffering one.

Petrarch's emphasis on *patientia* and *constantia* in his moral conclusion separates the example of Griselda from what seems to us its most obvious application, which is to encourage obedience in wives. Petrarch could have denied this literal application while encouraging men's *obedientia* to God, but his own inability to commit himself to a religious order as well as his love of ancient Latin writers make *patientia* and *constantia* more attractive virtues to him. His choice is also more attractive to us. Whether female or male, most of us resist obedience politically, many of us resist it spiritually (whatever our religious tradition encourages), and many of us, male as well as female, resist it domestically. It is a virtue whose practice requires dependence in a world that seems, at least to most modern inheritors of

281

the Christian Latin West, to value independence. While relatively few of our contemporaries will seek likeness to Christ through suffering, the fourteenth-century understanding of this relationship as an analogy in which men and women aim to equal the human Christ has resonance for us as dependency does not. In spite of Petrarch's indifference to women as readers, his interpretation of Griselda's virtue takes it outside the limits of wifely dependence and into the larger world where distinctions in human gender are not the issue; rather, the issue is the appropriate human response to a common human vulnerability to misfortune and pain.

The almost continuous engagement of the Euro-American audience with the story of Griselda as it was fashioned by Petrarch must be ascribable to the way that this compelling tale precariously balances alternative readings—*either* patience and women *and* men, *or* obedience and women. Petrarch tries to control us through his moral conclusion, though *Sen.* 17.4 records one reader's refusal to accept that interpretation or to like the story, rather to Petrarch's annoyance. Mostly, the earliest readers of the story responded positively to it, whether they made a strongly gendered response to Griselda as obedient and devoted wife or a non-gender-specific response to her as an example of patience. In their closing strategies, both Petrarch and Chaucer attempt to deflect readers from a strongly gendered reading of Griselda's example to a non-gender specific reading. Chaucer, comically and ironically, proposes even more responses: in the Envoy and the Host stanza, he satirizes two strongly gendered readings of Griselda, in the process obscuring his own attitude to the story. Chaucer has some moral and intellectual fun exposing different purposes this story may serve, depending on the reader.

Modern readers divide between a hostile or a favorable response to Griselda, depending on whether they perceive her as a weak and submissive wife—a reading encouraged by the *obedientia/fides* rubric,

282

the most common twentieth-century reading—*or* whether they perceive her as strong in maintaining composure, and love, in the face of terrible blows—a reading encouraged by the *patientia/constantia* rubrics and common in the nineteenth century. Because Griselda believes that her husband is murdering their children yet does not protest (she has agreed to accept his will without complaint), her story gives obedience and wifely devotion a bad name in twentieth-century culture that believes a woman has a greater duty to her children than to her husband. Readers before the Romantic era do not register this conflict of duties, but it has led post-Romantic admirers of the story, most of them responding to Chaucer's translation of Petrarch's Latin rather than directly to the Latin tale, to be defensive. One of the least defensive recent readings is Elizabeth Kirk's, a reading that takes Griselda's patience to be a fitting response to the God of late medieval nominalists, who define a universe existentially much like our own.

The many types of manuscript rubrics accompanying Petrarch's Griselda encourage recognition of the openness of this story to alternative interpretations; further, acknowledging the variety of the rubrics can help us to evade what Martin Irvine has called "the interpretive coercion of the editorial title." But since for us single short titles seem to be necessary, we must call Petrarch's Griselda by some, preferably one, name. Our interpretations will be least coerced by adopting what must have been the most common late medieval short title for the story, the simple *Historia Griseldis*. Rubrics that select for us Griselda's virtues have a stronger effect on our interpretation than their brevity would imply. It is probably not accidental that the period of greatest hostility to the Petrarchan version of the tale of Griselda, from the late nineteenth through the first half of the twentieth century, follows upon the widespread use of the Basle title praising Griselda for her obedience and wifely devotion.

What to Call Petrarch's Griselda

NOTES

1. Throughout this essay, I use the terms *scribe* and *scribal* to designate the activities of copyists and supervisors of copyists. Some of their activities were editorial and some authorial; for example, scribes or their supervisors chose to compose, to retain, or to change rubrics, or to have no rubrics at all. I reserve the terms *editor* and *editorial* to describe the activities of people engaged in preparing books for printing.

2. Editors of the Census of Petrarch manuscripts refer to introductory rubrics as titles, no doubt because the only other handy term for designating such material is *incipit*, a term that Petrarchan scholars reserve for the first words of the letter proper. I have consistently used the term *introductory rubric* to designate headings preceding Petrarch's letter to Boccaccio, *Sen.* 17.3, "Librum tuum" or the tale contained in it or abstracted from it, "Est ad Ytalie." I have sometimes called a *closing rubric* by the alternative term *explicit*.

3. The only manuscript for which I am not relying on a published description in classifying rubrics is Cambridge, Peterhouse MS. 81, which I have examined. I have relied on the Italian Ministry of Public Instruction's survey of Petrarch MSS. in the Biblioteche Governative (BG) or on Foligno's survey of MSS. in Milanese libraries, *F. Petrarcha e la Lombardia* (PeL), for six Italian MSS., where these works give full accounts of the introductory rubrics (these surveys are inconsistent). I have used Santoro's catalogue of the Trivulziana for two MSS. and Jordan and Wool for some MSS. in the Ambrosiana. I will cite these works by abbreviations BG, CS, JW, and PeL and, except for JW, page numbers. In other cases, except as noted, I have relied on Severs or the editors of the Censimento dei Codici Petrarcheschi, i.e., the Census.

I have not noted where MSS. are incomplete for loss of leaves or distinguished MSS. that contain the full letter *Sen.* 17.3 from those that contain only the tale. I have included AS34, a Latin epitome, and two other MSS. where the evidence uncertainly represents the MS. rubric for the tale, namely Metz, Bib. Mun. MS. 296 [P6.289]), destroyed in World War II and known from a catalogue, and Eichstätt, Staatsbib. MS. 417 [AS20], incomplete for loss of leaves but with a list of contents.

284

4. Although Fracassetti printed *Sen.* 17.3–4 as one letter, numbered 17.3, he acknowledged the separation of the two letters in older editions in a mid-page note before his translation of "Ursit amor" (2.564); he presumably refers to the Venice 1516 edition and the two MSS. he used, one from Florence's Laurenziana and the other from Venice's Marciana (1.Pref). To Fracassetti, the letter "Ursit amor" seemed not to be a separate letter, but a continuation of the third (2.564). Bernardo reports Fracassetti's view without disapproval (56).

5. Wilkins suggests that the missive form of *Sen.* 17.4 ended before "Promiseram memini in quadam ordinis huius epistola," with possibly another brief closing omitted from the collected form of the letter, and with the date. He believes that Petrarch then added the "Promiseram memini" passage. Finally, he added the farewells of the explicit: "They are almost certainly the last words that Petrarch wrote for the *Seniles*: they may indeed have been the last words that he ever wrote" (314).

6. Ricci explains that the Paduan Humanists who prepared the *Seniles* for circulation found no text of the *Posteritati* with the *Seniles*, and that the manuscript of the *Posteritati* to which the note referred was a problematic working draft of an incomplete text (not extant) requiring considerable editorial interpretation (5).

7. Severs 290. Subsequent citations for *Seniles* 17.3 will be to Severs's edition: for "Librum tuum," preface and line number, and for "Est ad ytalie," by part and line number. For *Seniles* 17.4, see Golenistcheff-Koutouzoff's edition.

8. Hirsh lists seven incunabula editions of Petrarch's Griselda (58). Four offer introductory rubrics containing "de Historia Griseldis mulieris maxime constantie et patientie. In preconium omnium laudabilium mulierum" (from Zell 1470). Three present "de insignis obedientia et fides uxoria."

9. Manuscripts will be referred to by their numbers in these descriptive lists, preceded by the first letter(s) of the editor's name, e.g., Ij1 (Ijsewijn, No. 1 in his list); M7 (Mann, No. 7). I make the following exceptions: Pellegrin's supplement to Vattasso

will be VP; Santoro will be C5 and Sottili will be AS to distinguish them from Severs (S). Pellegrin, who does not number manuscripts in her census for France, will be listed by initial, volume number, and page number, e.g., P4.373 (similarly, Kristeller will be K2.214a). See also note 3, above, Appendices I–III, and Bibliography I.

Early parts of the Censimento, or Census, were published in *Italia medieovale e umanistica*. In vol. 22 (1979) E. V. Bernadskaja published a census for the libraries of Leningrad (USSR), reporting no manuscripts of Petrarch's Griselda.

10. Scholars have drawn attention to two corrections in Branca's list. Sottili says that Branca's shelfmark (MS. 112) for Bamberg is in error (10: 453), the Griselda being only in Bamberg, Staatliche Bib. MS. Class. 93 (AS5). The manuscript Branca lists for Mikulov is probably the manuscript now owned by Phyllis Goodhart Gordan, New York City (U63, D87), which was "once MS. 52 in a library, probably that of Prince Dietrichstein of Nikolasburg, Moravia" (Dutschke 219). Pellegrin includes the Montpellier MS. listed by Branca.

11. According to Golenistcheff-Koutouzoff, Paris, BN MS. Lat. 8521, containing only *Sen.* 17.3, begins with an illumination that seems to dramatize Petrarch's debate with the Veronese in *Sen.* 17.4 and shows Petrarch defending *historia*. Above the "title" in this manuscript ("De insigni obedientia et fide uxoria"), one sees "une curieuse miniature qui représente Pétrarque parlant avec un ami. Le poète couronné est vêtu d'un long vêtement rouge et coiffé d'un bonnet également rouge, doublé de fourrure blanche. Il est assis dans un fauteuil rose, en face de son interlocuteur assis dans un fauteuil d'or. Entre eux, sur un pupitre, on remarque un livre ouvert. Au-dessus d'eux, sortant de tourelles violettes, deux hommes barbus font des gestes énergiques qui signifient 'oui' et 'non.' Il semble qu'ils discutent de la vraisemblance de l'histoire, puisque sur les bandelettes qui les entourent on lit du côté de Pétrarque: *Possible*, et du côté de son interlocuteur: *Impossible*." (15n2)

12. I have examined all the editions in the British Library of Foresti's *Supplementum chronicarum*. The following Latin editions and translations contain the epitome of Griselda's story (see Johnson 273 and the *British Library Catalogue*):

Supplementum chronicarum

Brescia 1485 (*BLC* IB.31089), f. 246

Venice 1486 (*BLC* IB.22311), f. 212^r (imperf.)

Venice 1490 (*BLC* IB.20536(2)), f. 178

Venice 1492/93 (*BLC* IB.22654), ff. 175^v–176^r

Cronicha de Tuto el Mondo Vulgare.

Venice 1491 (*BLC* IB.22651), f. 208

Supplementum supplementi de le chroniche vulgare. Trans. Francesco C. Fiorentino.

Venice 1520 (*BLC* 9006.i.10), f. 213

Venice 1524 (*BLC* C.64.g.9), ff. 211^r–213^v

Venice 1535 (*BLC* 9006.i.11), f. 213

Venice 1540 (*BLC* 216.d.11), ff. 208^v–209^r

Venice 1553 (*BLC* 581.i.1), f. 207

Sopplimento delle croniche vniuersali del mondo, trans. F. Sansovino.

Venice 1581 (*BLC* 580.e.10), ff. 390^r–391^v

Suma da todas las Cronicas del mondo. Trans. N. Viñoles.

Valencia 1510 (*BLC* C.63.k.17), ff. CCCIX^v–CCCX^v

Foresti also included an abbreviated version of the story of Griselda in his *De plurimis claris . . . mulieribus* (*BLC* 167.h.17), ff. 133^v–134^v.

13. Vattasso and Severs do not agree on the reading of the rubric in Vatican MS. Lat. 3355 (V23, S12): what Severs reads as *Fidem*, Vattasso interprets as *F<ranciscus> idem.*

14. AS104, AS155, AS181, AS198, AS218, AS256, D14, M19, M227, P4.373, P4.396, P6.304, PeL282, S2, V4, V65, V88.

15. Also BG115, D78 *var.*, Ij27, Ij49, M103, P6.301a *var.*, V91, V94.

16. See Philippe de Mézières, *Prol.* 23–54, in Golenistcheff-Koutouzoff 153–54; and Morse 77–79.

What to Call Petrarch's Griselda

APPENDIX I: Classifiable MSS. Containing Petrarch's *Historia Griseldis*

For a key to the abbreviations used, see Bibliography I and nn. 3 and 9.

AS5; K3.462b	Bamburg, Staatsbib. MS. Class. 93, ff. 173^v–180^v
AS10	Bonn, Universitätsbib. MS. 365, ff. 155^r–165^v
AS14	Darmstadt, Hessiche Landes-und Hochschulbib. MS. 679, ff. 114^r–118^r
AS18	Donaueschingen, Fürstlich-Fürstembergische Hofbib. MS. 412, ff. 204^r–216^v
AS20	Eishstätt, Staatsbib. MS. 417, [f. 20]: Table of contents
AS29	Erpernburg bei Brenken (Paderborn), Bib. des Freiherrn von Brenken MS. B 9, ff. 47^r–56^r
AS34	Fulda, Hessische Landesbib., MS. 4° C.10, ff. 107^r–108^r
AS40	Harburg, Fürstlich Oettingen-Wallerstein'sche Bib. und Kunstsammlung MS. II Lat. 1 4° 33, ff. 267^v–275^r
AS55	Cologne, Erzbischöfliche Diözesan-Bib. MS. 92, pp. 273a–295b
AS56	Cologne, Historisches Archiv der Stadt Köln MS. GB f 188, ff. 35^{v}a–40^{v}a
AS59	Cologne, Historisches Archiv der Stadt Köln MS. GB 4° 214, ff. 42^r–49^v
AS75	Mainz, Stadtbib. MS. 471a, ff. 43^r–52^v
AS87; S21	Munich, Bayerische Staatsbib. MS. 78, ff. 90^v–95^r
AS96; S43	Munich, Bayerische Staatsbib. MS. 361, ff. 146^r–152^v
AS104; S44	Munich, Bayerische Staatsbib. MS. 504, ff. 53^r–59^v
AS118; S6	Munich, Bayerische Staatsbib. MS. 5311, ff. 245^r–253^r
AS120	Munich, Bayerische Staatsbib. MS. 5350, ff. 219^v–222^v
AS122; S45	Munich, Bayerische Staatsbib. MS. 5377, ff. 219^r–224^v
AS126; S46	Munich, Bayerische Staatsbib. MS. 5683, ff. 262^r–267^r
AS128; S47	Munich, Bayerische Staatsbib. MS. 6379, ff. 148^r–151^v
AS140	Munich, Bayerische Staatsbib. MS. 14134, ff. 162^v–166^r
AS154	Munich, Bayerische Staatsbib. MS. 23820, ff. 213^{v}a–217^{v}b

AS155; S48	Munich, Bayerische Staatsbib. MS. 24504, ff. 104^v–114^r
AS162	Munich, Universitätsbib. 2° Cod. MS. 667, ff. 14^r–17^r
AS167	Munich, Universitätsbib. 4° Cod. MS. 806, ff. 243^v–251^r
AS173	Stuttgart, Württembergische Landesbib. MS. HB XII Poet.lat.4, ff. 258^v–265^v
AS181	Trier, Stadtbib. MS. 596/2038 4°, ff. 30^{r}a–34^{v}a
AS186	Trier, Stadtbib. MS 1879/74 8°, ff. 140^r–147^v
AS198	Wolfenbüttel, Herzog-August-Bib. MS. 45.6 Aug., ff. 40^r–42^v & 47^r–48^r
AS218	W.Berlin, Staatsbib. MS. Theol. Lat. fol. 194, ff. 102^{v}b–105^{v}b
AS224	W.Berlin, Staatsbib. MS. Lat. fol. 29, ff. 13^r–17^r
AS230	W.Berlin, Staatsbib. MS. Lat.qu.277, ff. 35^r–50^v
AS234	W.Berlin, Staatsbib. MS. Lat.qu.389, pp. 1–14
AS236	W.Berlin, Staatsbib. MS. Lat.qu.432, ff. 175^r–184^v
AS238	W.Berlin, Staatsbib. MS. Lat.qu.468, ff. 1^r–7^v
AS241	W.Berlin, Staatsbib. MS. Lat.qu.936, ff. 91^r–92^r
AS256	Eichstätt, Staatsbib. MS. 186 (formerly 387), ff. 263^r–268^v
B11	Basel, Universitätbib. MS. F.VIII.18, ff. 98^r–106^v
B17; S68	Bern, Burgerbib. MS. Cod. 531, ff. 213^r–224^v
B18; S69	Bern, Burgerbib. MS. Cod. 550, ff. 83^v–93^v
B33	Zurich, Zentbib. MS. Car. C 26, ff. 32^r–33^r
B37	Zurich, Zentbib. MS. Car. VI 60, ff. 1^r–5^v
BG50; S52	Florence, Laur. MS. Strozzi 91, ff. 164^r–170^v
BG114; S58	Milan, Brera MS. AD XI 43, ff. 1^r–14^v
BG115; S57	Milan, Brera MS. AD XI 23, ff. 100^r–108^v
BG164	Pavia, Bib. Universitaria MS. CXXX.D.21, ff. 167–74
CS162; PeL314^2	Milan, Bib. Trivulziana MS. 704, ff. 193^r–2014
CS184; PeL314^3	Milan, Bib. Trivulziana MS. 761, ff. 36^r–42^r

289

D14; U8	Bloomington IN, Indiana Univ. Lilly Lib. Poole MS. 26, ff. 46ʳ–52ʳ
D77; U54	New Haven CT, Yale Univ. Beinecke MS. a 17 (Osborn Shelves), ff. 83ᵛ–93ʳ
D78; U56	New Haven CT, Yale Univ. Beinecke MS. 197, ff. 1ʳ–7ʳ
Ij1	Brugge, Grootseminarie MS. 113/78, ff.191ʳa–198ʳb
Ij4	Brussels, Bib. Royale MS. 859 (858–61), ff. 804–83ᵛ
Ij13; S66	Brussels, Bib. Royale MS. 5116 (5113–5120), ff. 171ʳ–172ᵛ
Ij27; S67	Brussels, Bib. Royale MS. 15008 (1503–15048), ff. 60ʳ–64ᵛ
Ij33	Brussels, Bib. Royale MS. II 1159, ff. 37ʳ–40ᵛ
Ij46	Liège, Grand Séminaire MS. 6.F.13, ff. ff. 1ʳ–7ᵛ
Ij49	Liège, Grand Séminaire MS. 6.L.21, ff. 224ʳ–233ʳ M7; S25
JW	Milan, Ambrosiana MS. A 136 sup., ff. 113ʳ–120ᵛ
M7; S25	Cambridge, Corpus Christi MS. 177, ff. 76ᵛ–80ᵛ (now 52ᵛ–56ᵛ)
M8; S13	Cambridge, Corpus Christi MS. 275, ff. 163ʳ–168ᵛ
M9; S18	Cambridge, Corpus Christi MS. 458, ff. 108ʳ–121ᵛ
M19; S26	Cambridge, Peterhouse MS. 81 (*Seniles*), ff. 185ʳ–187ᵛ
M33	Glasgow, Glasgow Univ. Lib. MS. Gen. 1125, ff. 218ʳ–220ʳ
M39	Glasgow, Glasgow Univ. Lib. MS. Hunter 480, ff. 1ʳ–5ᵛ
M49; S27	London, BL MS. Add. 10094, ff. 67ʳ–73ᵛ
M85; S28	London, BL MS. Cotton Vespasian E.XII, ff. 77ᵛ–85ʳ
M94; S29	London, BL MS. Harley 2268, ff. 6ᵛ–10ᵛ
M96; S19	London, BL MS. Harley 2492, ff. 288ᵛ–293ᵛ
M103; S30	London, BL MS. Harley 2678, ff. 89ʳ–92ᵛ
M131; S31	London, BL MS. Royal 8 B.VI, ff. 33ᵛ–43ʳ
M132; S32	London, BL MS. Royal 12 C.xx, ff. 58ᵛ–65ᵛ
M155; S35	Oxford, Balliol MS. 146B, ff. 54ʳ–59ᵛ
M208; S33	Oxford, Bodleian MS. Canonici misc. 297, ff. 98ʳ–108ʳ
M210; S34	Oxford, Bodleian MS. Canonici misc. 352, ff. 14ʳ–21ʳ

M225; S15	Oxford, Bodleian MS. Lat. misc. d.34, ff. 46^r–53^v
M227; S36	Oxford, Bodleian MS. Laud misc. 743, ff. 84^r–89^v
M241; S14	Oxford, Magdalen MS. 39, ff. 24^v–34^r
P4.373; S40	Paris, BN MS. Lat. 5919 B, ff. 21^r–26^v
P4.396; S41	Paris, BN MS. Lat. 8521, ff. 2^r–24^r
P4.400; S42	Paris, BN MS. Lat. 8571 (*Seniles*), ff. 191^v–196^v; see Golen-istcheff-Koutouzoff 14, 248n1
P4.407; S16	Paris, BN MS. Lat. 11291, ff. 11^v–18^r
P4.409	Paris, BN MS. Lat. 14582, ff. 265^r–271^r
P4.413; S20	Paris, BN MS. Lat. 16232, ff. 99^r–103^r
P4.418; S39	Paris, BN MS. n.a. lat. 134, ff. 51^v–60^r
P4.421	Paris, BN MS. n.a. lat. 967, ff. 25^r–41^v
P6.284	Lille, Bib. Municipale MS. 624 (418), ff. 221^r–225^r
P6.285; S37	Lyon, Bib. Municipale MS. 128 (60), ff. 204^v–211^v
P6.286; S38	Lyon, Bib. Municipale MS. 168 (100), ff. 137^r–143^v
P6.289	[Metz, Bib. Municipale MS. 296: destroyed in WWII]: catalogue entry
P6.291	Montpellier, Bib. Fac. Medicine MS. 432, ff. 130^r–143^v
P6.294	St.Omer, Bib. Municipale MS. 327, ff. 60^v–67^v
P6.301a	Strasbourg, Bib. Nat. & univ. MS. 92 (lat. 89), ff. 1^r–9^r
P6.304	Vendôme, Bib. Municipale MS. 112, 35^r–39^v
PeL277; S54	Milan, Ambrosiana MS. B 116 sup., ff. 138^r–142^v
PeL282; S55	Milan, Ambrosiana MS. H 192 inf., pp. 103–13.
PeL281; S56	Milan, Ambrosiana MS. O 57 sup., ff. 70^r–81^r
S2	Florence, Laurenziana MS. 78.3 (*Seniles*), ff. 221^v–227^v
S3	Florence, Laurenziana MS. a.d. 266 (*Seniles*), ff. 151^v–154^v
S4	Florence, Laurenziana MS. 78.2, ff. 112^r–118^v
S5	London, BL MS. Harley 3081, ff. 223^r–228^v
S10	Florence, BN Cent. MS. Magliabechiano II, IV, 109, ff. 21^r–25^r

| S11 | Florence, Bib. Ricciardana MS. 805, ff. 13ᵛ–19ʳ |
| S17 | Paris, BN MS. Lat. 17165, ff. 191ʳ–193ʳ |

V4; S1	Vatican, Bib. Apos. MS. Vat. Lat. 1666, ff. 17ʳ–21ᵛ
V23; S12	Vatican, Bib. Apos. MS. Vat. Lat. 3355, ff. 129ᵛ–136ᵛ
V33; S64	Vatican, Bib. Apos. MS. Vat. Lat. 4518, ff. 50ʳ–53ʳ
V65; S65	Vatican, Bib. Apos. MS. Vat. Lat. 6875, ff. 285ʳ–292ʳ
V84; S60	Vatican, Bib. Apos. MS. Pal. Lat. 608, ff. 169ʳ–172ᵛ
V88; S61	Vatican, Bib. Apos. MS. Pal. Lat. 1585, ff. 192ᵛ–202ʳ
V91; S22	Vatican, Bib. Apos. MS. Pal. Lat. 1625, ff. 248ʳ–256ᵛ
V94; S62	Vatican, Bib. Apos. MS. Pal. Lat. 1794, ff. 146ᵛ–153ʳ
V117; S63	Vatican, Bib. Apos. MS. Reg. Lat. 1992, ff. 32ʳ–36ᵛ
VP2; K2.490	Vatican, Bib. Apos. Archiv. San Pietro, MS. C.133, ff. 88ᵛ–90ᵛ
VP12; K2.484	Vatican, Bib. Apos. MS. Chigi I.VI.215, ff. 127ʳ–131ᵛ
VP31; S24	Vatican, Bib. Apos. MS. Chigi L.VII.262, ff. 69ᵛ–74ʳ
VP52	Vatican, Bib. Apos. MS. Rossi 526 (IX 216), ff. 178ᵛ–182ᵛ
VP56	Vatican, Bib. Apos. MS. Rossi 717 (X 97), 14ʳ–16ʳ
VP 80	Vatican, Bib. Apos. MS. Vat. Lat. * 11507, ff. 97aᵛ–99ᵛ

Unclassifiable MSS. of the *Historia Griseldis* in the Census

AS25	Erlangen,Universitätsbib. MS. 641, *Seniles*
AS119	Munich, Bayerische Staatsbib. MS. 5340, *Seniles*
AS166	Munich, Universitätsbib. 4° Cod. MS. 768, ff. 35ᵛ–40ʳ
AS253	Ansbach, Staatliche Bib. MS. Lat. 73, *Seniles*
AS272	Ottobeuren, Bib. der Abtei MS. O.22 (II 353), ff. 247ʳ–253ʳ

| D87 | New York City, Phyllis Goodhart Gordan MS. 33, ff. 110ᵛ–118ʳ |

| P6.281 | Carcasonne, Bib. Municipale MS. 38, *Seniles* |
| P6.301b | Toulouse, Bib. Municipale MS. 818, *Seniles* |

APPENDIX II: Severs MSS. Correlated with Census MSS.

S1	V4	S38	P6.286
S6	AS118	S39	P4.418
S12	V23	S40	P4.373
S13	M8	S41	P4.396
S14	M241	S42	P4.400
S15	M225	S43	AS96
S16	P4.407	S44	AS104
S18	M9	S45	AS122
S19	M96	S46	AS126
S20	P4.413	S47	AS128
S21	AS87	S48	AS155
S22	V91	S52	BG50
S24	VP31	S54	PeL277
S25	M7	S55	PeL282
S26	M19	S56	PeL281
S27	M49	S57	BG115
S28	M85	S58	BG114
S29	M94	S60	V84
S30	M103	S61	V88
S31	M131	S62	V94
S32	M132	S63	V117
S33	M208	S64	V33
S34	M210	S65	V65
S35	M155	S66	Ij13
S36	M227	S67	Ij27
S37	P6.285	S68	B17
		S69	B18

Note that S2, S3, S4, S5, S10, S11, and S17 are included in Appendix I. S49, S50, S51, S53, and S59 are among the unclassifiable MSS. S7, S8, S9, S23, S70, S71, and S72 are printed editions.

What to Call Petrarch's Griselda

APPENDIX III: Further MSS. Containing Petrarch's *Historia Griseldis*

Branca (226n7) lists thirty-two MSS. of Petrarch's *Historia Griseldis*, only three of which are included in the Census (AS5, D87, P6.291).

A cursory, not an exhaustive survey of Kristeller's *Iter Italicum*, a finding list that does not include manuscript rubrics, has yielded a further twenty-seven manuscripts plus one of the "Librum tuum," which I present by country, with volume and page number for Kristeller in parentheses:

AUSTRIA
Fiecht bei Schwaz, Stiftsbib. MS. 132 (3.12b); Göttweig, Stiftsbib. MS. 455, now 510 (3.15b); Kremsmünster, Stiftsbib. MS. 375 (3.23b); St. Paul im Lavanttal, Stiftsbib. MS. 27/4, formerly XXVIII b 79 and 28.4.9, with *Sen.* 17.3–4 (3.48a); Seitenstetten, Stiftsbib. MS. 19, the *Seniles* (3.51a); Vienna, Dominikanerkloster MS. 30/30 (3.52b).

CZECHOSLOVAKIA
Olomouc, Státni Archiv MS. CO 418 (3.158a); Id. MS. CO 509 (3.158b).

GERMANY
Leipzig, Univ. MS. 1279 (3.418a); Id. MS. 1269 (3.422).

ITALY
Bergamo, Bib. Civ. MS. Lambda I 20 (1.13b); Genoa, Bib. Civ. Berio MS. 10.6.65 (1.239b); Milan, Ambros., MS. Cimelii C 141 inf. (1.319b); Venice, Marc. MS. 478 (1661) (2.214a); Id., MS. Lat. Classe XI 17 (4517), the *Seniles* (2.234a).

NETHERLANDS
Cuyk-Sint-Agatha, Kruisheerenklooster MS. C 19 (4.339a); Rotterdam, Bib. en Leeszalen der Gemeente MS. 96 C 9 (4.380a).

POLAND

Cracow, Bib. Jag. MS. 42 (4.403b); Id. MS. 126 (4.404a); Id. MS. 173 (4.494b); Wroclaw, Bib Univ. MS. IV F 61 (4.425a); Id. MS. IV Q 18 (4.426a), "Librum tuum" only; Bib. Ossol. MS. 601/I (4.440a).

SPAIN

Madrid, BN MS. 5779 (Q 107), the *Seniles* (4.528b); Id. MS. 19358 (4.578b); Salamanca, Bib. Univ. MS. 148, the *Seniles* (4.604a); Valencia, Bib. Cat. MS. 220, formerly 260 (4.650a); Bib. Univ. MS. 440 (4.653a).

I found no listings of Petrarch's Griselda under PORTUGAL. In the 1981 edition of *Boccaccio medievale* (348) Branca adds a number of MSS. to those listed in his original note, but most of these are included in Severs, the Census, Kristeller, or Branca's original note: the added note contains many careless errors. It may be that the following four MSS. contain Petrarch's Latin Griselda; if so, they should be added to the list of 188 MSS: Florence, Bib. Riccardiana MS. 991; Lille, Bib. Mun. MS. 128 (60); Venice, Bib. Naz. Marciana MS. lat. XI 101 (3939); and Pamplona, Bib. de la Catedral MS. 23. Milan, Bib. Ambros. MS. D 116 is a mistake for MS. B 116 sup. (see Jordan and Wool). Jordan and Wool add Milan, Bib. Ambros. MS. A 136 sup.

APPENDIX IV: Classifiable and Unclassifiable MSS.

Classifiable MSS.:

 60 from Severs (S)

 56 from the Census

 2 from Caterina Santoro (CS)

 1 from Jordan and Wool (JW)

 119 TOTAL

Unclassifiable MSS.:

 5 from Severs (S)

 8 from the Census

 29 from Branca

 27 from Kristeller (K)

 69 TOTAL

Charlotte Cook Morse

BIBLIOGRAPHY I: MSS. of the *Historia Griseldis*

These descriptive lists of manuscripts contain works by Petrarch (see also Branca and Golenistcheff-Koutouzoff, Bibliography III), several of them published for the Censimento dei Codici Petrarcheschi (CCP; also cited as Census) under the general editorship of Giuseppe Billanovich. Each work is preceded by the letter(s) of abbreviation used to identify it in this essay.

B =   Besomi, Ottavio. "Codici Petrarcheschi nelle biblioteche svizzere." *Italia medioevale e unmanistica* 8 (1965): 369–429. Monograph: CCP 3. Padua: Antenore, 1967.

D =   Dutschke, Dennis. *Census of Petrarch Manuscripts in the United States.* CCP 9. Padua: Antenore, 1986.

PeL =   Foligno, C., *et al.* "I Codici Petrarcheschi delle Biblioteche Milanesi." *F. Petrarca e la Lombardia.* Ed. A. Annonni *et al.* Società Storica Lombarda. Milan: Ulrico Hoepli, 1904. 263–341.

Ij =   Ijsewijn, Gilbert Tournoy-Jozef. *I Codici del Petrarca nel Belgio.* CCP 10. Padua: Antenore, 1988.

JW =   Jordan, Louis, and Susan Wool, eds. *Inventory of Western Manuscripts in the Biblioteca Ambrosiana . . . The Frank M. Folsom Microfilm Collection.* University of Notre Dame Pubs. in Medieval Studies 22/1 and 22/2. Notre Dame: U of Notre Dame P, 1984, 1986.

K =   Kristeller, Paul Oskar. *Iter Italicum: A Finding List of Uncatalogued or Incompletely Catalogued Humanistic Manuscripts of the Renaissance in Italian and Other Libraries.* 4 vols., 1 part. London: Warburg Institute, and Leiden: E. J. Brill, 1963–89.

M =   Mann, N. "Petrarch manuscripts in the British Isles." *Italia medioevale e umanistica* 18 (1975): 139–527. Monograph: CCP 6. Padua: Antenore, 1975.

What to Call Petrarch's Griselda

BG =   Ministero dell'Istruzione pubblica [Italy]. *I Codici petrarcheschi delle Biblioteche Governative del Regno*. Compiled by E. Narducci. Rome, 1874.

VP =   Pellegrin, E. "Manuscrits de Pétrarque à la Bibliothèque Vaticane. Supplément au catalogue de Vattasso." *Italia medioevale e umanistica* 18 (1975): 73–138; 19 (1976): 493–97. Monograph: CCP 5. Padua: Antenore, 1976.

P =   Pellegrin, E. "Manuscrits de Pétrarque dans les bibliothèques de France." *Italia medioevale e umanistica* 4 (1961): 341–431; 6 (1963): 371–464; 7 (1964): 405–522. Monograph: CCP 2. Padua: Antenore, 1966.

CS =   Santoro, Caterina. *I Codici medioevali della Biblioteca Trivulziana*. Milan: Biblioteca Trivulziana, 1965.

S =   Severs. "Manuscripts of Petrarch's Latin Tale of Griseldis (SEN. XVII 3)." *Literary Relationships* 41–58 (see Bibliography III) .

AS =   Sottili, Agostino. "I codici del Petrarca nella Germania Occidentale." *Italia medioevale e umanistica* 10 (1967): 411–91; 11 (1968): 345–448; 12 (1969): 335–476; 13 (1970): 281–467 (Monograph: CCP 4. Padua: Antenore, 1971); 14 (1971): 313–402; 15 (1972): 361–423; 18 (1975): 1–72; 19 (1976): 429–92. Monographs: CCP 4, 7. Padua: Antenore, 1971, 1978.

V =   Vattasso, Marco. *I Codici Petrarcheschi della Biblioteca Vaticana*. Studi e Testi, 20. Rome: Vatican, 1908.

U =   Ullman, Bernard L. "Petrarch Manuscripts in the United States." *Italia medieovale e umanistica* 5 (1962): 443–70. Monograph: CCP 1. Padua: Antenore, 1964.

Z =   Zamponi, Stefano. *I Manoscritti Petrarcheschi della Biblioteca Civica di Trieste*. CCP 8. Padua: Antenore, 1984.

Charlotte Cook Morse

BIBLIOGRAPHY II: Latin texts of *Seniles* 17.3, 17.4

Furnivall, F. J., et al., eds. *Originals and Analogues of Some of Chaucer's Canterbury Tales*. Chaucer Soc., Pt. II, Vol. 10. London 1875. 151–70, *Sen.* 17.3; 170–72, *Sen.* 17.4.

Golenistcheff-Koutouzoff, Elie. *L'Histoire de Griselidis en France au XIVe et XVe siècle*. Paris: E. Droz, 1933. 249–74, *Sen.* 17.3–4, based on Paris BN MS. lat. 8571.

Petrarch, Francis. [*Opera*]. 2 vols. Venice 1501. 2.13iij^v–[13vj], *Sen.* 17.3–4.

Petrarch, Francis. [*Opera*]. Venice 1503. 2.CCii–[CCiv^v], *Sen.* 17.3–4.

Petrarch, Francis. *Opera . . . omnia*. 4 vols. in 1. Basle 1554. 1.600–607, *Sen.* 17.3–4. 2.812–1070, *Rerum senilium libri*, ending with 17.2 numbered 16.2.

Petrarch, Francis. *Opera . . . omnia*. 4 vols. in 1. Basle 1581. 1.540–47, *Sen.* 17.3–4. 2.735–968, *Rerum senilium libri*, ending with 17.2 numbered 16.2.

Severs, J. Burke. *Literary Relationships* (see Bibliography III).

What to Call Petrarch's Griselda

BIBLIOGRAPHY III: General

Allen, Judson Boyce. *The Friar as Critic: Literary Attitudes in the Later Middle Ages.* Nashville: Vanderbilt UP, 1971.

Barber, Marjorie. "Petrarch: De Insigni Obedientia et Fide Uxoris." *The Clerk of Oxford's Tale.* Ed. Barber. London: Macmillan, 1956. 67–80.

Bernardo, Aldo S. "Petrarch's Autobiography: Circularity Revisited." *Annali d'Italianistica* 4 (1986): 45–72.

Boccaccio, Giovanni. *Il Decamerone.* Ed. Vittore Branca. Florence: Presso l'Accademica della Crusca, 1976.

———. *Opere latine minore.* Ed. Aldo Francesco Massèra. Scrittori d'Italia. Bari: Gius. Laterza, 1928. [Vol. 9 of *Opere.* 14 vols. Bari: Laterza, 1918–38.]

Bornstein, Diane, ed. *Distaves and Dames: Renaissance Treatises For and About Women; Facsimile Reproductions.* Delmar NY: Scholars' Facsimiles & Reprints, 1978. v–xx.

———. *The Lady in the Tower: Medieval Courtesy Literature for Women.* Hamden CT: Archon, 1983.

Branca, Vittore. *Boccaccio medievale.* Florence: Sansoni, 1956. 4th ed., 1975.

Burnley, J. D. *Chaucer's Language and the Philosophers' Tradition.* Chaucer Studies, no. 2. Cambridge: D. S. Brewer; Totowa NJ: Rowman and Littlefield, 1979.

Bynum, Caroline Walker. "'. . . And Woman His Humanity': Female Imagery in the Religious Writing of the Later Middle Ages." *Gender and Religion: On the Complexity of Symbols.* Ed. Caroline Walker Bynum, Steven Harrell, and Paula Richman. Boston: Beacon, 1986. 257–88.

300

————. *Holy Feast, Holy Fast: The Religious Significance of Food to Medieval Women.* Berkeley: U of California P, 1987.

Chaucer, Geoffrey. "The Clerk's Prologue and Tale." *The Riverside Chaucer.* 3rd ed. General ed. Larry D. Benson. Boston: Houghton Mifflin, 1987. 137–53.

Foresti, Jacobus Philippus, Bergamensis. *De plurimis claris . . . mulieribus.* Venice? 1497.

————. *Supplementum cronicarum.* Brescia, 1485. See also n. 12 above.

Fracassetti, Giuseppe, ed. *Lettere Senili.* By Francesco Petrarca. 2 vols. Florence: Successori Le Monnier, 1869, 1870.

French, Robert Dudley. "A Fable of Wifely Obedience and Devotion." *A Chaucer Handbook.* New York: F. S. Crofts, 1927. 291–311. 2d ed., 1947. 291–311.

Hanna, Ralph, III. "Some Commonplaces of Late Medieval Patience Discussions: An Introduction." *The Triumph of Patience: Medieval and Renaissance Studies.* Ed. Gerald J. Schiffhorst. Orlando: UP of Florida, 1978. 65–87.

Hirsh, Rudolf. "Francesco Petrarca's *Griseldis* in Early Printed Editions, ca. 1469–1520." *Gutenberg Jahrbuch* (Mainz), 1974. 57–65. Rpt. in *The Printed Word: Its Impact and Diffusion,* No. 1. London: Variorum Reprints, 1978.

Johnson, A. F. et al. *Short Title Catalogue of Books Printed in Italy and of Italian Books Printed in Other Countries from 1465 to 1600 Now in the British Museum.* London: British Museum, 1958. *Supplement* by D. E. Rhodes, 1986.

Kadish, Emile P. "Petrarch's *Griselda*: An English Translation." *Mediaevalia* 3 (1977): 1–24.

301

Kellogg, Alfred L. "The Evolution of the *Clerk's Tale*: A Study in Connotation." *Chaucer, Langland, Arthur: Essays in Middle English Literature.* New Brunswick, NJ: Rutgers UP, 1972. 276–329.

Kieckhefer, Richard. *Unquiet Souls: Fourteenth-Century Saints and Their Religious Milieu.* Chicago: U of Chicago P, 1984.

Kirk, Elizabeth D. "Nominalism and the Dynamics of the *Clerk's Tale*: *Homo Viator* as Woman." In *Chaucer's Religious Tales*. Ed. C. David Benson and Elizabeth Robertson. Cambridge UK: D. S. Brewer, 1990. 111–20.

Kolve, V. A., and Glending Olson, eds. *The* Canterbury Tales: *Nine Tales and the General Prologue [by] Geoffrey Chaucer.* Norton Critical Edition. New York: Norton, 1989. Tale, trans. French, 378–88; Preface and Sen. 17.4, trans. Robinson and Rolfe, 388–91.

Mann, Jill. "Satisfaction and Payment in Middle English Literature." *Studies in the Age of Chaucer* 5 (1983): 17–48.

Martellotti, G., et al., eds. *Prose.* By Francesco Petrarca. La letteratura italiano. Storia e testi, 7. Milan and Naples: Riccardo Ricciardi, 1955.

Middleton, Anne. "The Clerk and His Tale: Some Literary Contexts." *Studies in the Age of Chaucer* 2 (1980): 121–50.

Miller, Robert P., ed. *Chaucer: Sources and Backgrounds.* New York: Oxford, 1977. Tale, trans. French, 140–52; Preface and *Sen.* 17.4, trans. Robinson and Rolfe. 136–52.

Morse, Charlotte C. "Exemplary Griselda." *Studies in the Age of Chaucer* 7 (1985): 51–86.

Ong, Walter J. *Ramus, Method, and the Decay of Dialogue: From the Art of Discourse to the Art of Reason.* Cambridge MA: Harvard UP, 1958.

Parkes, Malcolm. "The Influence of the Concepts of *Ordinatio* and *Compilatio* on the Development of the Book." *Medieval Learning and Literature: Essays presented to Richard William Hunt.* Ed. J. J. G. Alexander and M. T. Gibson. Oxford: Clarendon, 1976. 115–41.

Ricci, Pier Giorgio. "Sul Testo della *Posteritati.*" *Studi petrarcheschi* 6 (1956): 5–21.

Robinson, James Harvey, and Henry Winchester Rolfe. *Petrarch: The First Modern Scholar and Man of Letters.* New York: G. P. Putnam's Sons, 1898. 191–96, 53–55. 2d ed., 1914. Rpt. Greenwood Press, 1968. Preface ("Librum tuum"), 191–94; moral conclusion ("Hanc historiam"), 194; and *Sen.* 17.4 ("Ursit amor"), 194–96, 53–55. No translation of the tale.

Severs, J. Burke. *The Literary Relationships of Chaucer's* Clerkes Tale. Yale Studies in English, 96. New Haven: Yale UP, 1942. *Sen.* 17.3, with facing edition of French *Livre*, 254–92. Tale also in *Sources and Analogues of Chaucer's* Canterbury Tales, ed. W. F. Bryan and Germaine Dempster (1941; rpt. New York: Humanities, 1958), 296–331.

Weinstein, Donald, and Rudolph M. Bell. *Saints & Society: The Two Worlds of Western Christendom, 1000–1700.* Chicago and London: U of Chicago P, 1982.

Wilkins, Ernest H. *Petrarch's Later Years.* Mediaeval Academy of America, 70. Cambridge MA: Mediaeval Academy of America, 1959.

'Thys ys my mystrys boke': English Women as Readers and Writers in Late Medieval England[1]

Josephine Koster Tarvers

Could English women read and write in the late Middle Ages? If they could, what did they read and write? Depending on which learned tomes one consults, women were either totally ignorant; or barely able to read and write; or able to compose works of rhetorical sophistication but unable to write them down; or able to compose, write out, copy, and perhaps supervise the distribution of their works. Are any of these—or all of these—positions valid? We know some details about *men's* literacy: approximately how they learned to read and write, what they wrote, and how their manuscripts were copied and passed on. But what of their sisters? How did they learn to read and write?[2] Where did they fit into the literary and literate picture? In what ways did they participate in the manuscript culture of England in the late fourteenth and early fifteenth centuries?

The canonical assumption in literary criticism—one might cynically call it phallogocentric—is that women *do* not fit into the picture, that they did not participate in the rise of vernacular literacy and the consequent explosion of works produced in the late fourteenth and early fifteenth centuries. As evidence to support this position, scholars advance the arguments that Eileen Power made almost seventy years ago with little reassessment. They assert that women could not attend the grammar schools run by the Church and thus lacked access to learning; that nunneries were frequently cited by ecclesiastical

305

authorities in the fifteenth century for the decline of their learning; and that for all the attempts to prove otherwise, the canon of English women writers in the late Middle Ages—if the term is not regarded as an oxymoron—must be limited to Julian of Norwich, Margery Kempe, and Dame Juliana Verners (the last of whom was actually Master Julian Verner, if the latest editor of the *Boke of St. Albans* is correct in assessing the scribal evidence [Hands lv–lx]).

As examples of how this assumption has affected critical assessment of the period, consider just three recent instances. One scholarly text on medieval readers and writers, written by an eminent woman critic, devotes a detailed forty-page chapter to vernacular literacy and education—and mentions only four women in it (Coleman ch. 2). (Two bequeathed manuscripts, a third provided patronage for a male author, and the fourth endowed a grammar school.) Another collection of essays on women in the Middle Ages and Renaissance includes only two essays about women who lived before 1500: one on Margery Kempe, the other on women religious who died to protect their chastity (Rose). Even the *Norton Anthology of Literature by Women* (Gilbert and Gubar) limits the Middle English canon to Julian and Margery, and turns to Queen Elizabeth and the Renaissance with great relief. Here the old saws about women's literacy are repeated without re-examination, a particularly distressing circumstance given the context:

> It is significant . . . that all the writers who flourished in these periods [the Middle Ages and Renaissance] were men. When we turn to the literary history of women in these nine hundred years, we find no texts in the Old English period that have been definitively identified as composed by women, hardly any works by medieval women, and very few indeed by Renaissance women. . . . It is likely, though, that most women did not write, first, because few had access to either the education or the social authority that would facilitate such activity, and second, because, mostly confined to

the home—whether farm, castle, or convent—and constrained by cultural definitions of femininity, most had neither the experience of public life nor the expectation of an audience that would foster creativity. (1)

As Annette Kolodny has aptly observed, we find in literary texts and periods what we expect to find there (151–58). If we believe women lived in only these three communities, we will not look for women writers in the middle or manorial classes. If we believe women only wrote 'creatively,' we will not search the numerous didactic and exegetical texts which survive, often obscurely catalogued, in manuscript. If we believe in the canonical literary histories, we will not look beyond them. If we believe there is little evidence of women's engagement with the literary and literate worlds, we will not expect to find it—and so we are not surprised when we do not.

But what if we change our expectations, discarding these long-ingrained canonical biases? Judson Allen properly argued that we must understand the medieval ways of responding to texts—both reading and, by extension, composing—"way[s] dependent on manuscripts, and further, on the manuscripts which happened to be available . . . in a culture in which books were relatively rare, vastly rarer than they are now" (359). What happens to our assessment of women's literacy when we actually examine the surviving manuscripts produced in medieval England? A different character of evidence emerges then, evidence that women wrote both complete works and letters, copied or had them copied, considered them their property, and proudly indicated their ownership of these texts. Manuscript evidence strongly suggests that women participated in the learned community, though perhaps not to the same extent as men. The character of that historical evidence, which I wish to survey briefly here, may lead us to construct a far different argument from what the canonical critical position predicts. Let me make it clear at the outset that this is by no means a compre-

hensive survey but rather an attempt to organize observations made
while working on other projects. Nearly every medievalist to whom I
have described this essay has been able to expand this list based on
observations of his or her own. Clearly, far more documentation for the
arguments I will advance is available than can be rehearsed in this
space.

First there are those women authors who have been identified—Julian and Margery. Julian's literacy and scholarship are
unquestionable; she is an accomplished stylist, confident, able to call
on a wide range of sources.[3] Her spiritual predecessor, Hildegard of
Bingen, tells us that when *she* began to write, the monk who was her
magister sternly ordered her to keep her writings hidden; only when his
abbot approved did the monk cooperate with Hildegard in her writing:

> Ista cuidam monacho magistro meo intimavi, qui bone conversationis et
> diligentis intencionis ac veluti peregrinus a sciscitationibus morum
> multorum hominum erat, unde et eadem miracula libenter audiebat. Qui
> admirans michi iniunxit, ut ea absconse scriberem, donec videret que et
> unde essent. Intelligens autem quod a deo essent, abbati suo intimavit,
> magnoque desiderio deinceps in his mecum laboravit.
>
> (*Vita*, PL 197; qtd. in Dronke 232)

Julian appears not to have had such strictures placed upon her; she
wrote freely. Margery, the "pore creature," relied on amanuenses (one
of whom apparently exceeded Chaucer's own Adam Scriveyn in
obscurity) to record and read back her dictation for correction (*Book*
3–6; 214–16; 219–20). This may have been a function of her social
status rather an indication of her inability to record her own thoughts;
employment of a scribe was a sign of prestige, not necessarily an
indication of illiteracy. The learned anchoress and the 'illiterate'
housewife: these are the canonical figures of the women writer.

Beyond these two known authors, what else do we know of

medieval English women writers? As is typical with most medieval texts, authorial holograph manuscripts are the exception rather than the rule. More common are copies women ordered to be made for them or for women in their charge. Barking Abbey had a tradition of manuscript-making dating back to Asser's *Vita Alfredi*; the Barking Ordinary preserves a text once removed from its authoress, Katherine of Sutton, Abbess of Barking from 1363–76, who wrote three "animated" liturgical dramas (the term is Karl Young's [1: 167]) in Latin for the nuns of Barking. Her *Depositio, Elevatio*, and *Visitatio* dramatically develop the gospel accounts of the Adoration of the Cross in realistic and innovative fashion. In the colophon to Oxford Univ. Coll. MS. 169 the unnamed copyist notes that the Lady Sibilla de Felton, Katherine's successor, ordered the original to be recopied about 1404, the date of the Barking Ordinary. Sibilla also zealously supervised the *eleccio*, an annual distribution of books among the nuns, suggesting that a considerable portion of the community was literate. And Bodley MS. Holkham Misc. 41 preserves a copy of a prayer cycle composed by a woman, probably reclused, around 1400, for the use of women living together in a community (Tarvers).

Likewise a Kirklees Priory manuscript, now CUL MS. K.k.I.6, compiled by the amateur bibliophile Richard Fox (fol. 245ᵛ), contains a translation from French and Latin to English of the seven penitential Psalms, along with commentary, by Alyanore or Alinor Hull, a widow who ended her life in the Benedictine Priory at Cannington, Somersetshire, about 1460. We know that Alyanore was a book owner; her will leaves to her confessor both her large and small breviaries, her Psalter, and her "blue byble of Latin"—one of the rare copies of the Vulgate in medieval England (Barratt 88). Along with her confessor, the intriguingly-named Roger Huswyf, she donated a four-volume copy of Nicholas of Lyra's *Postilles on the Bible* to St. Albans in 1457 (Ker 301). Alyanore presumably made her translations in the second quarter of the fifteenth century, and one scholar who has closely examined them contends that they were written for an audience, not limited to women, which read French and Latin as well as English (Barratt 95, 100).

Alyanore Hull's is not the only Benedictine woman's work of this period. Library of Congress MS. 4 preserves a translation of the Benedictine Rule into Middle English, probably from the alien Benedictine priory of Lyminster, made after 1415 by a woman scribe whose last name may have been Crane (Krochalis 29–30). An acerbic colophon (fol. 36ʳ) scolding women who mishandle books also makes clear that Lyminster had a large enough library, and literate population, to follow the Rule's prescription to distribute a book to each member each year, for private reading:

> nameliche, of these younge ladies, that thei be nought negligent for to leue here bokes to hem assigned behynde hem in the quer, neyther in cloystre, nether leye here bokes open other vnclosed, ne withoute kepinge, neither kitte out of no book leef ne quaier, neyther write thereinne neyther put out, without leve, neyther leve no book out of the place. Ho so vnwitinge or [sic] his negligence of [sic] mysgouernaunce lest or alieneth [some text omitted; no gap in ms.] bote al so clene and enter that thei ben kept, and in same numbre and in the same state, or in bettre, yif it may, that they be yolde vp agayne in to the librarie, as thei were afore in yer resseyued.

This colophon implies an active, if badly-behaved, group of women readers, who habitually wrote in and corrected their books, as well as cutting out leaves and whole quires of those texts which most engaged them. The call to return books in their original state, "or in bettre," implies a community much concerned about these valuable properties and their preservation. And the scribal errors in that text suggest that it may have been copied from a warning issued to some other group of women readers.

310

Other women's translations of the Rule survive from this period: the Northern metrical version (BL MS. Cott. Vesp. A. 25) was translated "tyll women to make it couth / that leris no latyn in thar youth" (fol. 66ʳ). A Northern prose version of the Rule (BL MS. Lansdowne 378) was copied from a version written for men; the copyist occasionally confuses the pronouns. (This manuscript also contains a rite for administering the Eucharist to nuns.) And nuns play roles in other works; the recently-published *Revelation of Purgatory* (Harley) preserves a fifteenth-century woman's dream-vision of the pains of the nun Margaret after death. One can examine the catalogue of nearly any collection of late-medieval English manuscripts and find similar examples.

Works also survive which were written explicitly for women readers. Into this category fall not only early works such as *Ancrene Wisse* and Richard Rolle's *Form of Living* but Walter of Bibbesworth's *Tretiz de Langage*, composed for Dyonise de Mountechensi to enable her to teach her children French; the text had English glosses: "tut dis troverez-vous primes / le frCnceis e puis le engleise amount" (*Prol.* 20–21). *The Pilgrimage of the Soul*, a fifteenth-century translation into English of DeGuilleville's *Pelerinage de la Vie Humaine* was also intended for female instruction. New York Public Library MS. Spencer 19 of the *Pilgrimage* includes a translator's colophon, signed by one 'AK,' which indicates that the translation was intended for a noble lady.[4] *Disce Mori*, a catechetical treatise, is addressed to "my best-beloved Suster dame Alice," probably a nun of Sion (Patterson ch. 4). The prose *Life of St. Jerome* in Yale UL Beinecke MS. 317, "an unprepossessing little volume of Latin and English devotional writings," was prepared for Margaret, Duchess of Clarence; and the author, Symon Wynter, encouraged her "that hit sholde lyke your ladyship first to rede hit & to do copye hit for yoursilf, & syth to lete oþer rede hit & copye hit, who so wyll" (Keiser, 32, 41). Another manuscript of this work, MS. Lambeth Palace Library 432, expands on Wynter's instructions:

> that not only ye shuld knowe hit the more clerely to your gostely profecte [sic], but also hit shuld mow abyde and turne to edificacion of othir that wold rede hit and do to copy hit for youre selfe, and sith to let other rede hit and copy hit, who so will.

The Chastysing of God's Children may have been written for a nun of Barking; *The Myroure of our Ladye* was translated for the nuns of Sion.

Likewise, *The Orcherd of Syon*, a translation of the *Dialogues* of St. Catherine of Siena, was prepared for the "religyous modir & deuote sustren clepid & chosen bisily to laboure at the hous of Syon" (Hodgson and Liegey, 1). BL MS. Royal 18 A.x includes a form of confession for a woman. MS. Sidney Sussex College (Camb.) 74 contains a treatise on the *Ave Maria* addressed to gentlewomen. MS. Bodley 416 contains the long but acephalous *Boke to a Mother*, as well as a meditation explaining why women should behave on the Sabbath and holy days. Two nuns of Barking, Matilda Hayle and Mary Hastings, once owned BL Addit. 10596, a collection of devotional materials with the Wycliffite versions of the stories of Susanna and Tobias. Many of these manuscripts of pious readings later passed into male hands, according to ownership inscriptions; but their initial audience was literate women.

Women of course had held a place in the educational curriculum of the West since Plato's academy, and their activities as teachers in the early Christian period are well-documented; the names of Hild, Hrotsvitha, Heloise, and Hildegard figure prominently in the spread of Christian education. In fact the institutionalization of learning in monasteries, often double ones, further established a place for women at what Sister Prudence Allen calls "the centre of Christian philosophical activity," albeit in the theoretical rather than practical sense of the phrase. Allen argues strongly that it was the shift from monastic to university-based education, a shift in which women were excluded as teachers and students, which accelerated the separation of men's and women's "tracks" of education (414–15). Nevertheless, some evidence suggests that English women remained active in education. The notarial roles for Boston in 1404 list as a member of the Corpus Christi gild one Maria Mereflete, *magistra scolarum*—that is, mistress of a Latin grammar school; her own writing apparently does not survive (Adamson 59; Orme, 59, calls her 'Matilda'). Mereflete also provides a strong argument that some women were taught Latin grammar; how else could she teach it? An 'E. Scolemaysteresse' received a legacy from a London grocer in 1408; and an 'Elizabeth Scolemaystres' was active in the same city in 1441 (Orme, 55). Although fewer references to English schoolmistresses survive than to continental women teachers at the same time, clearly some English women were active as teachers outside convent walls.

One locus for such women teachers was in the Lollard movement. Among the names of women questioned and sometimes imprisoned for their literate activities are Alice Dexter, the anchoress Matilda, Anna Palmer, Agnes Nowers, Christina More, Agnes Tickhill, Dame Anne Latimer, Dame Alice Sturry, and Katherine Dertford (Cross 360–62). Often they shared their activities with their husbands and children, and wives seem to have carried on their teaching after the imprisonment or death of their husbands. An anonymous homilist in the late fourteenth century lamented that women as well as men served as preachers of the Gospel: "Ecce iam videmus tantam disseminacionem evangelii quod simplices viri et mulieres et in reputacione hominum laici ydiote scribunt et discunt evangelium et quantum possunt et sciunt docent et seminant verbum dei" (CUL MS. I.i.3.8, fol. 149[r]). Margaret Deanesly likewise identified a number of women active as teachers in the Lollard

313

movement; these women faced severe punishment, even death, for such public exercise of their literacy (357–58; 364; 367–79).

Then there are women's letters—substantial in number though again few in holograph. The Paston and Cely letters, for instance are often cited as evidence of women's inability to write, since these upper-middle class women employed scribes and only infrequently endorsed the letters. But employment of a scribe reflected the family's social status—and the ladies of these families, as well as of the Stonors and Plumptons, were indeed very conscious of their rank and consequence as members of the up-and-coming merchant class. They used secretaries as a sign of their social standing—and, if the twenty-nine men who wrote for Margaret Paston are any indication, they were not easy employers. There are several unchallenged women's holographs in the Paston letters, including Elyzabeth Brews' hasty request for armed men to protect her cows against repossession by the sheriff's men (Davis no. 820). The Duchess of Suffolk's intimate and imperative note to the youngest John Paston survives, asking for the loan of his lodgings for several days for a still-unknown reason (no. 798); Elizabeth Mundford's (no. 657) and Elizabeth Clere's (no. 724) correspondence about pending lawsuits include the latter's request for the loan of "j roll callyd domysday" in a real estate dispute. Clere's letter to John Paston I about his mother's abuse of his sister Elizabeth (no. 446) is frequently quoted; but while the part of the letter about the younger Elizabeth's "broken head" is often repeated, few note that her cousin Clere asked John to burn the letter to preserve secrecy or that it was "wretyn in hast on Seynt Peterys Day be candel lyght" in her own hand. Other women's holographs include Margery Cely's "sympyll letter" announcing her first pregnancy to her husband (Hanham no. 222), and Elyzabeth Stonor Rich's letter concerning her "crayzed" daughter Catherine and Elyzabeth's attempts to acquire some of the family silver by subterfuge (Kingsford no. 168). These women all habitually used secretaries and expected scribal copies of their manuscripts to be produced. However, it is equally clear that they could produce manuscripts of their own when circumstances and their own temperaments so moved them, although occasional self-deprecating comments indicate their awareness of their letters' 'unprofessional' appearance. Asta Kihlbohm comments that Elizabeth Rich "could write very well if she chose, though her bold impatient hand—by no means bad—and several smudges of ink indicate that writing was a task she did not particularly relish" (xvi).

Testamentary evidence also shows that women such as Alyanore Hull owned manuscripts and frequently bequeathed them to other women. On the continent at this time books were considered part of a woman's *gerade*—the household goods she would normally inherit from her mother, such as "geese, small farm animals, beds, household furniture, linens, clothing, [and] kitchen utensils" (Bell 155). M. B. Parkes has suggested to me that the "residue" of an estate in England was likewise likely to contain the books; thus, he argues, books are likely to be mentioned in wills only when they are bequeathed separately from the residue. So testamentary evidence of book ownership will reveal exceptions and special cases, not the great majority of book inheritance. Such a situation parallels the case in Germany, where all books connected with pious matters were expected to be inherited by women: "alle Bucher die zum Gottedienste gehore [sic]" and "Bucher die Fraue phlege zu lese [sic]" (Bell 157).

Indeed, all the mentions of books I have yet found in women's wills specify bequests to testators other than the daughters who would receive the remenaunt. Elizabeth, Lady Clare, left all her books to the foundation of Clare College, Cambridge, in 1360 (LaFarge 92). In 1395 Lady Alice West left "a peyre Matyns bookis" to her son Thomas and "a masse book, and alle the bokes that I haue of latyn, englisch, and frensch" to her daughter-in-law Johane (Furnivall 5). Lady Peryne

Clanbowe in 1422 left a massbook to her brother, Sir Robert Whitney, and "a booke of Englyssh, cleped 'pore caytife'" to Elizabeth Joye (Furnivall 49–50). The will of Eleanor Purdeley of London lists "libros Anglicanos, videlicet the Storie of Josep [sic], Patrikek [sic] purgatore, and þe sermon of altqṵyne" in 1433 (Furnivall 2). Manuscripts of *Piers Plowman* frequently descend on the distaff side, suggesting that this great but difficult religio-political poem was considered suitable for female readers; the first known owner of a copy of the poem, William Palmere, received it from a woman (Wood). Deanesly (220–24; 335–43) presents evidence that Wycliffite Bibles and related materials were also bequeathed from woman to woman.[5]

Another canonical assumption about medieval women is that they owned only illustrated manuscripts, since they could not be expected to read the texts. Again the actual physical evidence presents another picture; manuscripts which bear traces of passing through women's hands frequently are without illustration. Sometimes there are scribal colophons to show us these passings, but more often the evidence takes the form of *ex libris* or *ex dono* inscriptions telling us who owned the manuscript and approximately when. The Simeon Manuscript, made around 1400 and intimately related to the great Vernon Manuscript, may have been compiled for Joan Bohun, grandmother of Henry V, and was eventually owned by an "Awdri Norwood."[6] Its contents range widely, from devotional treatises and religious lyrics to romances and contemporary political poetry. Like the Vernon Manuscript it was made for an audience with wide-ranging tastes and multi-lingual ability; the contents of both are in English, French, and Latin, and the decoration of Vernon may also indicate a feminine audience. A. I. Doyle argues that

> an amply-grounded presumption, in England and throughout Europe at this time in the later middle ages, would be that any collection of vernacular

316

religious literature of comparable scope was probably made for nuns or other devout women (anchoresses, vowesses or ladies of similar piety and spiritual counsel). (*Vernon* 14)

Doyle admits that some items in the massive manuscript may indicate lay, male, or mixed readership, but identifies several religious communities of appropriate size and resources to commission Vernon. Moreover, he adduces the case of the related University College Oxford MS. 97, whose scribe regularly dropped the phrase "or womman" from texts where Vernon retains it, to suggest that the earlier Vernon was designed for woman readers (9, 14–15).

There are many other extant examples of manuscripts which passed through the hands of women; the following selection will suggest their variety. The mid fifteenth-century Bodley MS. Ex musaeo 23, a copy of the Middle English religious prose compilation *Aventure and Grace*, came to the ownership of one Thomas Kyngwood in the late fifteenth century "ex dono magistra Anne Bulkeley." Whoever this learned lady was, she owned more than one book, for an autograph prayer signed by her survives in BL MS. Harley 494, and her descendant, Katherine Bulkeley, inherited that manuscript as Abbess of Godstowe around 1533. Another Bodley manuscript, Ex musaeo 232, a compilation made by John Flemmyn[g] of Rolle's meditation on the passion, Gregory on humility, the *Mirror of St. Edmond*, and a number of prayers, bears the ownership marks of two women. An 'Annes Helperby' signed her name several times as owner; and another woman, 'Elyzabethe Stoughton,' also recorded her name. Bodley MS. Laud misc. 416, a miscellany of devotional materials and Middle English poetry, was owned by two nuns of Sion, Anne Colyvylle and Clemencia Thaseburght (Doyle, *A Survey* 2:44). Bodley MS. Rawlinson C. 882, a copy of the *Pore Caitiff*, bears two ownership inscriptions by women: the slightly awkward "Iste liber constat Domina Margarete

Erloy, cum magno gaudio et honore Ihesu Christi", and the more pragmatic "iste liber constat Domina Agnese Lye[ll]; hoo thys boke stelyth, schall have cryst curse and myne." Bodley MS. misc. liturg. 104, made around 1340, is a handsome Latin Psalter with late fourteenth- and early fifteenth-century prayers added in Latin, English, and French. Latin prayers to St. Anne and St. Christopher led Frederic Madan to conclude that the manuscript "had passed into the hands of a husband and wife named Christopher and Anna" (fol. ii^v). And indeed the name of an Anne is preserved in the manuscript; "Anne Cobell" wrote her name in an early fifteenth-century script near the end of the Psalter (fol. 110^v). The ink and inscription very much resemble the handwriting of some of the added prayers, but seven letter forms are not enough to argue with confidence that Anne herself copied some of this material.

One last Bodley manuscript shows with some clarity how fifteenth-century manuscripts passed from woman to woman. Bodley MS. Hatton 73 contains Gower's *Confessio Amantis* and short English poems by Chaucer and Lydgate, along with a few Latin prayers. Its first identifiable owner, if we can correctly decipher its confusing sequence of ownership inscriptions, was a woman named "Katherine," who wrote a few Latin phrases in a mid fifteenth-century hand (fol. 122^v). Then we find "This is my lady more boke. And sumtym it was Quene Margarete boke" (fol. 121^v). The Queen Margaret in question is likely Margaret of Anjóu (1430–82), queen to Henry VI, whose role as patroness of learning is well known. Another inscription tells us that Lady More was "domina margareta more" (1505–44), daughter of Sir Thomas More. From her the book passed to "domina elyzabeth wyndesore" (fol. 1^r). This lady, yet another colophon tells us "quod Clarke," died on January 18, 1513 (fol. 123^r), and the book then passed to Gartrude Powlet (fol. 1^r). According to the *Dictionary of National Biography*, the Mores's home in Chelsea passed to Sir William Paulet, first Marquis of Winchester, in 1537, in return for Paulet's services as one of More's judges. Gartrude, undoubtedly one of Sir William's kinswomen, and a woman named 'Marya' leave their signatures in the book as well (fol. 9ᵛ). Here we have an instance of a book passing from middle-class woman to royalty to gentry, documented chiefly in the women's own hands.

These instances could probably be easily duplicated by any scholar examining a fairly representative collection of late Middle English manuscripts. But once one decides to look for such information, evidence of women's participation in the manuscript culture appears with increasing regularity. A Huntington Library manuscript of Hoccleve and Lydgate (HM EL 26.A.13) contains the handwriting of Elyzabeth Gaynesford and the draft of the beginning of a letter to her sister (fol. 3ᵛ). The elaborate Ellesmere psalter (HM EL 9.H.17) was commissioned by a woman for other women; its colophon records that "domina isabella de vernun dedit istud psalterium conventum de hampul;" and a miniature of Lady Isabella presenting the Psalter to the Virgin and Child is included. A processional of the late fourteenth century (HM EL 34.B.7) is marked "This booke longeth to Dame Margery Byrkenhed of Chestre" (fol. 85ᵛ).

The Huntington Library also includes one of the most remarkable instances indicating a woman's ownership of a manuscript. HM 136 is a rather common manuscript of *The Brut*, covering events up to 1422. But what distinguishes it is the evidence of its ownership by a Mistress Dorothy Helbartun. She signs her name or initials not once, not twice, but more than sixty times. She comes alive again as one turns the pages and finds evidence of her—and of some "servant" of hers—asserting across the years her delight and pride in ownership. She begins simply enough with her initials and short inscriptions such as "dorethe helbartun's boke" but branches out to such variations as "Be yt known to al men thys ys dorethes boke;" "God save her that do owe thys boke, DH"; "Thys ys dorethe helbartun boke And she wyll apon yu loke"; and the aggressively assertive "Wyll yow say thys ys not mystrys dorethes boke? Then yow lye." She even tells us how she obtained it: "Mystrys Barnarde gave her thys boke"; and "Who gave her thys boke? Mare her mother." A servant—perhaps even a suitor—assisted her, recording among other assertions that "I am he that wyll here recorde thys ys my mystrys buke." Ironically, in keeping with the Index of Middle English Prose's bibliographical policy, Ralph Hanna III's admirable handlist of the Huntington manuscripts does not mention any authorship marks in the volume. Dorothy's reaction to such an omission can only be imagined.

Clearly, then, when we put aside our conditioned critical assumption that English women did not participate in the manuscript culture of their world, and look at the manuscripts themselves, we find a different picture from what we had been led to expect. It is clear that some English women, like some English men, did compose literary and didactic works; and, as in the case of their male counterparts, we are fortunate when a woman writer's name is preserved for us. We know that social pretensions aside, women of the upper middle class could and did write letters on subjects ranging from the extremely personal to the moderately larcenous. We know that women inherited Middle English manuscripts containing works at all levels of sophistication; that the contents of these ranged widely, including not only devotional material but poetry and history, in both English and the more "learned" languages of French and Latin. Women considered manuscripts prize possessions, and made dispositions of them, frequently to other women, in their wills. We know too that they indicated their pride of possession in manuscript ownership not only with their signatures but with anathemas against dispossessors. They called themselves *domina* and *magistra*, appellations which attested to their perception of their learning. In short, these women thought of themselves as learned, as

320

participants in a world of reading, writing, and manuscript production.

It is difficult to establish from the surviving records just what percentage of the English population—male and female—could read and write at this period. We know as little about education in this period as we do at any time in English history. We do not know if the alleged "unlettered" condition of women referred to all kinds of learning, or whether, as has been speculated, it meant a decline in the reading of French and all but rudimentary Latin.[7] We do not know why the incidence of women's letters and signatures seems to increase in the 1440s, and why that increase continues throughout the century. All of these areas require further serious inquiry by scholars not only of literature but of history, economics, and gender theory as well. But we know enough to assume that when we talk about reading and writing in England, particularly in the fifteenth century, we have to mention women more than four times, to look not only at Julian of Norwich and Margery Kempe but beyond, to assume that some women authors lived and worked in the period between Margery and Queen Elizabeth. We need to ask not if English women *were* readers and writers, but *what* they read and wrote. In short, we can no longer be content with mouthing the canonical misperceptions of the past; we have to extend the literary and literate history of the late English Middle Ages to include women as well as men.

NOTES

1. An earlier version of this paper was presented at the Twenty-Second International Congress on Medieval Studies, Kalamazoo, 1987. My first acquaintance with many of the manuscripts I discuss here came contemporaneously with my first acquaintance with Judson Allen, in Oxford in the summer of 1983. Those discussions and Judson's friendship remain a great source of inspiration to me. I am deeply indebted to Professor Germaine Greer, then of the University of Tulsa, for providing me with a Tulsa Center

for the Study of Women's Literature Summer Bursary that enabled me to work in Bodley. The manuscripts in the Huntington Library were examined with the generous assistance of a Rutgers University Faculty Summer Research Grant. I am especially indebted to Professors M. B. Parkes, Jeanne Krochalis, and George R. Keiser for suggestions useful in the development of this paper.

2. To begin to appreciate the confusion that surrounds this issue, one need only consult the very different accounts in Orme 52–55 and Ferrante 9–42. It may well be that economic historians will provide the key to understanding this complex situation.

3. Among the many surveys of Julian's learning, a recent concise account may be found in Jones 272–74.

4. I am indebted for knowledge of the Spencer manuscript to Professor Rosemarie McGerr of Yale University, who is preparing an edition of the *Pilgrimage of the Soul*.

5. George Kane first made the suggestion about *Piers Plowman* manuscripts to me. J. I. Catto has been studying the bequests of manuscripts in women's wills; when his work appears it will undoubtedly shed further light on this subject.

6. A. I. Doyle, "Introduction" 15–16. Doyle's identification of "Awdri Norwood" as an Elizabethan signature (16) would seem to negate Janet Coleman's argument that this woman was a contemporary kinswoman of the Cistercian poet/compiler John Northwood (Coleman 78).

7. M. B. Parkes has advanced the latter opinion in "The Literacy of the Laity" 555–77.

MANUSCRIPTS CITED

Cambridge. University Library. MS. I.i.3.8

——————. ——————. MS. K.k.I.6

——————. Sidney Sussex College. MS. 74

London. British Library. MS. Additional 10596

——————. ——————. MS. Cotton Vespasian A. 25

——————. ——————. MS. Harley 494

——————. ——————. MS. Lansdowne 378

——————. ——————. MS. Royal 18 A.x

——————. Lambeth Palace Library. MS. 432

Oxford. Bodleian Library. MS. Bodley 416

——————. ——————. MS. Ex musaeo 23

——————. ——————. MS. Ex musaeo 232

——————. ——————. MS. Hatton 73

——————. ——————. MS. Holkham misc. 41

——————. ——————. MS. Laud Misc. 416

——————. ——————. MS. Misc. liturg. 104

——————. ——————. MS. Rawlinson C. 882

————. University College. MS. 169

San Marino, CA. Huntington Library. MS. EL 9.H.17

————. ————. MS. EL 26.A.13

————. ————. MS. EL 34.B.7

————. ————. MS. HM 136

WORKS CITED

Adamson, John William. *'The Illiterate Anglo-Saxon' and Other Essays*. Cambridge: Cambridge UP, 1946.

Allen, Judson Boyce. "Langland's Reading and Writing: *Detractor* and the Pardon Passus." *Speculum* 59.2 (1984): 342–62.

Allen, Prudence, R.S.M. *The Concept of Woman: The Aristotelian Revolution 750 BC–AD 1250*. Montreal: Eden P, 1985.

Barratt, Alexandra. "Dame Eleanor Hull: A Fifteenth-Century Translator." *The Medieval Translator*. Ed. Roger Ellis. Cambridge: D. S. Brewer, 1989.

Bell, Susan Groag. "Medieval Women Book Owners: Arbiters of Lay Piety and Ambassadors of Culture." *Women and Power in the Middle Ages*. Ed. Mary Erler and Maryanne Kowaleski. Athens: U of Georgia P, 1988.

Coleman, Janet. *Medieval Readers and Writers*. English Literature in History 1350–1400. London: Hutchinson, 1981.

Cross, Claire. "'Great Reasoners in Scripture': The Activities of Women Lollards 1380–1530." *Medieval Women*. Ed. Derek Baker. Oxford: Oxford UP for the Ecclesiastical History Society, 1978.

Davis, Norman, ed. *Paston Letters and Papers of the Fifteenth Century*. Oxford: Oxford UP, 1971–76.

Deanesly, Margaret. *The Lollard Bible*. Cambridge: Cambridge UP, 1920.

Doyle, A. I. "Introduction." *The Vernon Manuscript: A Facsimile of Bodleian Library, Oxford, MS. Eng. Poet. A. 1*. Cambridge: D. S. Brewer, 1987.

———. "A Survey of the Origins and Circulation of Theological Writings in English in the 14th, 15th, and Early 16th Centuries, with Special Consideration of the Part of the Clergy Therein." 2 vols. Diss. Cambridge 1936.

Dronke, Peter. *Women Writers of the Middle Ages: A Critical Study of Texts from Perpetua (203) to Margarete Porete (1310)*. Cambridge: Cambridge UP, 1984.

Ferrante, Joan M. "The Education of Women in the Middle Ages in Theory, Fact, and Fantasy." *Beyond Their Sex: Learned Women of the European Past*. Ed. Patricia H. Labalme. NY: New York UP, 1984.

Furnivall, Frederick J., ed. *The Fifty Earliest English Wills in the Court of Probate, London*. EETS o.s. 78. London: Trubner, 1882.

Gilbert, Sandra M., and Susan Gubar, eds. *The Norton Anthology of Literature by Women*. NY: Norton, 1985.

Hands, Rachel, ed. *English Hawking and Hunting in* The Boke of St. Albans. Oxford: Oxford UP, 1975.

Hanham, Alison, ed. *The Cely Letters 1472–1488*. EETS o.s. 273. London: Oxford UP, 1975.

Hanna III, Ralph. *Index of Middle English Prose Handlist I: A Handlist of the Manuscripts Containing Middle English Prose in the Henry E. Huntington Library*. Cambridge: D.S. Brewer, 1984.

Harley, Marta Powell, ed. *A Revelation of Purgatory by an Unknown, Fifteenth-Century Woman Visionary*. Studies in Women and Religion 15. Lewiston, NY: Edwin Mellen, 1985.

Hodgson, Phyllis and Gabriel M. Liegey, eds. *The Orcherd of Syon*. EETS o.s. 258. London: Oxford UP, 1966.

Jones, Catherine. "The English Mystic: Juliana of Norwich." *Medieval Women Writers*. Ed. Katharina M. Wilson. Athens: U of Georgia P, 1984.

Keiser, George R. "Patronage and Piety in Late Medieval England: Margaret, Duchess of Clarence, Symon Wynter, and Beinecke MS. 317." *Yale University Library Gazette* 60 (Oct. 1985): 32–46.

Kempe, Margery. *The Book of Margery Kempe*. Ed. Sanford B. Meech and Hope Emily Allen. EETS o.s. 212. London: Humphrey Milford, 1940.

Ker, N. R. *Medieval Libraries of Great Britain*. 2nd ed. London: Royal Historical Society, 1964.

Kihlbohm, Asta. "A Contribution to the Study of Fifteenth Century English." Diss. Uppsala, 1926.

Kingsford, Charles Lethbridge, ed. *The Stonor Letters and Papers 1290–1483*. Camden Society 3rd series, no. 30. London: Camden Society, 1919.

Kolodny, Annette. "Dancing Through the Minefield: Some Observations on the Theory, Practice, and Politics of a Feminist Literary Criticism." *The New Feminist Criticism: Essays on Women, Literature, and Theory*. Ed. Elaine Showalter. NY: Pantheon, 1985.

Krochalis, Jeanne. "The Benedictine Rule for Nuns: Library of Congress, MS. 4." *Manuscripta* 30.1 (1986): 21–34.

LaFarge, Margaret Wade. *A Small Sound of the Trumpet: Women in Medieval Life*.

Boston: Beacon, 1986.

The Myroure of our Ladye. Ed. John Henry Blunt. EETS e.s. 19 (1873); rpt. Millwood, NY: Kraus, 1973.

Orme, Nicholas. *English Schools in the Middle Ages.* London: Methuen, 1973.

Parkes, M. B. "The Literacy of the Laity." *The Medieval World.* Ed. David Daiches and Anthony Thorlby. London: Aldus, 1973.

Patterson, Lee. *Negotiating the Past: The Historical Understanding of Medieval Literature.* Madison: U of Wisconsin P, 1987.

Power, Eileen. *Medieval English Nunneries.* 1922; rpt. NY: Burt Franklin, 1964.

Rose, Mary Beth, ed. *Women in the Middle Ages and Renaissance: Literary and Historical Perspectives.* Syracuse: Syracuse UP, 1986.

Tarvers, Josephine Koster. "'The Festis and the Passion of oure Lord Ihesu Christ': A Middle English Prayer Sequence for Women." Forthcoming.

Walter de Bibbesworth. *Le Tretiz.* Ed. William Rothwell. Anglo-Norman Text Society Plain Text Ser., 6. London: Anglo-Norman Text Society, 1980.

Wood, R. A. "A Fourteenth-Century Owner of *Piers Plowman.*" *Medium Aevum* 53 (1984): 83–90.

Young, Karl. *The Drama of the Medieval Church.* 2 vols. Oxford: Clarendon, 1933.

Publications by
Judson Boyce Allen (1968–85)

Books

The Friar as Critic: Literary Attitudes in the Later Middle Ages.
Nashville: Vanderbilt UP, 1971.

*A Distinction of Stories: The Medieval Unity of Chaucer's Fair Chain
of Narratives for Canterbury.* Columbus: Ohio State UP, 1981.
With Theresa Anne Moritz.

*The Ethical Poetic of the Later Middle Ages: A Decorum of Convenient
Distinction.* Toronto: U of Toronto P, 1982.

Articles

"The Style and Content of Baptist Sermons in Seventeenth-Century
England." *Furman Studies* 15 (May 1968): 1–21.

"The Ironic Fruyt: Chauntecleer as Figura." *Studies in Philology* 66
(1969): 25–35.

"The Library of a Classicizer: the Sources of Robert Holkot's Mytho-
graphic Learning." *Arts libéraux et philosophie au Moyen Âge:
Actes du quatrième Congrès international de philosophie médiévale.* Montréal and Paris, 1969. 722–29.

Publications by Judson Boyce Allen

"Medieval Studies, An Intellectual Model for Evangelical Ecumenism." *Review and Expositor* 66 (Summer 1969): 299–311.

"Edward Taylor's Catholic Wasp: Exegetical Convention in 'Upon a Spider Catching a Fly.'" *English Language Notes* 7 (June 1970): 257–60.

"An Unrecorded *Ars Predicandi.*" *Wake Forest University Library Newsletter* I (October 1969): 2–4.

"Alisoun Through the Looking Glass, Or Every Man His Own Midas." *Chaucer Review* 4 (1970): 99–105. With Patrick Gallacher.

"An Anonymous Twelfth-Century 'De natura deorum' in the Bodleian Library." *Traditio* 26 (1970): 352–64.

"Utopian Literature: The Problem of Literary Reference." *Cithara* II (May 1972): 40–55.

"The Old Way and the Parson's Way: An Ironic Reading of the *Parson's Tale.*" *The Journal of Medieval and Renaissance Studies* 3 (1973): 255–71.

"Commentary as Criticism: Formal Cause, Discursive Form, and the Late Medieval Accessus." *Acta Conventus Neo-Latini Lovaniensis*. Ed. J. Isewijn and E. Kessler. Munich: Fink Verlag, 1973. 29–48.

"The Education of the Public Man: A Medieval View." *Renascence* 26 (Summer 1974): 171–88. Rpt. in *Medieval Studies in North America, Past, Present, and Future*. Ed. Francis G. Gentry and Christopher Kleinhenz. Kalamazoo, Michigan: Medieval Institute Publications, 1982. 179–99.

"Hermann the German's Averroistic Aristotle and Medieval Poetic Theory." *Mosaic* 9 (1976): 67–81.

"God's Society and Grendel's Shoulder Joint: Gregory and the Poet of the 'Beowulf.'" *Neuphilologische Mitteilungen* 78 (1977): 239–40.

"The *Grand Chant Courtois* and the Wholeness of the Poem: The Medieval *Assimilatio* of Text, Audience, and Commentary." *L'Esprit Créateur* 18 (Fall 1978): 5–17.

"Commentary as Criticism: The Text, Influence, and Literary Theory of the Fulgentius Metaphored of John Ridewall." *Acta Conventus Neo-Latini Amstelodamensis.* Ed. P. Tuynman, G. C. Kuiper, and E. Kessler. Munich: Fink Verlag, 1979. 25–47.

"The Medieval Unity of Malory's *Morte Darthur.*" *Medievalia* 6 (1980): 279–309.

"The Chalice in Dante's *Paradiso.*" *Quaderni d'italianistica* 2 (1981): 71–77.

"Contemporary Literary Theory and Chaucer." *The Chaucer Newsletter* 3 (Summer 1981): 1–2.

"*Accessus ad auctores.*" *Dictionary of the Middle Ages.* Ed. Joseph R. Strayer. New York: Charles Scribner's Sons, 1982. 1:34–35.

"Grammar, Poetic Form, and the Lyric Ego: A Medieval A Priori." *Vernacular Poetics in the Middle Ages.* Ed. Lois Ebin. Kalamazoo, Michigan: Medieval Institute Publications, 1984. 199–226.

"Langland's Reading and Writing: *Detractor* and the Pardon Passus." *Speculum* 59.2 (April 1984): 342–62.

"Reading and Looking Things Up in Chaucer's England." *The Chaucer Newsletter* 7 (Spring 1985): 1–2.

"Malory's Diptych *Distinctio*: The Closing Books of his Work." *Studies in Malory*. Ed. James W. Spisak. Kalamazoo, Michigan: Medieval Institute Publications, 1985. 237–55.

Reviews

Orpheus in the Middle Ages, by John Block Friedman. *Journal of English and Germanic Philology* 71 (April 1972): 241–43.

Rhetoric in the Middle Ages: A History of Rhetorical Theory from St. Augustine to the Renaissance, by James J. Murphy. *Speculum* 52 (April 1977): 411–14.

The Gothic Visionary Perspective, by Barbara Nolan. *Christianity and Literature* 27 (Summer 1978): 63–64.

Chaucerian Fiction, by Robert B. Burlin. *Speculum* 54 (January 1979): 116–18.

The Pattern of Judgment in the Queste *and* Cleanness, by Charlotte C. Morse. *Journal of English and Germanic Philology* 79 (January 1980): 105–07.

Verses in Sermons: "Fasciculus morum" and Its Middle English Poems, by Siegfried Wenzel. *Speculum* 56 (1981): 660–61.

Publications by Judson Boyce Allen

Medieval Imagination: Rhetoric and the Poetry of Courtly Love, by Douglas Kelly. *Clio* 11:2 (1982): 213–15.

A Commentary on Seneca's "Apocolocyntosis diui Claudii" or "Glose in Librum de ludo Claudi Annei Senece,*"* ed. Richard E. Clairmont. Critical edition with facing English translation, commentary, notes, indices, and facsimile of Cod. Balliol 130. *Speculum* 58 (1983): 844.

Contributors

Christopher Baswell (Ph.D. Yale University) has taught at the University of Geneva and is now at Barnard College. He is preparing a fascicle for the *Catalogus translationum et commentariorum* on Virgil 900–1200. His book, *Figures of Olde Werk: Virgil's* Aeneid *and Medieval England,* will appear in Spring 1993 (Cambridge UP). He has published articles and reviews and co-edited a volume of essays, *The Politics of Myth: Medieval and Renaissance* (forthcoming 1992).

Cynthia Renee Bland (Ph.D. University of North Carolina, Chapel Hill) has worked for the *Middle English Dictionary* and taught at The College of Our Lady of the Elms (Massachusetts); she now teaches at Ohio Wesleyan University. She has published *The Teaching of Grammar in Late Medieval England: An Edition with Commentary of Oxford, Lincoln College MS. Lat. 130* (1991).

Marianne G. Briscoe (Ph.D. Catholic University of America) has worked for the Newberry Library, Chicago, and the University of Chicago; she is now Vice President for Advancement at St. Mary's College of California. She specializes in medieval English drama, preaching, and preaching theory. She is co-editor of *Contexts of Early English Drama* and editor of the records for Oxford and Oxfordshire for the Records of Early English Drama.

Contributors

Penelope Reed Doob (Ph.D. Stanford University) teaches at York University, Toronto, where she has also served as Associate Vice-President, Faculties. She has published reviews and articles on dance, especially ballet, and on medieval literature. She is now working on a study of dance in the Middle Ages, having already written on madness and on labyrinths: *Nebuchadnezzar's Children: Conventions of Madness in Middle English Literature* (1974) and *The Idea of the Labyrinth from Classical Antiquity through the Middle Ages* (1990).

John M. Fyler (Ph.D. University of California, Berkeley) teaches at Tufts University, where he has recently served a stint as chair of the English Department. He edited the *House of Fame* for *The Riverside Chaucer*; he has published numerous articles and *Chaucer and Ovid* (1979).

Martin Irvine (Ph.D. Harvard University) has taught at Wayne State University and now teaches at Georgetown University. He has published articles on Old English literature, Chaucer, medieval Latin, and literary theory. He has a book forthcoming, *Grammatica: Literary Theory and Textual Culture in the Early Middle Ages*, the first part of a two-part study of *grammatica* and literary theory.

Kathryn Kerby-Fulton (D.Phil. Centre for Medieval Studies, University of York, England) teaches at the University of Victoria, Victoria, Canada. She has published a study of Langland's use of apocalyptic thought, entitled *Reformist Apocalypticism and Piers Plowman* (1990), and various articles on medieval visionary writers, especially Hildegard of Bingen.

336

Alastair J. Minnis (Ph.D. Queen's University of Belfast) has taught at the Universities of Belfast and Bristol and now co-directs the Centre for Medieval Studies at the University of York (England). He has edited four anthologies of critical essays and is general editor of *Cambridge Studies in Medieval Literature*, joint general editor of *Publications of the John Gower Society*, and editor of a new series which publishes the proceedings of the York Manuscripts Conferences. His own work centers on medieval literary theory and includes numerous articles and several books: *Chaucer and Pagan Antiquity* (1982); *Medieval Theory of Authorship: Scholastic Literary Attitudes in the Later Middle Ages* (1984; 2nd ed. 1988); and, with A. Brian Scott, *Medieval Literary Theory and Criticism c.1100–c.1375: The Commentary Tradition* (1988; rev. 1991).

Charlotte Cook Morse (Ph.D. Stanford University) has taught at Yale University and worked for a year at the National Endowment for the Humanities; she now teaches at Virginia Commonwealth University. She is editing Chaucer's *Clerk's Tale* for the Variorum Chaucer. She has published several articles and *The Pattern of Judgment in the* Queste *and* Cleanness (1976).

R. Allen Shoaf (Ph.D. Cornell University) has taught at Yale University and is now Alumni/ae Professor of English at the University of Florida, Gainesville. He is the founding editor of *Exemplaria: A Journal of Theory in Medieval and Renaissance Studies*. He has written or edited five books on Dante, Chaucer, and Milton and written numerous articles and reviews.

Josephine Koster Tarvers (Ph.D. University of North Carolina, Chapel Hill), who taught at Rutgers University, New Brunswick, is president of in*Scribe Communications, Rock Hill, South Carolina. She does consulting work in English with several major corporations as well as with smaller businesses. She has read papers and published articles on rhetoric and composition as well as on medieval English literature and manuscripts. She is currently working on studies of late medieval prayer and women's literacy in late medieval England.

Marjorie Curry Woods (Ph.D. University of Toronto, Centre for Medieval Studies) has taught at Oberlin College and the University of Rochester; she now teaches at the University of Texas at Austin. Her work centers on medieval poetics and rhetoric and ranges from the study of manuscripts and editing to practical criticism, literary theory, and the history of pedagogy. She is active in international associations concerned with rhetoric and with Neo-Latin studies. She has published articles and *An Early Commentary on the* Poetria nova *of Geoffrey of Vinsauf* (1985).